IRELAND

TOP SIGHTS, AUTHENTIC EXPERIENCES

Neil Wilson, Isabel Albiston, Fionn Davenport,
Damian Harper, Catherine Le Nevez

2

Contents

Christ Church Cathedral (p63), Dublin
DAVID SOANES PHOTOGRAPHY/GETTY IMAGES ©

Plan Your Trip
Ireland's Top 12

Dublin
Capital city and the home of Guinness

Ireland's largest city (p34) by some stretch is the main gateway into
the country, and it has enough distractions to keep visitors engaged
for at least a few days. From world-class museums and entertainment, superb dining and top-grade hotels, Dublin has all the baubles
of a major international metropolis. But the real clinchers are Dubliners themselves, who are friendlier, more easygoing and welcoming
than the burghers of virtually any other European capital.

1

Connemara

Gorgeous coast and wild mountains

Wandering Connemara's (p122) characterful roads brings you from one village to another, each with traditional pubs and restaurants serving seafood chowder cooked from recipes that are family secrets. Inland, the scenic drama is even greater. In fantastically desolate valleys, green hills, yellow wildflowers and wild streams reflecting the blue sky provide elemental beauty.

Top: Seafood chowder; Bottom: Connemara (p122), County Galway

2

ROLF G. WACKENBERG/SHUTTERSTOCK ©

Glendalough

Ancient churches scattered amid scenic splendour

When St Kevin chose a remote cave on a lake nestled in a forested valley as his monastic retreat, he inadvertently founded a settlement (p98) that would later prove to be one of Ireland's most dynamic universities and, in our time, one of the country's most beautiful ruined sites. The remains of the settlement (including an intact round tower), coupled with the stunning scenery, are unforgettable.

Above: Round Tower, Glendalough (p98), County Wicklow,

3

Dingle

Picturesque peninsula strewn with ancient ruins

Dingle (p213) is the name of both the peninsula jutting into the Atlantic and its delightful main town, the peninsula's beating heart. Fishing boats unload fish and shellfish that couldn't be any fresher if you caught it yourself, many pubs are untouched since their earlier incarnations as old-fashioned shops, artists sell their creations (including beautiful jewellery with Irish designs) at intriguing boutiques, and toe-tapping trad sessions take place around roaring pub fires.

Right: Harbour in Dingle (p213), County Kerry

Galway City

Ireland's liveliest city hums through the night

One word to describe Galway City (p118)? Craic! Discover music-filled pubs where you can hear three old guys playing spoons and fiddles or a hot, young band. Join the locals as they bounce from place to place, never knowing what fun lies ahead but certain of the possibility. Add in local bounty such as the famous oysters and nearby adventure in the Connemara Peninsula and the Aran Islands and the fun never ends.

Right: High St, Galway City (p118)

Brú na Bóinne

Mysterious prehistoric passage tombs

Ancient and yet eerily futuristic, Newgrange's immense, round, white stone walls topped by a grass dome is an extraordinary sight. Part of the vast Neolithic necropolis Brú na Bóinne (Boyne Palace; p84), it contains Ireland's finest Stone Age passage tomb, predating the Pyramids by some six centuries. Most extraordinary of all is the tomb's precise alignment with the sun at the time of the winter solstice.

Megalithic art, Newgrange (p85), County Meath

6

Cliffs of Moher

Iconic seacliffs of jaw-dropping beauty

Bathed in the golden glow of the late afternoon sun, the Cliffs of Moher (p140) are but one of the splendours of County Clare. From a boat bobbing below, the towering stone faces have a dramatic ruggedness that's enlivened by thousands of seabirds, including cute little puffins. Down south in Loop Head, pillars of rock towering above the sea have abandoned stone cottages whose very existence is inexplicable.

7

Antrim Coast

Dramatic coastal scenery with geological wonders

County Antrim's Causeway Coast (p152) is a scenic backdrop for *Game of Thrones* filming locations. Put on your walking boots by the swaying Carrick-a-Rede rope bridge, then follow the rugged coastline for 16.5 spectacular kilometres, passing Ballintoy Harbour (aka the Iron Islands' Lordsports Harbour) and the famous Giant's Causeway's outsized basalt columns, as well as cliffs and islands, sandy beaches and ruined castles, before finishing with a dram at the Old Bushmills Distillery.

Right: Carrick-A-Rede (p165)

Cork City

Gourmet delights in Ireland's foodie capital

The Republic's second city (p184) is second only in terms of size – in every other respect it will bear no competition. A tidy, compact city centre is home to an enticing collection of art galleries, museums and – most especially – places to eat. From cheap cafes to top-end gourmet restaurants, Cork City excels. At the heart of it is the simply wonderful English Market, a covered produce market that is an attraction unto itself.

Far left: English Market (p180), Left. Cork City Gaol (p185)

Belfast

Victorian architecture, top museums and lively pubs

Northern Ireland's capital city (p218) is buzzing, having reinvented itself as a major tourist hot spot. Historical attractions range from Titanic Belfast, a multimedia celebration of the world's most famous ocean liner (built and launched here in 1911), to the grimly fascinating corridors of Crumlin Road Gaol, and black-taxi tours of West Belfast's political murals, a reminder of the strife that scarred the city in the last decades of the 20th century. Top: Crumlin Road Gaol (p227); Bottom left: Posters in Titanic Belfast (p222); Bottom right: Taxi tour of Belfast's murals (p225)

10

Kilkenny City

Arts, crafts and medieval monuments

From its regal castle to its soaring medieval cathedral, Kilkenny (p238) exudes a permanence and culture that makes it an unmissable stop. Its namesake county boasts scores of artisans and craftspeople and you can browse their wares at Kilkenny's boutiques. Chefs eschew Dublin to be close to the source of Kilkenny's wonderful produce and you can enjoy the local brewery's beer at scores of delightful pubs.

Ring of Kerry

Classic road trip through spectacular scenery

Driving around the Ring of Kerry (p200) is an unforgettable experience, but you don't need to limit yourself to the main route – there are countless opportunities for detours. Near Killorglin, it's a short hop up to the little-known Cromane Peninsula. Between Portmagee and Waterville, you can explore the Skellig Ring. The peninsula's interior offers mesmerising mountain views, so don't forget your camera!

Above: Valentia Island (p200), Ring of Kerry

Plan Your Trip
Need to Know

When to Go

Belfast
GO May–Sep

Galway
GO May–Sep

Dublin
GO Any time;
lots of indoor
attractions

Kerry
GO May–Sep

Cork
GO May–Sep

High Season (Jun–mid-Sep)

○ Weather at its best.

○ Accommodation rates at their highest (especially in August).

○ Tourist peak in Dublin, Kerry, southern and western coasts.

Shoulder (Easter–May, mid-Sep–Oct)

○ Weather often good, sun and rain in May; 'Indian summers' and often warm in September.

○ Summer crowds and accommodation rates drop off.

Low Season (Nov–Feb)

○ Reduced opening hours from October to Easter; some destinations close. Big city attractions operate as normal.

○ Cold and wet weather throughout the country; fog can reduce visibility.

Currency

Republic of Ireland: euro (€)
Northern Ireland: pound sterling (£)

Language

English, Irish

Visas

Not required by most citizens of Europe, Australia, New Zealand, USA and Canada.

Money

Visa and MasterCard credit and debit cards are widely accepted; American Express is only accepted by the major chains, and virtually no one will accept Diners or JCB.

Mobile Phones

All European and Australasian phones work in Ireland and Northern Ireland; some North American (non-GSM) phones don't. Check with your provider. Prepaid SIM cards cost from €10.

Time

Western European Time (UTC/GMT November to March; plus one hour April to October).

Daily Costs

Budget: Less than €80

○ Dorm bed: €12–20

○ Cheap meal in cafe or pub: €8–15

○ Intercity bus travel (200km trip): €12–25

○ Pint: €5–6.50

Midrange: €80–150

○ Double room in hotel or B&B: €80–180 (more expensive in Dublin)

○ Main course in restaurant: €15–30

○ Car rental (per day): from €30

○ Three-hour train journey: €60

Top end: More than €150

○ Four-star hotel stay: from €200

○ Three-course meal in good restaurant: €70

○ Top round of golf (midweek): €100

Useful Websites

Entertainment Ireland (www.entertainment. ie) Countrywide listings for every kind of entertainment.

Failte Ireland (www.discoverireland.ie) Official tourist board website – practical info and a huge accommodation database.

Lonely Planet (www.lonelyplanet.com/ireland) Destination information, hotel bookings, traveller forum and more.

Northern Ireland Tourist Board (www.nitb. com) Official tourist site.

Opening Hours

Banks 10am to 4pm Monday to Friday (to 5pm Thursday).

Pubs 10.30am to 11.30pm Monday to Thursday, 10.30am to 12.30am Friday and Saturday, noon to 11pm Sunday (30 minutes 'drinking up' time allowed); closed Christmas Day and Good Friday.

Restaurants Noon to 10.30pm; many close one day of the week.

Shops 9.30am to 6pm Monday to Saturday (to 8pm Thursday in cities), noon to 6pm Sunday.

Arriving in Ireland

Dublin Airport Private coaches run every 10 to 15 minutes to the city centre (€7). Taxis take 30 to 45 minutes and cost €20 to €25.

Dublin Port Terminal Buses are timed to coincide with arrivals and departures; costs €3 to the city centre.

Belfast International Airport Airport Express 300 bus runs hourly from Belfast International Airport (one way/return £7.50/10.50, 30 to 55 minutes). A taxi costs around £30.

George Best Belfast City Airport Airport Express 600 bus runs every 20 minutes (one way/return £2.50/3.80, 15 minutes). A taxi costs around £10.

Getting Around

Transport in Ireland is efficient and reasonably priced to and from major urban centres; smaller towns and villages along those routes are well served.

Train A limited (and expensive) network links Dublin to all major urban centres, including Belfast in Northern Ireland.

Car The most convenient way to explore Ireland's every nook and cranny. Cars can be hired in every major town and city; drive on the left.

Bus An extensive network of public and private buses make them the most cost-effective way to get around; there's service to and from most inhabited areas.

Bike Dublin operates a bike-share scheme with over 100 stations spread throughout the city.

For more on **getting around**, see p301

Plan Your Trip
Hot Spots For...

HONEY CLOVERZ/GETTY IMAGES ©

Irish Cuisine

Ireland's foodie revolution kicked off in County Cork in the 1970s and has now spread all over the country, with fine food and farmers markets everywhere.

Cork (p178)
The gourmet capital of Ireland, Cork is home to countless restaurants and the legendary English Market.

Best Dish
The Producers' Platter at Nash 19 (p187).

Dublin (p34)
Ireland's biggest city is a hotbed of modern Irish cuisine, with several Michelin star-rated restaurants.

Best Dish
Tartare of veal and mushroom at Chapter One (p73).

Kinsale (p191)
This historic harbour town is famous for fine dining, and is the best place to sample fresh Irish seafood.

Best Dish
Lobster with wild garlic butter at Finn's Table (p193).

LUCKY TEAM STUDIO/SHUTTERSTOCK ©

Coastal Scenery

Much of Ireland's most spectacular scenery is to be found around its wave-battered coastline, from beaches of golden sand to towering cliffs and sea stacks.

Ring of Kerry (p200)
This 179km circular tour winds past beaches, ruins and loughs, with views of the island-dotted Atlantic.

Caherdaniel
Grandstand island views from Beenarourke ridge (p201).

Antrim Coast (p152)
Black basalt and white chalk cliffs plus stretches of golden sand make up the beautiful Antrim Coast.

Giant's Causeway
Hexagonal columns form the coast's centrepiece (p156).

County Clare (p136)
Sculpted over aeons by Atlantic breakers, Clare's coast is a cornucopia of spectacular scenery.

Cliffs of Moher
Hauntingly beautiful 200m-high cliffs (p140).

Traditional Music

Western Europe's most vibrant folk music is Irish traditional music, best enjoyed in the convivial company of an old-fashioned pub.

IMAGEBROKER/ALAMY STOCK PHOTO ©

Doolin (p149)
This west coast village is a major centre of Irish folk music, with daily sessions in its trio of pubs.

Gus O'Connor's
Atmospheric 19th-century hostelry (p150).

Galway City (p118)
Traditional pubs offer live music, while street performers belt out traditional classics.

Tig Cóilí
Authentic old pub (p115) with live *céilidh* every day.

Derry (Londonderry; p170)
Friendly, atmospheric pubs, with live music happening somewhere every night of the week.

Peadar O'Donnell's
Rowdy traditional music sessions (p174) every night.

Monastic Sites

The 'land of saints and scholars' was a cradle of early Christianity, which has left a legacy of amazing ancient monastic sites.

DESIGN PICS/PATRICK SWAN/GETTY IMAGES ©

Skellig Michael (p202)
Ireland's most spectacular monastic site, perched on top of a jagged rock pinnacle.

Beehive Cells
6th-century drystone housing for monks (p202).

Rock of Cashel (256)
Medieval ruins atop a fortified, rock-girt hill dominate the landscape for miles around.

Cormac's Chapel
Houses Ireland's oldest mural paintings (p257).

Glendalough (p98)
Nestled between two lakes, haunting Glendalough is one of the most historic spots in the country.

St Kevin's Kitchen
11th-century church (p101) with a distinctive bell tower.

Plan Your Trip
Local Life

ARNDALE/SHUTTERSTOCK ©

Activities

There's no better way of experiencing this wildly beautiful country than by exploring its varied landscapes – and the rewards can be spectacular. From majestic craggy mountains to lush lakeside woods, from broad sandy beaches to blankets of wild bog stretching as far as the eye can see, Ireland's great outdoors will never disappoint.

Shopping

Selling souvenirs to visitors is big business in Ireland, and many visitor attractions are accompanied by the inevitable gift shop. But look beyond the tourist kitsch of *shillelaghs* (Irish fighting sticks), cuddly leprechauns and shamrock key rings and you'll find plenty of good-value, high-quality items. Traditional Irish products such as crystal, knitwear and tweed remain popular choices, but a new wave of young Irish designers and craftspeople are turning out innovative ceramics, textiles and jewellery.

Entertainment

The big cities of Dublin, Belfast, Cork, Limerick and Galway offer a thriving entertainment scene. Big-name bands and singers play at venues like the **3 Arena** (☑01-819 8888; www.3arena.ie; East Link Bridge, North Wall Quay; tickets €30-90; ⊘6.30-11pm; ☒The Point) in Dublin and the **SSE Arena** (Map p228; www.ssearenabelfast.com; 2 Queen's Quay; ☒Station St) in Belfast, while any number of pubs and clubs host live performances by local and Irish bands.

More distinctively Irish are the traditional-music sessions that enliven many an evening in pubs the length and breadth of the country.

Eating

In the last couple of decades Ireland has 'rediscovered' its own native cuisine. A host of chefs and producers have led a foodie revolution that, at its heart, is about bringing to the table the kind of meals that have long been taken for

ATTILA JANDI/SHUTTERSTOCK ©

granted on well-run Irish farms. This 'local food' movement has gone from strength to strength, with farmers markets showcasing local produce, and restaurants all over the country increasingly highlighting local sourcing of ingredients.

Drinking & Nightlife

Famed around the world for Guinness and whiskey, Ireland has a well-deserved reputation as a place to enjoy a drink or six. Every town and hamlet has at least one pub, usually several, and a visit to the pub is the best way to get a handle on what makes the country tick.

The traditional Irish pub is often the hub of a community, whether urban or rural, a meeting place and venue for quiz nights and live music. What makes the Irish pub scene unique is the survival of the 'spirit grocery', a combined pub and grocer's shop that emerged in the 19th century when a growing temperance movement forced many pub landlords

to diversify their businesses in order to remain solvent.

In the last decade there has been a swing away from the big international brands in favour of beers made by small, local breweries – so-called 'craft beers'. Many of these have their own pubs, or even combine pub and brewery in one place.

★ **Best Traditional Pubs**

Stag's Head (p75)

Monroe's Tavern (p115)

McGann's (p143)

Sin É (p188)

Crown Liquor Saloon (p226)

From left: Avoca Handweavers, Avoca village, County Wicklow (p106); Crown Liquor Saloon (p226), Belfast

Plan Your Trip
Month by Month

February

Bad weather makes February the perfect month for indoor activities.

✯ Audi Dublin International Film Festival

Most of Dublin's cinemas participate in the capital's film festival, a two-week showcase for new films by Irish and international directors, which features local flicks, arty international films and advance releases of mainstream movies.

☆ Six Nations 7

The Irish national rugby team (www. irishrugby.ie) plays its three home matches at the Aviva Stadium in the southern Dublin suburb of Ballsbridge. The season runs from February to April.

March

Spring is in the air, and the whole country is getting ready for arguably the world's most famous parade.

✯ St Patrick's Day

Ireland erupts into one giant celebration on 17 March (www.stpatricksday.ie), but Dublin throws a five-day party around the parade (attended by 600,000), with gigs and festivities that leave the city with a giant hangover.

April

The weather is getting better, the flowers are beginning to bloom and the festival season begins anew.

☆ Circuit of Ireland International Rally

Northern Ireland's most prestigious rally race – known locally as the 'Circuit' (www. circuitofireland.net) – sees over 130 competitors throttle and turn through some 550km of Northern Ireland and parts of the Republic over two days at Easter.

☆ Irish Grand National

Ireland loves horse racing, and the race that's loved the most is the Grand National, the showcase of the national hunt season that takes place at Fairyhouse in County Meath on Easter Monday.

☆ World Irish Dancing Championships

There's far more to Irish dancing than *Riverdance*. Every April, some 4500 competitors from all over the world gather to test their steps and skills against the very best. The location varies from year to year; see www.irishdancingorg.com.

May

The May Bank Holiday (on the first Monday) sees the first of the busy summer weekends as the Irish take to the roads to enjoy the budding good weather.

☆ North West 200

Ireland's most famous road race is also the country's biggest outdoor sporting

★ Best Festivals

St Patrick's Day, March

Galway International Arts Festival, July

Dublin Fringe Festival, September

All-Ireland Finals, September

Belfast International Arts Festival, October

event; 150,000-plus people line the triangular route to cheer on some of the biggest names in motorcycle racing. Held in mid-May.

🎵 Fleadh Nua

The third week of May sees the cream of the traditional music crop come to Ennis, County Clare, for one of the country's most important festivals (p144).

From left: St Patrick's Day revelry in Temple Bar, Dublin; Fleadh Cheoil na hÉireann (p24)

June

The bank holiday at the beginning of the month sees the country spoilt for choice as to what to do.

☆ Irish Derby

Wallets are packed and fancy hats donned for the best flat-race festival in the country (www.curragh.ie), run during the first week of the month.

✿ Bloomsday

Edwardian dress and breakfast of 'the inner organs of beast and fowl' are but two of the elements of the Dublin festival celebrating 16 June, the day on which Joyce's *Ulysses* takes place; the real highlight is retracing Leopold Bloom's steps.

July

There isn't a weekend in the month that a major festival doesn't take place, while visitors to Galway will find that the city is in full swing for the entire month.

✿ Galway International Arts Festival

Music, drama and a host of artistic endeavours are on the menu at the most important arts festival (p119) in the country, which sees Galway go merriment mad for the last two weeks of the month.

✿ Longitude

A mini-Glastonbury in Dublin's Marlay Park, Longitude packs them in over three days in mid-July for a feast of EDM, nu-folk, rock and pop. In 2017 Stormzy, The Weeknd and Mumford & Sons were the headliners.

August

Schools are closed, the sun is shining (or not!) and Ireland is in holiday mood.

☆ Galway Race Week

The biggest horse-racing festival west of the Shannon is not just about the horses, it's also a celebration of Irish culture, sporting gambles and elaborate hats.

✿ Fleadh Cheoil na hÉireann

The mother of all Irish music festivals (www.fleadhcheoil.ie), held at the end of the month, attracts in excess of 400,000 music lovers and revellers to whichever town is playing host (for the last couple of years it's been Ennis, County Clare).

✿ Rose of Tralee

The country's biggest beauty pageant divides critics between those who see it as embarrassing and those who see it as a harmless throwback to older days. Wannabe Roses plucked from Irish communities throughout the world compete for the ultimate prize.

September

Summer may be over, but September weather can be surprisingly good, so it's often the ideal time to enjoy the last vestiges of the sun as the crowds dwindle.

✿ Dublin Fringe Festival

Upwards of 100 different performances take the stage, the street, the bar and the car in the fringe festival that is unquestionably more innovative than the main theatre festival that follows it.

☆ All-Ireland Finals

The second and fourth Sundays of the month see the finals of the hurling and Gaelic football championships respectively, with 80,000-plus crowds thronging into Dublin's Croke Park for the biggest sporting days of the year.

October

The weather starts to turn cold, so it's time to move the fun indoors again. The calendar is still packed with activities and distractions.

✿ Belfast International Arts Festival

Northern Ireland's top arts festival attracts performers from all over the world for the second half of the month; on offer is everything from visual arts to dance.

Plan Your Trip
Get Inspired

Read

Dubliners (James Joyce; 1914) A collection of short stories still as poignant and relevant today as when they were written.

Room (Emma Donoghue; 2010) A harrowing but beautiful account of a boy and his mother being held prisoner, told from the boy's perspective.

The Secret Scripture (Sebastian Barry; 2008) The story of a 100-year-old patient of a mental hospital who writes her autobiography; now a 2015 film directed by Jim Sheridan.

The Gathering (Anne Enright; 2007) Powerful account of alcoholism and domestic abuse in an Irish family.

Watch

Bloody Sunday (2002) Unmissable account of events in Derry in 1972.

The Dead (1987) John Huston brings James Joyce's story to life in his last film, with powerful performances by Donal McCann and Anjelica Huston.

'71 (2014) Excellent film about a British soldier separated from his unit during a Belfast riot in 1971.

What Richard Did (2012) A killing among privileged youths prompts serious soul-searching; loosely based on real events that occurred in 2000.

Listen

Astral Weeks (Van Morrison; 1968) The beguiling poetry is matched by the brilliant musicianship on this extraordinary record.

Achtung Baby (U2; 1991) The band at their creative, rock and roll best.

Loveless (My Bloody Valentine; 1991) This alt-rock groundbreaker defined the effects-laden, shoe-gazer style of mid-1990s sound.

The Lion and the Cobra (Sinéad O'Connor; 1987) O'Connor's debut album is as brilliant today as it was on its release.

Above: James Joyce statue, Dublin

Plan Your Trip
Five-Day Itineraries

Dublin to Wicklow & Meath

Dublin has enough to entertain you for at least three days, leaving you two to devote to day trips from the capital. Even on a quick trip here you'll see some of the country's top highlights.

County Meath (p80) On day five, head north into County Meath and visit Brú na Bóinne, Tara and the site of the Battle of the Boyne.

Dublin (p34) Spend two days in the capital, enjoying the top sights and restaurants, and perhaps a theatre performance.
🚗 1 hr to Powerscourt

County Wicklow (p92) Spend a day exploring the delights of Enniskerry and Powerscourt, and another touring the Wicklow Mountains and Glendalough.
🚗 1½ hrs to Brú na Bóinne

Northern Delights

Link Northern Ireland's two vibrant and historic cities with a scenic tour of the Antrim Coast and the iconic Giant's Causeway, taking in a string of locations made famous as settings for TV saga *Game of Thrones*.

Causeway Coast (p160) Spend a day exploring the Glens of Antrim, Carrick-a-Rede Rope Bridge and the Giant's Causeway.
🚗 1 hr to Derry

Derry (Londonderry) (p170) Take in the sights, walk around the city walls, and view the Bogside murals.

Belfast (p218) Enjoy two days sightseeing, including a black-taxi tour. On the third take a *Game of Thrones* tour.
🚗 2 hrs to Giant's Causeway

Plan Your Trip
10-Day Itinerary

Dublin to Killarney

If you've only got 10 days and you must see the best of the country, you won't have time to linger too long anywhere, but if you manage it correctly, you'll leave with the top highlights in your memory – and on your memory card.

Dublin (p34) One day in the capital, including visits to Trinity College and the *Book of Kells*, the National Museum of Ireland – Archaeology and the Guinness Storehouse. 🚗 3 hrs to Galway

Galway (p108) Three nights based here provides time to soak up the city's cultural delights, followed by a day's scenic drive along the Connemara coastline. 🚗 4hrs (via Cliffs of Moher) to Ennis

Ennis (p144) Drive south from Galway to visit the Cliffs of Moher, before an overnight in Ennis, where you can enjoy a trad music session in one of its pubs. 🚗 3 hrs to Dingle

Dingle (p213) Explore Dingle town the afternoon you arrive; the next day take a harbour cruise to see Fungie the dolphin, then motor around Slea Head Drive. 🚗 1 hr to Killarney

Killarney (p208) Stay for two nights and explore Killarney National Park, then drive (or take a coach tour) around the scenic splendours of the famous Ring of Kerry (180km).

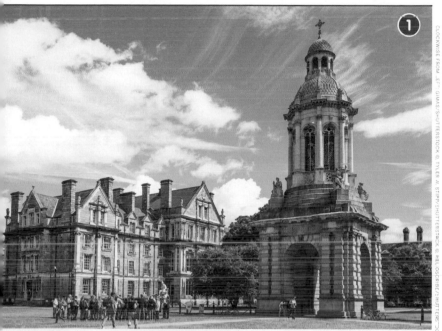

Plan Your Trip
Two-Week Itinerary

Belfast to Galway

This trail takes in many of Ireland's most famous attractions and passes through spectacular countryside. It's almost 1500km in length, so you could dash around it in under a week, but what's the point of rushing? You won't be disappointed on this route.

Belfast (p218) **& County Antrim** (p152) Two nights in Belfast. Spend one day exploring the city's sights and one on a driving tour to the Giant's Causeway.
🚗 2 hrs or 🚆 2¼ hrs to Dublin

Galway (p108) Drive north to Galway via the Cliffs of Moher, and spend three nights there; discover the sights on a Connemara coastal tour.

Dublin (p34) A one-day whistle-stop tour of the capital should include Trinity College, the National Museum of Ireland – Archaeology and the Guinness Storehouse.
🚗 1½ hrs or 🚆 1¾ hrs to Kilkenny

Killarney (p208) Two nights based in Killarney, exploring nearby Killarney National Park, and taking a tour around the Ring of Kerry (180km).
🚗 5 hrs via Cliffs of Moher or 🚆 4 hrs (direct) to Galway

Kilkenny (p238) Take a day to explore Kilkenny's medieval heritage – castle, cathedral, and city walls, plus art and crafts shops and riverside walks.
🚗 2½ hrs to Cork

Kinsale (p191) Indulge yourself with a day of shopping, eating and lounging around in the lovely yachting harbour of Kinsale.
🚗 1½ hrs to Killarney

Cork (p176) Take in Cashel and Blarney on the way to Cork, and spend the next day seeing the city's sights, including Spike Island.
🚗 40 mins or 🚆 50 mins to Kinsale

Plan Your Trip
Family Travel

Ireland loves kids. Everywhere you go you'll find locals to be enthusiastic and inquisitive about your beloved progeny. However, this admiration hasn't always translated into child services such as widespread and accessible baby-changing facilities, or high chairs in restaurants – especially in smaller towns and rural areas.

For further general information see Lonely Planet's *Travel with Children guide* . Also check out www.eumom.ie for advice for pregnant women and parents with young children, as well as www.babygoes2.com, a travel site about family-friendly accommodation worldwide.

Restaurants & Pubs

Although there are legal restrictions on children in pubs, restaurants technically should allow kids of all ages at all times. But in practice, many restaurants (especially in

the higher bracket, but not exclusively so) would prefer if you left the kids at home, especially at busy times, when high chairs are suddenly unavailable: if you're booking ahead, be sure to specify if you need one.

Feeding & Changing

Although breastfeeding is not a common sight (Ireland has one of the lowest rates of it in the world), you can do so with impunity pretty much everywhere without getting so much as a stare. Nappy-changing facilities are generally only found in the newer, larger shopping centres – otherwise you'll have to make do with a public toilet.

Sightseeing

When it comes to activities for the whole family, Ireland is much better placed than it was even a decade ago, as many

providers recognise the importance of catering to the whole family. Most activity centres offer kids' programs for all ages; many museums have kid-friendly exhibits and some even cater guided tours to suit younger ages.

As far as parks, gardens and green spaces go, Ireland has an abundance of them but very few amenities such as designated playgrounds and other exclusively child-friendly spots. In Dublin, St Stephen's Green has a popular playground in the middle of it, but it is the exception rather than the rule.

Getting Around

Under fives travel free on all public transport and most admission prices have an under-16s reduced fee. It's always a good idea to talk to fellow travellers with (happy) children and locals on the road for tips on where to go.

★ Best Sights & Activities
Phoenix Park (p55)
Muckross Traditional Farms (p206)
Titanic Belfast (p222)
Carrick-a-Rede Rope Bridge (p165)
Fungie the Dolphin (p215)

Car seats (around €50/£35 per week) are mandatory for children in hire cars between the ages of nine months and four years. Bring your own seat for infants under about nine months as only larger, forward-facing child seats are generally available. Remember not to place baby seats in the front if the car has an airbag.

From left: Muckross Traditional Farms (p206), Killarney National Park; Spotting Fungie the dolphin (p215), Dingle Bay

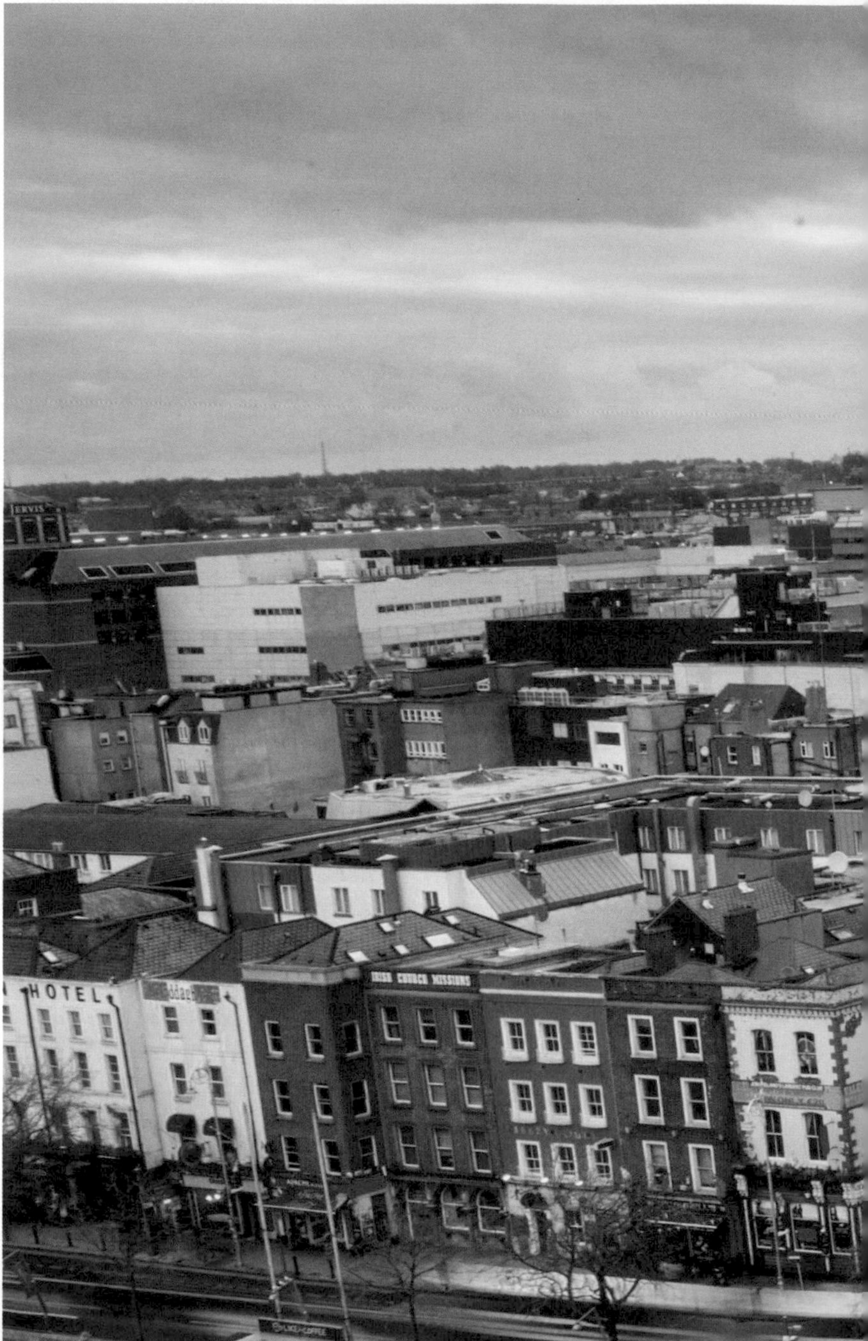
HOTEL
IRISH CHURCH MISSIONS

Irish Museum of Modern Art (p66)

Arriving in Dublin

Dublin Airport Buses to the city every 10 to 15 minutes between 6am and midnight; taxis (€20-25) take 30 to 45 minutes.

Dublin Port Terminal Buses (adult/child €3/1.50, 20 minutes) coincide with arrivals.

Busáras All Bus Eireann services arrive at Busáras; private operators have stops in different parts of the city.

Train Stations Main-line trains from all over Ireland arrive at Heuston or Connolly Stations.

Sleeping

The surge in tourist numbers and the relative lack of beds means hotel prices are higher than they were during the Celtic Tiger years. There are good midrange options north of the Liffey, but the biggest spread of accommodation is south of the river, from midrange Georgian townhouses to the city's top hotels. Budget travellers rely on the selection of decent hostels.

For more information on where to stay, see p79.

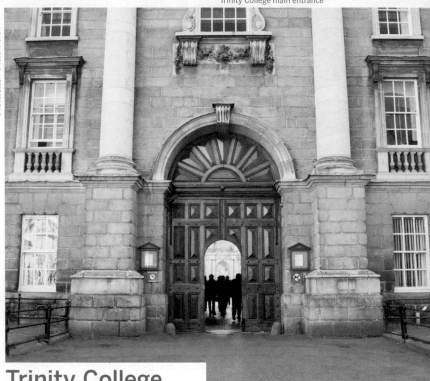
Trinity College main entrance

ATORMMFOTO/SHUTTERSTOCK ©

Trinity College

This calm retreat from the bustle of contemporary Dublin is Ireland's most prestigious university, a collection of elegant Georgian and Victorian buildings, cobbled squares and manicured lawns – a delightful place to wander.

Great For...

☑ **Don't Miss**

The Long Room, which starred as the Jedi Archive in the movie *Star Wars Episode II: Attack of the Clones.*

The college was established by Elizabeth I in 1592 on land confiscated from an Augustinian priory in an effort to stop the brain drain of young Protestant Dubliners, who were skipping across to continental Europe for an education and becoming 'infected with popery'. Trinity went on to become one of Europe's most outstanding universities, producing a host of notable graduates – how about Jonathan Swift, Oscar Wilde and Samuel Beckett at the same alumni dinner?

It remained completely Protestant until 1793, but even when the university relented and began to admit Catholics, the Catholic Church held firm; until 1970, any Catholic who enrolled here could consider themselves excommunicated.

The campus is a masterpiece of architecture and landscaping beautifully preserved in Georgian aspic. Most of the buildings and

The Long Room

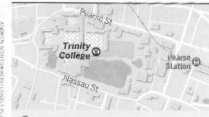

ⓘ Need to Know

Map p64; ☎01-896 1000; www.tcd.ie; College Green, 🚇College Green; ⊗8am-10pm, 🚊all city centre; **FREE**

✕ Take a Break

Fade Street Social (p72) is an excellent lunch spot just a few blocks southwest.

★ Top Tip

Student-led walking tours (Authenticity Tours, Map p64; www.tcd.ie/visitors/tours; Trinity College; tours €6, incl Book of Kells €14; h10.15am-3.40pm Mon-Sat, to 3.15pm Sun May-Sep, fewer midweek tours Oct & Feb-Apr) **depart from the Regent House entrance on College Green.**

statues date from the 18th and 19th centuries, each elegantly laid out on a cobbled or grassy square. The newer bits include the 1978 Arts & Social Science Building, which backs on to Nassau St and forms the alternative entrance to the college. Like the college's Berkeley Library, it was designed by Paul Koralek; it houses the Douglas Hyde Gallery of Modern Art.

To the south of Library Sq is the **Old Library** (Map p64; Library Sq; adult/student/ family €11/9.50/22, skip-the-queue tickets booked in advance €14/12/28; ⊗8.30am-5pm Mon-Sat, 9.30am-5pm Sun May-Sep, 9.30am-5pm Mon-Sat, noon-4.30pm Sun Oct-Apr), built in a severe style by Thomas Burgh between 1712 and 1732. It is one of five copyright libraries across Ireland and the UK, which means it's entitled to a copy of every book published in these islands – around five million books, of which only a fraction are stored here. You

can visit the library as part of a tour of the stunning 65m **Long Room**.

Trinity's greatest treasures are kept here. It houses about 200,000 of the library's oldest volumes, including the **Book of Kells**, a breathtaking illuminated manuscript of the four Gospels of the New Testament, created around AD 800 by monks on the Scottish island of Iona. Other displays include a rare copy of the Proclamation of the Irish Republic, which was read out by Pádraig (Patrick) Pearse at the start of the Easter Rising in 1916.

Also here is the so-called harp of Brian Ború, which was definitely not in use when the army of this early Irish hero defeated the Danes at the Battle of Clontarf in 1014. It dates from around 1400, making it one of the oldest harps in Ireland. Your entry ticket also includes admission to temporary exhibitions on display in the East Pavilion.

Trinity College, Dublin

STEP INTO THE PAST

Ireland's most prestigious university, founded on the order of Queen Elizabeth I in 1592, is an architectural masterpiece, a cordial retreat from the bustle of modern life in the middle of the city. Step through its main entrance and you step back in time, the cobbled stones transporting you to another era, when the elite discussed philosophy and argued passionately in favour of empire.

Standing in Front Square, the 30m-high ❶ Campanile is directly in front of you with the ❷ Dining Hall to your left. On the far side of the square is the Old Library building, the centrepiece of which is the magnificent ❸ Long Room, which was the inspiration for the computer-generated imagery of the Jedi Archive in *Star Wars Episode II: Attack of the Clones*. Here you'll find the university's greatest treasure, the ❹ Book of Kells. You'll probably have to queue to see this masterpiece, and then only for a brief visit, but it's very much worth it.

Just beyond the Old Library is the very modern ❺ Berkeley Library, which nevertheless fits perfectly into the campus' overall aesthetic. Directly in front of it is the distinctive ❻ Sphere Within a Sphere, the most elegant of the university's sculptures.

DON'T MISS

➡ Douglas Hyde Gallery, the campus' designated modern-art museum.

➡ A cricket match on the pitch, the most elegant of pastimes.

➡ A pint in the Pavilion Bar, preferably while watching the cricket.

➡ A visit to the Science Gallery, where science is made completely relevant.

Campanile
Trinity College's most iconic bit of masonry was designed in the mid-19th century by Sir Charles Lanyon; the attached sculptures were created by Thomas Kirk.

RPEDROSA/GETTY IMAGES ©

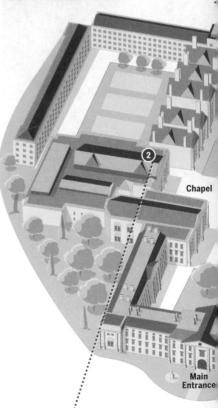

Chapel

Main Entrance

Dining Hall
Richard Cassels' original building was designed to mirror the Examination Hall directly opposite on Front Square: the hall collapsed twice and was rebuilt from scratch in 1761.

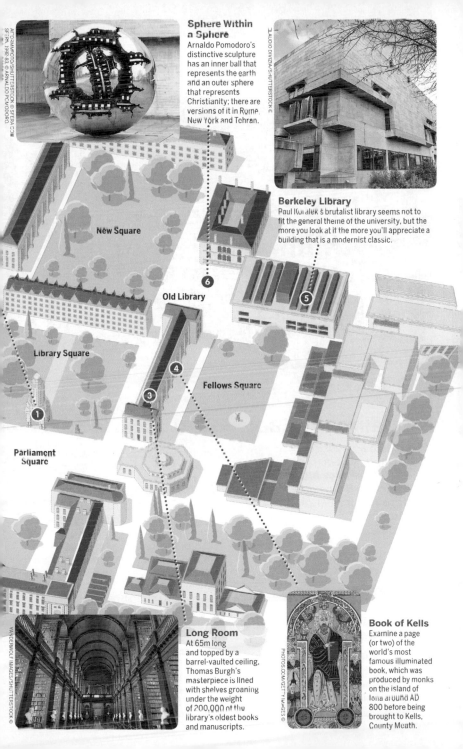

Sphere Within a Sphere

Arnaldo Pomodoro's distinctive sculpture has an inner ball that represents the earth and an outer sphere that represents Christianity; there are versions of it in Rome, New York and Tehran.

Berkeley Library

Paul Koralek's brutalist library seems not to fit the general theme of the university, but the more you look at it the more you'll appreciate a building that is a modernist classic.

New Square

Old Library

Library Square

Fellows Square

Parliament Square

Long Room

At 65m long and topped by a barrel-vaulted ceiling, Thomas Burgh's masterpiece is lined with shelves groaning under the weight of 200,000 of the library's oldest books and manuscripts.

Book of Kells

Examine a page (or two) of the world's most famous illuminated book, which was produced by monks on the island of Iona around AD 800 before being brought to Kells, County Meath.

RODRIGO GARRIDO/SHUTTERSTOCK ©

Kilmainham Gaol

If you have any desire to understand Irish history – especially the juicy bits about resistance to British rule – then a visit to this former prison is an absolute must.

Great For...

☑ **Don't Miss**

Kilmainham houses an outstanding museum dedicated to Irish nationalism and prison life.

This threatening grey building, built between 1792 and 1795, played a role in virtually every act of Ireland's painful path to independence and even today, despite closing in 1924, it still has the power to chill.

It took four years to build, and the prison opened – or rather closed – its doors in 1796. The Irish were locked up for all sorts of misdemeanours, some more serious than others. A six-year-old boy spent a month here in 1839 because his father couldn't pay his train fare, and during the Famine it was crammed with the destitute imprisoned for stealing food and begging. But it is most famous for incarcerating 120 years of Irish nationalists, from Robert Emmet in 1803 to Éamon de Valera in 1923. All of Ireland's botched uprisings ended with the leaders' confinement here, usually before their execution.

MATHI/SHUTTERSTOCK ©

Inchicore Rd

Kilmainham Gaol 🔵

Cammock

S Circular Rd

ℹ️ Need to Know

Map p68; 📞01-453 2037; www.kilmainham-gaolmuseum.ie; Inchicore Rd; adult/child €8/4; ⏰9.30am 6.45pm Jul & Aug, to 5.30pm rest of year; 🚌69, 79 from Aston Quay, 13, 40 from O'Connell St

✕ Take a Break

The Old Royal Oak pub (p75), dating from 1845, is just east of Kilmainham Gaol.

★ Top Tip

Tours can sell out and are not bookable in advance – arrive early to avoid disappointment.

It was the treatment of the leaders of the 1916 Easter Rising that most deeply etched the gaol into the Irish consciousness. Fourteen of the rebel commanders were executed in the stone breakers' yard, including James Connolly who was so badly injured at the time of his execution that he was strapped to a chair at the opposite end of the yard.

The gaol's final function was as a prison for the newly formed Irish Free State, an irony best summed up with the story of Ernie O'Malley, who escaped from the gaol when incarcerated by the British but was locked up again by his erstwhile comrades during the Civil War. This chapter is played down on the tour, and even the passing comment that Kilmainham's final prisoner was the future president, Éamon de Valera, doesn't reveal that he had been imprisoned by his fellow Irish citizens. The gaol was decommissioned in 1924.

An excellent audiovisual introduction to the building is followed by a thought-provoking tour of the eerie prison, the largest unoccupied building of its kind in Europe. Sitting incongruously outside in the yard is the *Asgard*, the ship that successfully ran the British blockade to deliver arms to nationalist forces in 1914. The tour finishes in the gloomy yard where the 1916 executions took place.

Chapel Royal and Record Tower

ROB WILSON/SHUTTERSTOCK ©

Dublin Castle

This mostly 18th-century creation – more hotchpotch palace than medieval castle, though a 13th-century tower survives – was the stronghold of British power in Ireland for 700 years.

The castle is now used by the Irish government for meetings and functions, and the best bits are only visible as part of a 70-minute guided tour (departing every 20 to 30 minutes, depending on numbers).

It was officially handed over to Michael Collins, representing the Irish Free State, in 1922, when the British viceroy is reported to have rebuked Collins on being seven minutes late. Collins replied, 'We've been waiting 700 years, you can wait seven minutes'.

As you walk into the grounds from the main Dame St entrance, there's a good example of the evolution of Irish architecture. On your left is the Victorian **Chapel Royal** (occasionally part of the Dublin Castle tours), decorated with more than 90 heads of various Irish personages and saints carved out of Tullamore limestone.

Great For...

☑ **Don't Miss**

The view over Dublin from the top of the Bedford Tower.

Bedford Tower

DAVID SOANES/SHUTTERSTOCK ©

Lord Edward St

Dame St

Dublin Castle

S Great George's St

ⓘ Need to Know

Map p64; ☑01-677 7129; www.dublincastle. ie; Dame St; guided tours adult/child €10/4, self-guided tours €7/3; ☺9.45am-5.45pm, last admission 5.15pm; ⓹all city centre

✕ Take a Break

Head across the street to Queen of Tarts (p71) for great cakes and coffee.

★ Top Tip

There's a self-guided tour option, but it only includes the State Apartments.

Beside this is the Norman **Record Tower** with its 5m-thick walls. It's currently closed to the public pending a long-awaited revamp. On your right is the Georgian **Treasury Building**, the oldest office block in Dublin, and behind you, yikes, is the uglier-than-sin Revenue Commissioners Building of 1960.

Heading away from that eyesore, you ascend to the Upper Yard. On your right is a figure of Justice with her back turned to the city – an appropriate symbol for British justice, reckoned Dubliners. Next to it is the 18th-century **Bedford Tower**, from which the Irish Crown Jewels were stolen in 1907 and never recovered. Opposite is the entrance for the tours.

The guided tours are pretty dry, but you get to visit the **State Apartments**, many of which are decorated in dubious taste.

You will also see **St Patrick's Hall**, where Irish presidents are inaugurated and foreign dignitaries toasted, and the room in which the wounded James Connolly was tied to a chair while convalescing after the 1916 Easter Rising, so that he could be executed by firing squad.

The highlight is a visit to the **medieval undercroft** of the old castle, discovered by accident in 1986. It includes foundations built by the Vikings (whose long-lasting mortar was made of ox blood, egg shells and horse hair), the hand-polished exterior of the castle walls that prevented attackers from climbing them, the steps leading down to the moat and the trickle of the historic River Poddle, which once filled the moat on its way to join the Liffey.

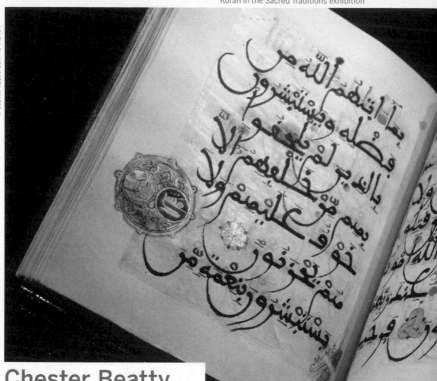

Koran in the Sacred Traditions exhibition

LONELY PLANET/GETTY IMAGES ©

Chester Beatty Library

The world-famous Chester Beatty Library, housed in the Clock Tower at the back of Dublin Castle, is not just Ireland's best small museum, but one of the best you'll find anywhere in Europe.

Great For...

☑ Don't Miss

Fragments of the Christian gospels written on papyrus, dating from around AD 200.

Sir Alfred Chester Beatty

An avid traveller and collector, the American mining magnate Beatty was fascinated by different cultures and amassed more than 20,000 manuscripts, rare books, miniature paintings, clay tablets, costumes and any other objets d'art that caught his fancy and could tell him something about the world. Fortunately for Dublin, he also happened to take quite a shine to the city and made it his adopted home. In return, the Irish made him their first honorary citizen in 1957.

Art of the Book

The collection is spread over two levels. On the ground floor you'll find the **Art of the Book**, a compact but stunning collection of artworks from the Western, Islamic and East Asian worlds. Highlights include the finest collection of Chinese jade books

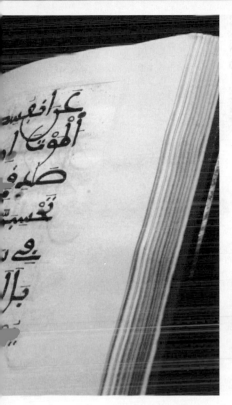

ℹ Need to Know

Map p64; 📞01-407 0750; www.cbl.ie; Dublin Castle; ⏰10am-5pm Mon-Fri, 11am-5pm Sat, 1-5pm Sun year-round, closed Mon Nov-Feb, free tours 1pm Wed, 2pm Sat & 3pm Sun; 🚌all city centre; **FREE**

✕ Take a Break

The library's own Silk Road Café (p71) is a great place for lunch.

★ Top Tip

The library regularly holds specialist workshops, exhibitions and talks on everything from origami to calligraphy.

---

in the world and illuminated European texts featuring exquisite calligraphy that stand up in comparison with the *Book of Kells*. Audiovisual displays explain the process of bookbinding, paper making and printing.

Sacred Traditions

The 2nd floor is home to **Sacred Traditions**, a wonderful exploration of the world's major religions through decorative and religious art, enlightening text and a cool cultural-pastiche video at the entrance. The collection of Korans dating from the 9th to the 19th centuries (the library has more than 270 of them) is considered by experts to be the best example of illuminated Islamic texts in the world. There are also outstanding examples of ancient papyri, including renowned Egyptian

love poems from the 12th century BC and some of the earliest illuminated Gospels in the world, dating from around AD 200. The collection is rounded off with some exquisite scrolls and artwork from China, Japan, Tibet and Southeast Asia, including the two-volume Japanese *Chogonka Scroll*, painted in the 17th century by Kano Sansetu.

The Building

As if all of this wasn't enough for one visit, the library also hosts temporary exhibits that are usually too good to be missed. Not only are the contents of the museum outstanding, but the layout, design and location are also unparalleled, from the marvellous Silk Road Café and gift shop, to the rooftop terrace and the beautiful landscaped garden out the front. These features alone would make this an absolute Dublin must-do.

FINDS FROM
IRISH WETLANDS

National Museum of Ireland

The mother of all Irish museums and the country's most important cultural institution was established in 1977 as the primary repository of the nation's treasures.

Great For...

☑ Don't Miss

The extraordinary hoard of prehistoric gold objects in the archaeology museum.

The collection is so big that it is spread across three separate museums – the archaeology museum in Kildare St, the decorative arts museum at Collins Barracks and a country life museum in County Mayo, on Ireland's west coast. They're all fascinating, but the star attractions are to be found in the archaeology museum. It has Europe's finest collection of Bronze and Iron Age gold artefacts, the most complete collection of medieval Celtic metalwork in the world, fascinating prehistoric and Viking artefacts, and a few interesting items relating to Ireland's fight for independence. If you don't mind groups, the themed guided tours will help you wade through the myriad exhibits.

National Museum of Ireland – Archaelogy

ANTOE.IVAN@~SHUTTERSTOCK ©

O'Connell-GPO
NMI Decorative Arts & History
Abbey Street
Jervis
Museum Smithfield Four Courts
Westmoreland
Pearse St
Dame St
Trinity
Thomas St High St
Dawson
NMI Archaelology
St Stephen's Green

ℹ Need to Know

NMI Archeology (Map p64; www.museum.ie; Kildare St; ⏲10am-5pm Tue-Sat, 2-5pm Sun; 🚌all city centre) **FREE**

NMI Decorative Arts (Map p68; www.museum.ie; Benburb St; ⏲10am-5pm Tue-Sat, 2-5pm Sun; 🚌25, 66, 67, 90 from city centre, 🚈Museum) **FREE**

✕ Take a Break

There are several good eateries on Merrion Row, just south of the archaeology museum.

★ Top Tip

You can travel between the two museum locations on a hop-on, hop-off tour bus.

NMI – Archaeology

Treasury

The Treasury is the most famous part of the collection, and its centrepieces are Ireland's best-known crafted artefacts, the **Ardagh Chalice** and the **Tara Brooch**. The 12th-century Ardagh Chalice is made of gold, silver, bronze, brass, copper and lead; it measures 17.8cm high and 24.2cm in diameter and, put simply, is the finest example of Celtic art ever found. The equally renowned Tara Brooch was crafted around AD 700, primarily in white bronze, but with traces of gold, silver, glass, copper, enamel and wire beading, and was used as a clasp for a cloak. It was discovered on a beach in Bettystown, County Meath, in 1850, but later came into the hands of an art dealer who named it after the hill of Tara, the historic seat

of the ancient high kings. It doesn't have quite the same ring to it, but it was the Bettystown Brooch that sparked a revival of interest in Celtic jewellery that hasn't let up to this day. There are many other pieces that testify to Ireland's history as the land of saints and scholars.

Ór-Ireland's Gold

Elsewhere in the Treasury is the *Ór-Ireland's Gold* exhibition, featuring stunning jewellery and decorative objects created by Celtic artisans in the Bronze and Iron Ages. Among them are the **Broighter Hoard**, which includes a 1st-century-BC large gold collar, unsurpassed anywhere in Europe, and an extraordinarily delicate gold boat. There's also the wonderful **Loughnashade bronze war trumpet**, which also dates from the 1st century BC. It is 1.86m long and made of sheets of bronze, riveted together, with an intricately designed disc at the mouth. It produces a sound similar to the Australian didgeridoo, though you'll have to take our word for it. Running alongside the wall is a **15m log boat**, which was dropped into the water to soften, abandoned and then pulled out 4000 years later, almost perfectly preserved in the peat bog.

Kingship & Sacrifice

One of the museum's biggest showstoppers is the collection of Iron Age 'bog bodies' in the *Kingship and Sacrifice* exhibit – four figures in varying states of preservation dug out of the midland bogs. The bodies' various eerily preserved details – a distinctive tangle of hair, sinewy legs and fingers with fingernails intact – are memorable, but it's the accompanying detail that will make you pause: scholars now believe that all of these bodies were victims of the most horrendous ritualistic torture and sacrifice – the cost of being notable figures in the Celtic world.

Other Exhibits

If you can cope with any more history, upstairs are **Medieval Ireland 1150–1550**, **Viking Age Ireland** – which features exhibits from the excavations at Wood Quay, the area between Christ Church Cathedral and the river – and our own favourite, the aptly named **Clothes from Bogs in Ireland**, a collection of 16th- and 17th-century woollen garments recovered from the bog. Enthralling stuff!

NMI – Decorative Arts & History

Once the world's largest military barracks, this splendid early neoclassical grey-stone building on the Liffey's northern banks

Collins Barracks, the National Museum of Ireland – Decorative Arts & History

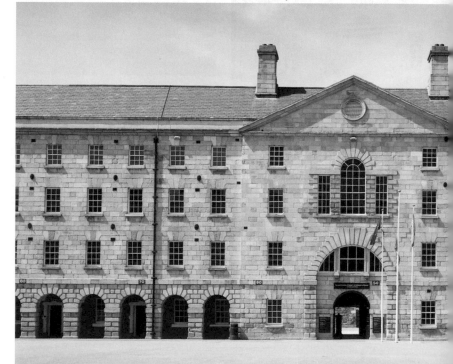

was completed in 1704 according to the design of Thomas Burgh (he of Trinity College's Old Library). It is now home to the Decorative Arts & History collection of the National Museum of Ireland, with a range of superb permanent exhibits ranging from a history of the Easter Rising to the work of iconic Irish architect and designer Eileen Gray (1878–1976).

The Building

The building's central square held six entire regiments and is a truly awesome space, surrounded by arcaded colonnades and blocks linked by walking bridges. Following the handover to the new Irish government in 1922, the barracks was renamed to honour Michael Collins, a hero of the struggle for independence, who was killed that year in the Civil War; to this day most Dubliners refer to the museum as the **Collins Barracks**. Indeed, the army coat he wore on the day of his death (there's still mud on the sleeve) is part of the **Soldiers and Chiefs** exhibit, which covers the history of Irish soldiery at home and abroad from 1550 to the 21st century.

The Exhibits

The museum's exhibits include a treasure trove of artefacts ranging from silver, ceramics and glassware to weaponry, furniture and folk-life displays. The fascinating **Way We Wore** exhibit displays Irish clothing and jewellery from the past 250 years. An intriguing sociocultural study, it highlights the symbolism jewellery and clothing had in bestowing messages of mourning, love and identity.

The old Riding School is home to **Proclaiming a Republic: The 1916 Rising**, which opened in 2016 as an enhanced and updated version of the long-standing exhibit dedicated to the rebellion. The exhibit explores the complicated sociohistorical background to the Rising and also includes visceral memorabilia such as first-hand accounts of the violence of the Black and Tans and post-Rising hunger strikes, and the handwritten death certificates of the Republican prisoners and their postcards from Holloway prison.

Some of the best pieces are gathered in the **Curator's Choice** exhibition, which is a collection of 25 objects hand-picked by different curators and displayed alongside an account of why they were chosen.

> ★ **Top Tip**
> If you want to avoid crowds, the best time to visit is weekday afternoons, when school groups have gone, and never during Irish school holidays.

BIFFBOFFE FF/GETTY IMAGES ©

> ★ **Top Tip**
> A 10-minute walk east along the Liffey from the decorative arts museum is the atmospheric Brazen Head (p76), reputedly Dublin's oldest pub.

National Museum of Ireland

NATIONAL TREASURES

Ireland's most important cultural institution is the National Museum, and its most important branch is the original one, housed in this fine neoclassical (or Victorian Palladian) building designed by Sir Thomas Newenham Deane and finished in 1890. Squeezed in between the rear entrance of Leinster House – the Irish parliament – and a nondescript building from the 1960s, it's easy to pass by the museum. But within its fairly cramped confines you'll find the most extensive collection of Bronze and Iron Age gold artefacts in Europe and the extraordinary collection of the Treasury. This includes the stunning ❶ **Ardagh Chalice** and the delicately crafted ❷ **Tara Brooch**. Amid all the lustre, look out for the ❸ **Broighter Gold Collar** and the impressively crafted ❹ **Loughnashade War Trumpet**, both extraordinary examples of Celtic art. Finally, pay a visit to the exquisite ❺ **Cross of Cong**, which was created after the other pieces but is just as beautiful.

As you visit these treasures – all created after the arrival of Christianity in the 5th century – bear in mind that they were produced with the most rudimentary of instruments.

VIKING DUBLIN

Archaeological excavations in Dublin between 1961 and 1981 unearthed evidence of a Viking town and cemeteries along the banks of the River Liffey. The graves contained weapons such as swords and spears, together with jewellery and personal items. Craftsmen's tools, weights and scales, silver ingots and coins show that the Vikings, as well as marauding and raiding, were also engaged in commercial activities. The Viking artefacts are now part of the National Museum's collection.

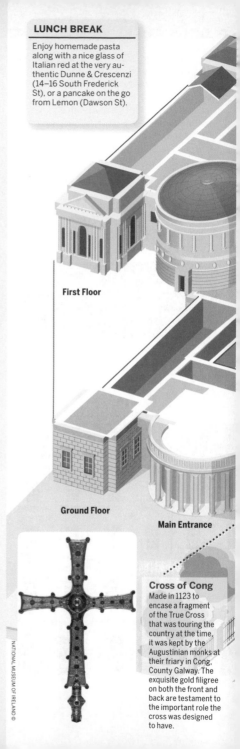

LUNCH BREAK

Enjoy homemade pasta along with a nice glass of Italian red at the very authentic Dunne & Crescenzi (14–16 South Frederick St), or a pancake on the go from Lemon (Dawson St).

First Floor

Ground Floor

Main Entrance

Cross of Cong

Made in 1123 to encase a fragment of the True Cross that was touring the country at the time, it was kept by the Augustinian monks at their friary in Cong, County Galway. The exquisite gold filigree on both the front and back are testament to the important role the cross was designed to have.

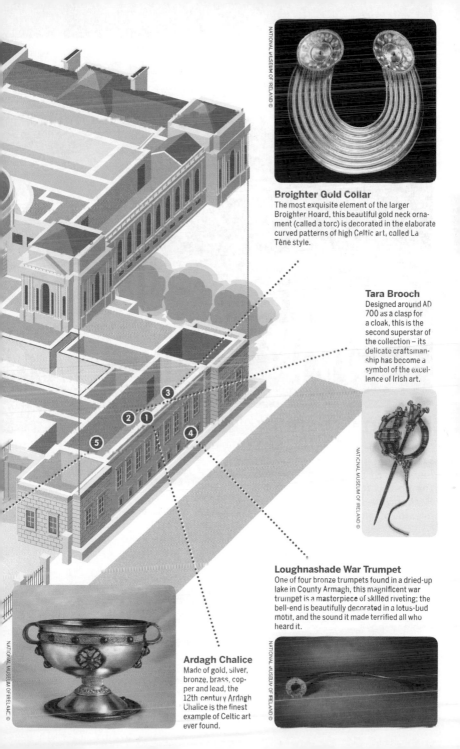

Broighter Gold Collar
The most exquisite element of the larger Broighter Hoard, this beautiful gold neck ornament (called a torc) is decorated in the elaborate curved patterns of high Celtic art, called La Tène style.

Tara Brooch
Designed around AD 700 as a clasp for a cloak, this is the second superstar of the collection – its delicate craftsmanship has become a symbol of the excellence of Irish art.

Loughnashade War Trumpet
One of four bronze trumpets found in a dried-up lake in County Armagh, this magnificent war trumpet is a masterpiece of skilled riveting; the bell-end is beautifully decorated in a lotus-bud motif, and the sound it made terrified all who heard it.

Ardagh Chalice
Made of gold, silver, bronze, brass, copper and lead, the 12th century Ardagh Chalice is the finest example of Celtic art ever found.

NATIONAL MUSEUM OF IRELAND ©

Herd of deer in Phoenix Park

DESIGN PICS/PATRICK SWAN/GETTY IMAGES ©

Dublin Greenery

Dublin is blessed with abundant green spaces, from the manicured lawns of St Stephen's Green to the sprawling acres of Phoenix Park, home to deer, the zoo, the president and the US ambassador.

Great For...

☑ **Don't Miss**

The famous statue of Oscar Wilde in Merrion Square.

St Stephen's Green

As you watch the assorted groups of friends, lovers and individuals splaying themselves across the nine elegantly landscaped hectares of Dublin's most popular green lung, **St Stephen's Green** (Map p64; ☉dawn-dusk; 🚌all city centre, 🚊St Stephen's Green), consider that those same hectares once formed a common for public whippings, burnings and hangings. These days, the harshest treatment you'll get is the warden chucking you off the grass for playing football or frisbee.

Spread across the green's lawns and walkways are some notable artworks; the most imposing of these is a monument to Wolfe Tone, the leader of the abortive 1798 rebellion. Occupying the northeastern corner of the green, the vertical slabs serving as a backdrop to the statue have

Oscar Wilde statue, Merrion Square

ATTILA JANDI/SHUTTERSTOCK ©

smoking jacket and reclines on a rock. Atop one of the plinths, daubed with witty one-liners and Wildean throwaways, is a small green statue of Oscar's pregnant mother.

Phoenix Park

Dubliners are rightly proud of this humongous **park** (Map p68; www.phoenixpark. ie; ⏰24hr; 🚌10 from O'Connell St, 25, 26 from Middle Abbey St) **FREE** at the northwestern edge of the city centre, a short skip from Heuston Station and the Liffey quays. The hugely impressive 709 hectares that comprise the park make up one of the largest set of inner-city green lungs in the world. To put it into perspective, it dwarfs the measly 337 hectares of New York's Central Park and is larger than all of the major London parks put together. The park is home to Áras an Uachtaráin (p57); the residence of the Irish president, as well as the American ambassador and a shy herd of fallow deer who are best observed – from a distance – during the summer months. It is also where you'll find Europe's oldest **zoo** (Map p68; www.dublinzoo.ie; adult/child/family €17.50/13/49; ⏰9.30am-6pm Mar-Sep, to dusk Oct-Feb), not to mention dozens of playing fields for all kinds of sport. How's that for a place to stretch your legs?

Chesterfield Ave runs northwest through the length of the park from the Parkgate St entrance to the Castleknock Gate. Near the Parkgate St entrance is the 63m-high **Wellington Monument** (Map p68) obelisk,

been dubbed 'Tonehenge'. At this entrance is a memorial to all those who died in the Potato Famine (1845–51).

Merrion Square

Arguably the most elegant of Dublin's Georgian squares, **Merrion Square** (Map p68; ⏰dawn-dusk; 🚌all city centre) is also the most prestigious. Its well-kept lawns and beautifully tended flower beds are flanked on three sides by gorgeous Georgian houses with colourful doors, peacock fanlights, ornate door knockers and, occasionally, footscrapers, used to remove mud from shoes before venturing indoors.

Just inside the northwestern corner of the square is a flamboyant **statue of Oscar Wilde**, who grew up across the street at No 1 (now used exclusively by the American University Dublin); Wilde wears his customary completed in 1861. Nearby is the **People's Garden** (Map p68), which dates from 1864, and the bandstand in the Hollow. Across Chesterfield Ave from the Áras an Uachtaráin – and easily visible from the road – is the massive **Papal Cross**, which marks the site where Pope John Paul II preached to 1¼ million people in 1979. In the centre of the park the **Phoenix Monument**, erected by Lord Chesterfield in 1747, looks so unlike a phoenix that it's often referred to as the Eagle Monument.

Iveagh Gardens

These beautiful gardens may not have the sculpted elegance of the other city parks, but they never get too crowded and the warden won't bark at you if you walk on the grass. They were designed by Ninian Niven in 1863 as the private grounds of Iveagh House and include a rustic grotto, cascade, fountain, maze and rosarium. Enter the gardens from Clonmel St, off Harcourt St.

Airfield

Once the home of eccentric philanthropist sisters Letitia and Naomi Overend, the **Airfield estate** (☎01-969 6666; www.airfield.ie; Upper Kilmacud Rd; adult/child €10/5; ☺9.30am-5pm Sep-Jun, to 6pm Jul & Aug; ☐11, 14, 14C, 44, 44B, 75, 116 from city centre) is now held in trust for public use. Though the house is closed to the public (except for the excellent cafe), the lovely 16-hectare grounds with walled gardens, pet farm, vintage car museum and medicinal garden are great for a stroll.

Glasshouse in the National Botanic Gardens

National Botanic Gardens

Founded in 1795, the 19.5-hectare **botanic gardens** (Botanic Rd; ☉9am-6pm Mon-Sat, 11am-8pm Sun Apr-Oct, 10am-4.30pm Mon-Sat, 11am-4.30pm Sun Nov-Mar, ☐13, 13A, 19 from O'Connell St, 34, 34A from Middle Abbey St) **FREE** are home to a series of curvilinear glasshouses, dating from 1843 to 1869, created by Richard Turner, who was also responsible for the glasshouse at Belfast Botanic Gardens and the Palm House in London's Kew Gardens. Within these Victorian masterpieces you will find the latest in botanical technology, including a series of computer-controlled climates reproducing environments of different parts of the world.

War Memorial Gardens

Hardly anyone ever ventures this far west, but they're missing the lovely landscaping of the **War Memorial Gardens** (www.heritageireland.ie; South Circular Rd, Islandbridge; ☉8am-dusk Mon-Fri, 10am-dusk Sat & Sun; ☐69, 79 from Aston Quay, 13, 40 from O'Connell St) **FREE** Designed by Sir Edwin Lutyens, the memorial commemorates the 49,400 Irish soldiers who died during WWI – their names are inscribed in the two huge granite book rooms that stand at one end.

Herbert Park

A gorgeous swath of green lawns, ponds and flower beds near the Royal Dublin Society Showground. Sandwiched between prosperous Ballsbridge and Donnybrook, the **park** (☉dawn-dusk; ☐5, 7, 7A, 8, 45, 46, ☒Sandymount, Lansdowne Rd) runs along the River Dodder. There are tennis courts and a kids' playground here too.

★Famous Addresses

Notable former residents of Merrion Sq include Oscar Wilde (1 North Merrion Sq), **WB Yeats** (52 East Merrion Sq) **and Daniel O'Connell** (58 East Merrion Sq).

PAWEL GAUL/GETTY IMAGES ©

★Áras an Uachtaráin

The residence of the Irish president is a Palladian **lodge** (www.president.ie; Phoenix Park; ☉guided tours hourly 10.30am-3.30pm Sat; ☐10 from O'Connell St, 25, 26 from Middle Abbey St) **FREE** built in 1751 and enlarged in 1816. Queen Victoria stayed here during her visit in 1849.

Gravity Bar at the top of the Guinness Storehouse

Guinness Storehouse

More than any other beer produced anywhere in the world, Guinness has transcended its own brand. This beer-lover's Disneyland is a multimedia homage to Ireland's most famous export.

Great For...

☑ Don't Miss

Enjoying the view from the Gravity Bar with your free pint of Guinness (price included with admission).

The mythology around Guinness is remarkably durable: it doesn't travel well; its distinctive flavour comes from Liffey water; it is good for you – not to mention the generally held belief that you will never understand the Irish until you develop a taste for the black stuff. All absolutely true, of course, so it should be no surprise that the Guinness Storehouse, in the heart of the St James's Gate Brewery, is the city's most-visited tourist attraction, an all-singing, all-dancing extravaganza that combines sophisticated exhibits, spectacular design and a thick, creamy head of marketing hype.

Guinness Storehouse Museum

The old grain storehouse, the only part of the massive, 26-hectare St James's Gate Brewery open to the public, is a suitable

Guinness Gate, Rainsford St

Guinness Storehouse ◎
S Market St Bellevue

Pim St

❶ Need to Know

Map p68; www.guinness-storehouse.com;
St James's Gate, South Market St, adult/
child €18/16.50, Connoisseur Experience
€48; ⏰9.30am-5pm Sep-Jun, to 6pm Jul &
Aug; 🚌21A, 51B, 78, 78A, 123 from Fleet St,
🚊James's

✕ Take a Break

Arthur's Pub (p75) on the 5th floor of
the building serves up delicious bar
lunches.

★ Top Tip

Avoid the queues (and save money) by
buying your ticket in advance, online.

cathedral in which to worship the black
gold. A stunning central atrium rises seven
storeys in the shape of a pint of Guinness,
with a dazzling array of audiovisual and interactive exhibits that cover most aspects of
the brewery's story and explain the brewing
process in overwhelming detail. The head is
represented by the glass-walled Gravity Bar,
which provides panoramic views of Dublin to
savour with your complimentary half-pint.

The Perfect Pour

As you work your way to the top and your
prize of arguably the nicest Guinness you
could drink anywhere, you'll explore the various elements that made the beer the brand
that it is and perhaps understand a little
better the efforts made by the company to
ensure its quasi-mythical status. From the
(copy of) the original 9000-year lease (in
a glass box embedded in the ground floor)
to the near-scientific lesson in how to pour
the perfect pint, everything about this place
is designed to make you understand that
Guinness isn't just any other beer.

Arthur Guinness

One fun fact you will learn is that genius
can be inadvertent: at some point in the
18th century, a London brewer acciden-
tally burnt his hops while brewing ale, and
so created the dark beer we know today.
Its name of 'porter' came because the
dark beer was very popular with London
porters. In the 1770s, Arthur Guinness,
who had until then only brewed ale, started
brewing the dark stuff to get a jump on all
other Irish brewers. By 1799 he decided
to concentrate all his efforts on this single
brew. He died four years later, aged 83, but
the foundations for world domination were
already in place.

Dublin Crawl Walking Tour

If there's one constant, it's that Dubliners will always take a drink. Come hell or high water, the city's pubs will never be short of customers.

Start Lower Camden St
Distance 2.5km
Duration One hour to two days

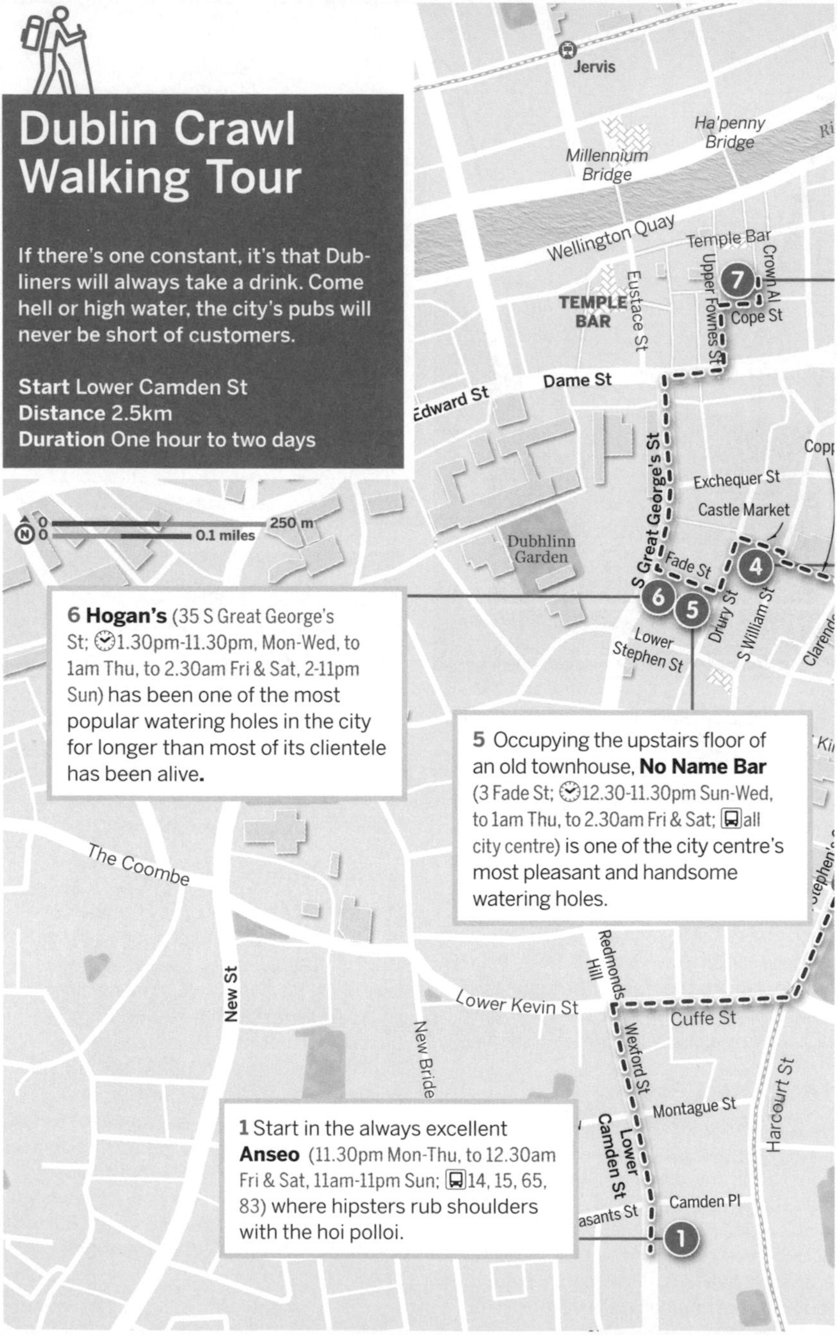

N
0   250 m
0   0.1 miles

Jervis

Ha'penny Bridge

Millennium Bridge

Wellington Quay

Temple Bar

Crown Al

7

Cope St

TEMPLE BAR

Eustace St

Upper Fowles St

Dame St

Edward St

Copp

S Great George's St

Exchequer St

Castle Market

Dubhlinn Garden

Fade St

4

6 Hogan's (35 S Great George's St; ☺1.30pm-11.30pm, Mon-Wed, to 1am Thu, to 2.30am Fri & Sat, 2-11pm Sun) has been one of the most popular watering holes in the city for longer than most of its clientele has been alive.

6 **5**

Lower Stephen St

Drury St

S William St

Clarend

Kil

The Coombe

5 Occupying the upstairs floor of an old townhouse, **No Name Bar** (3 Fade St; ☺12.30-11.30pm Sun-Wed, to 1am Thu, to 2.30am Fri & Sat; ⊟all city centre) is one of the city centre's most pleasant and handsome watering holes.

New St

New Bride

Redmonds Hill

Lower Kevin St

Cuffe St

Wexford St

Montague St

Harcourt St

Lower Camden St

1 Start in the always excellent **Anseo** (11.30pm Mon-Thu, to 12.30am Fri & Sat, 11am-11pm Sun; ⊟14, 15, 65, 83) where hipsters rub shoulders with the hoi polloi.

asants St

Camden Pl

1

7 Finally, ring the doorbell to access the **Vintage Cocktail Club** (www. vintagecocktailclub.com; Crown Alley; ☺5pm-1.30am Mon-Fri, 12.30pm-1.30am Sat & Sun; 🚌all city centre) If you've followed the tour correctly, you might not be able to find it. How many fingers?

Classic Photo: Grogan's Castle Lounge

4 Discuss the merits of that un-written masterpiece with a clutch of frustrated writers in **Grogan's Castle Lounge** (p75)

2 Become a character in *Mad Men* at the whiskey bar at trendy **37 Dawson St** (☎01-902 2908; www.37dawsonstreet.ie ☺10.30am-11.30pm Mon-Thu, to 12.30am Fri & Sat, noon-11pm Sun; 🚌all city centre)

3 Sink a glorious pint of plain (Guinness) in the atmospheric snug at **Kehoe's** (p75)

◉ SIGHTS

◉ Grafton St & Around

Little Museum of Dublin   Museum
(Map p64; ☑01-661 1000; www.littlemuseum.
ie; 15 St Stephen's Green N; adult/student €8/6;
⊙9.30am-5pm Mon-Wed & Fri, to 8pm Thu;
🚌all city centre, 🚋St Stephen's Green) This
award-winning museum tells the story of
Dublin over the last century via memorabilia, photographs and artefacts donated
by the general public. The impressive
collection, spread over the rooms of a
handsome Georgian house, includes a
lectern used by JFK on his 1963 visit to
Ireland and an original copy of the fateful
letter given to the Irish envoys to the treaty negotiations of 1921, whose contradic-
tory instructions were at the heart of the
split that resulted in the Civil War.

National Gallery   Museum
(Map p64; www.nationalgallery.ie; W Merrion Sq;
⊙9.15am-5.30pm Mon-Wed, Fri & Sat, to 8.30pm
Thu, 11am-5.30pm Sun; 🚌4, 7, 8, 46A from city
centre) FREE A magnificent Caravaggio and
a breathtaking collection of works by Jack

B Yeats – William Butler's younger brother
– are the main reasons to visit the National
Gallery, but not the only ones. Its excellent
collection is strong in Irish art, and there
are also high-quality collections of every
major European school of painting.

Museum of Natural History   Museum
(National Museum of Ireland – Natural History;
Map p64; www.museum.ie; Upper Merrion St;
⊙10am-5pm Tue-Sat, 2-5pm Sun; 🚌7, 44 from
city centre) FREE Dusty, weird and utterly
compelling, this window into Victorian times
has barely changed since Scottish explorer
Dr David Livingstone opened it in 1857 –
before disappearing into the African jungle
for a meeting with Henry Stanley. It is a fine
example of Victorian charm and scientific
wonderment, and its enormous collection is
a testament to the skill of taxidermy.

◉ Temple Bar

You can visit all of Temple Bar's attractions
in less than half a day, but that's not really
the point: this cobbled neighbourhood, for

St Patrick's Cathedral and Park

DAVID SOANES PHOTOGRAPHY/GETTY IMAGES ©

so long the city's most infamous party zone, is more about ambience than attractions. If you visit during the day, the district's bohemian bent is on display. Browse for vintage clothes, get your nipples pierced, nibble on Mongolian barbecue, buy organic food, pick up the latest musical releases and buy books on every conceivable subject. You can check out the latest art installations or join in a pulsating drum circle. By night – or at the weekend – it's a different story altogether, as the area's bars are packed to the rafters with revellers looking to tap into their inner Bacchus. It's loud, raucous and a lot of fun.

Christ Church Cathedral Church

(Church of the Holy Trinity; Map p64; www.
christchurchcathedral.ie; Christ Church Pl; adult/
student/child €6.50/4/2.50, with Dublinia
€14.50/12/7.50; ⏾9am-5pm Mon-Sat, 12.30
2.30pm Sun year-round, longer hours Mar-Oct;
🚍50, 50A, 56A from Aston Quay, 54, 54A from
Burgh Quay) Its hilltop location and eye-catching flying buttresses make this the most photogenic of Dublin's cathedrals. It was founded in 1030 and rebuilt from 1172, mostly under the impetus of Richard de Clare, Earl of Pembroke (better known as Strongbow), the Anglo-Norman noble who invaded Ireland in 1170 and whose monument has pride of place inside.

Guided tours (adult/family €4/12;
⏾12.10pm, 2pm & 4pm Mon-Fri, 2pm, 3pm & 4pm
Sat) include the belfry, where a campanologist explains the art of bell-ringing and you can even have a go.

From the main entrance, a bridge, part of the 1871–78 restoration, leads to **Dublinia** (📞01-679 4611; www.dublinia.ie; adult/student/
child €9.50/8.50/6, with Christchurch Cathedral
€14.50/12/7.50; 10am-5.30pm Mar-Sep, to 4.30pm
Oct-Feb) a lively and kitschy attempt to bring Viking and medieval Dublin to life

◉ Kilmainham & The Liberties

St Patrick's Cathedral Cathedral

(Map p64; www.stpatrickscathedral.ie; St Patrick's Close; adult/child €6.50/free; ⏾9.30am-
5pm Mon-Fri, 9am-6pm Sat, 9-10.30am &
12.30-2.30pm Sun; 🚍50, 50A, 56A from Aston

The Spire

The city's most visible landmark, **the Spire** (Map p74; O'Connell St, 🚍all city centre, 🚇Abbey) soars over O'Connell St and is an impressive bit of architectural engineering that was erected in 2001: from a base only 3m in diameter, it soars more than 120m into the sky and tapers into a 15cm-wide beam of light... it's tall and shiny and it does the trick rather nicely.

The brainchild of London-based architect Ian Ritchie, it is apparently the highest sculpture in the world, but much like the Parisian reaction to the construction of the Eiffel Tower, Dubliners are divided as to its aesthetic value and have regularly made fun of it. Among other names, we like 'the erection in the intersection', the 'stiletto in the ghetto', and the altogether brilliant 'eyeful tower'.

DAVID SOANES/SHUTTERSTOCK ©

Quay, 54, 54A from Burgh Quay) Ireland's largest church is St Patrick's Cathedral, built between 1191 and 1270 on the site of an earlier church that had stood here since the 5th century. It was here that St Patrick himself reputedly baptised the local Celtic chieftains, making this bit of ground some fairly sacred turf: the well in question is in the adjacent **St Patrick's Park**, which was once a slum but is now a lovely spot to sit and take a load off.

Temple Bar, Grafton St & St Stephen's Green

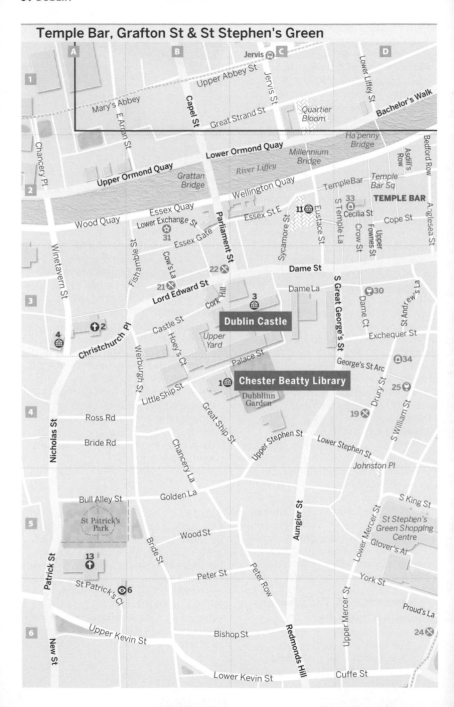

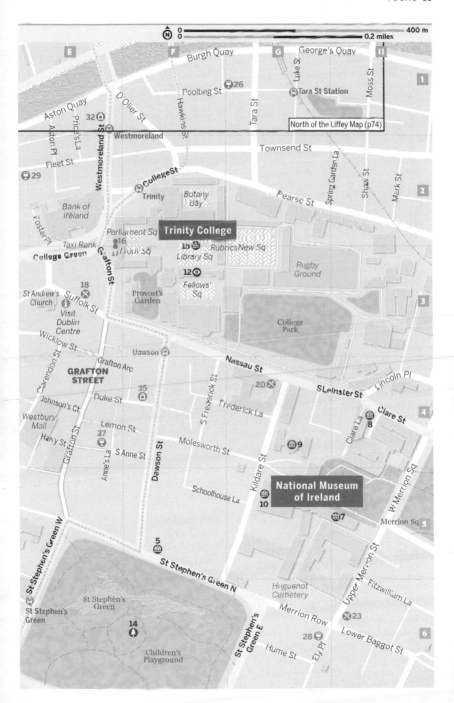

Temple Bar, Grafton St & St Stephen's Green

Irish Museum of Modern Art
Museum

(IMMA; Map p68; www.imma.ie; Military Rd; ◷11.30am-5.30pm Tue-Fri, 10am-5.30pm Sat, noon-5.30pm Sun, tours 1.15pm Wed, 2.30pm Sat & Sun; ⊟51, 51D, 51X, 69, 78, 79 from Aston Quay, ⊟Heuston) **FREE** Ireland's most important collection of modern and contemporary Irish and international art is housed in the elegant expanse of the Royal Hospital Kilmainham, designed by Sir William Robinson and built between 1684 and 1687 as a retirement home for soldiers. It fulfilled this role until 1928, after which it languished for nearly 50 years until a 1980s restoration saw it come back to life as a wonderful repository of art.

⊚ North of the Liffey

Dublin City Gallery – the Hugh Lane
Gallery

(Map p74; ☏01-222 5550; www.hughlane.ie; 22 N Parnell Sq; ◷9.45am-6pm Tue-Thu, to 5pm Fri & Sat, 11am-5pm Sun; ⊟7, 11, 13, 16, 38, 40, 46A, 123 from city centre) **FREE** Whatever reputation Dublin has as a repository of world-class art has a lot to do with the simply stunning collection at this exquisite gallery, housed in the equally impressive Charlemont House, designed by William Chambers in 1763. Within its walls you'll find the best of contemporary Irish art, a handful of Impressionist classics and Francis Bacon's relocated studio.

Old Jameson Distillery
Museum

(Map p68; www.jamesonwhiskey.com; Bow St; adult/student/child €18/15/9, masterclasses €55; ◷10am-5pm Mon-Sat, 10.30am-5pm Sun; ⊟25, 66, 67, 90 from city centre, ⊟Smithfield) Smithfield's biggest draw is devoted to *uisce beatha* (ish-kuh ba-ha, 'the water of life'); that's Irish for whiskey. To its more serious devotees, that is precisely what whiskey is, although they may be put off by the slickness of this museum (occupying part of the old distillery that stopped production in 1971), which shepherds visitors through a compulsory tour of the recreated factory (the tasting at the end is a lot of fun) and into the ubiquitous gift shop.

TOURS

Fab Food Trails — Walking

(☏01-497 1245 www.fabfoodtrails.ie; tours €55; ☺10am Sat) Highly recommended 2½-hour tasting walks through the city centre's choicest independent producers. You'll visit up to eight bakeries, cheesemongers, markets and delis, learning about the food culture of each neighbourhood you explore. There is also a Coffee Walk (exploring the best artisanal coffee shops) and a Food and Fashion walk. You meet in the city centre.

Green Mile — Walking

(Map p64; ☏01-661 1000; www.littlemuseum.ie; Little Museum of Dublin, 15 St Stephen's Green N; adult/student €7/5; ☺11am Sat & Sun; ☐all city centre, ☐St Stephen's Green) Excellent one-hour tour of St Stephen's Green led by local historian Donal Fallon. Along the way you'll hear tales of James Joyce, the park's history and the drafting of the Irish Constitution. Book ahead as tours fill up pretty quickly. The tour also includes admission to and a guided tour of the Little Museum of Dublin (p62).

Historical Walking Tour — Walking

(Map p64; ☏01-878 0227; www.historicaltours.ie; Trinity College Gate; adult/student/child €12/10/free; ☺11am & 3pm May-Sep, 11am Apr & Oct, 11am Fri-Sun Nov Mar; ☐all city centre) Trinity College history graduates lead this 'seminar on the street' that explores the Potato Famine, Easter Rising, Civil War and Partition. Sights include Trinity, City Hall, Dublin Castle and Four Courts. In summer, themed tours on architecture, women in Irish history and the birth of the Irish state are also held. Tours depart from the College Green entrance.

 Literary Dublin

Marsh's Library (Map p64; www.marshlibrary.ie; St Patrick's Close; adult/child €3/free; ☺9.30am-5pm Mon & Wed-Fri, 10am-5pm Sat; ☐50, 50A, 56A from Aston Quay, 54, 54A from Burgh Quay) This magnificently preserved scholars' library is one of Dublin's most beautiful open secrets. Atop its ancient stairs are beautiful, dark-oak bookcases, each topped with elaborately carved and gilded gables, and crammed with 25,000 books, manuscripts and maps dating back to the 15th century.

National Library (Map p64; www.nli.ie; Kildare St; ☺9.30am-7.45pm Mon-Wed, to 4.45pm Thu & Fri, 9.30am-12.45pm Sat; ☐all city centre) Suitably sedate and elegant, the National Library's extensive collection has many valuable early manuscripts, first editions and maps. Some areas are open to the public, including the domed reading room where Stephen Dedalus expounded his views on Shakespeare in James Joyce's *Ulysses*.

Dublin Writers Museum (Map p74; www.writersmuseum.com; 18 N Parnell Sq; adult/child €8/5; ☺9.45am-4.45pm Mon-Sat, 11am-4.30pm Sun; ☐3, 7, 10, 11, 13, 16, 19, 46A, 123 from city centre) Memorabilia aplenty and lots of literary ephemera line the walls and display cabinets of this elegant museum devoted to preserving the city's rich literary tradition up to 1970.

Central Dublin

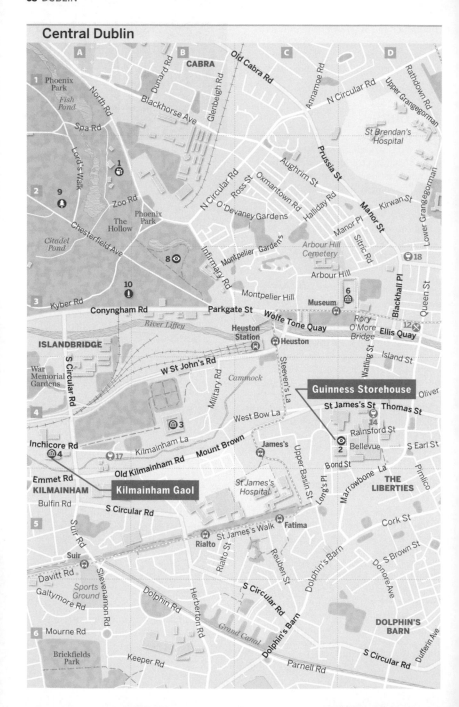

A **B** **C** **D**

1 Phoenix Park
Fish Pond
North Rd
CABRA
Old Cabra Rd
Annamoe Rd
N Circular Rd
Rathdown Rd
Upper Grangegorman

Dunard Rd
Blackhorse Ave
Glenbeigh Rd
St Brendan's Hospital

Spa Rd
Prussia St
Lower Grangegorman

Lord's Walk
Aughrim St

2 9
Zoo Rd
N Circular Rd
Ross St
Oxmantown Rd
Halliday Rd
Manor St
Kirwan St

Phoenix Park
The Hollow
O'Devaney Gardens
Manor Pl
Sitric Rd

Citadel Pond
Chesterfield Ave
8
Infirmary Rd
Montpelier Gardens
Arbour Hill Cemetery
Blackhall Pl
Queen St
18

Arbour Hill

3 Kyber Rd
Conyngham Rd
10
Montpelier Hill
Parkgate St
Montpelier Hill
Museum
6
Wolfe Tone Quay
Rory O'More Bridge
Ellis Quay
12

River Liffey
Heuston Station
Heuston

ISLANDBRIDGE
Island St

War Memorial Gardens
S Circular Rd
W St John's Rd
Military Rd
Cammock
Steeven's La
Watling St
Oliver

Guinness Storehouse

4
West Bow La
St James's St
Thomas St

3
14

Inchicore Rd
4
17
Kilmainham La
Mount Brown
James's
Rainsford St
Bellevue
S Earl St

Emmet Rd
KILMAINHAM
Old Kilmainham Rd
Upper Basin St
Bond St
THE LIBERTIES
Pimlico

Kilmainham Gaol
St James's Hospital
Long's Pl
Marrowbone La

Bulfin Rd
S Circular Rd

5 Suir Rd
Rialto
St James's Walk
Fatima
Cork St
S Brown St

Suir
Rialto St
Reuben St
Dolphin's Barn
S Brown St

Davitt Rd
Sports Ground
Slievenamon Rd
Dolphin Rd
Herberton Rd
S Circular Rd
Donore Ave

Galtymore Rd

6 Mourne Rd
Keeper Rd
Grand Canal
Dolphin's Barn
Parnell Rd
S Circular Rd
DOLPHIN'S BARN
Dufferin Ave

Brickfields Park

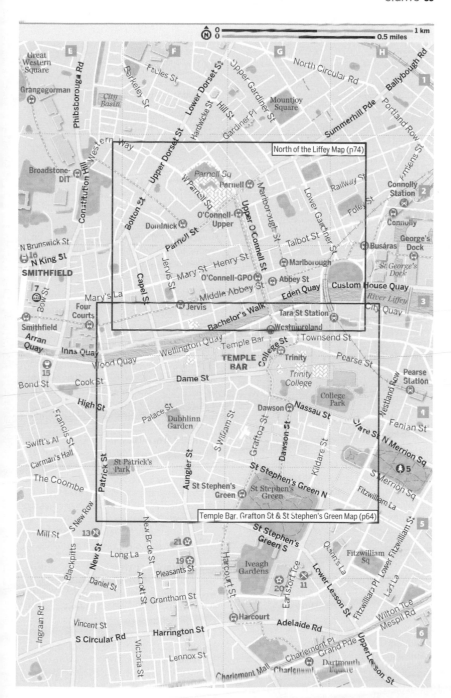

Central Dublin

Dublin Musical Pub Crawl Walking
(Map p64; ☑01-478 0193; www.discoverdublin.ie;
58-59 Fleet St; adult/student €14/12; ⊙7.30pm
daily Apr-Oct, 7.30pm Thu-Sat Nov-Mar; ▣all city
centre) The story of Irish traditional music
and its influence on contemporary styles is
explained and demonstrated by two expert
musicians in a number of Temple Bar pubs
over 2½ hours. Tours meet upstairs in the
Oliver St John Gogarty (Map p64; www.
gogartys.ie; ⊙10.30am-11.30pm Mon-Thu, to
12.30am Fri & Sat, noon-11pm Sun) pub and are
highly recommended.

🔒 SHOPPING

If it's made in Ireland – or pretty much
anywhere else – you can find it in Dublin.
Grafton St is home to a range of largely
British-owned high-street chain stores;
you'll find the best local boutiques in the
surrounding streets. On the north side,
pedestrianised Henry St has international chain stores, as well as Dublin's best
department store, Arnott's.

Avoca Handweavers Arts & Crafts
(Map p64; ☑01-677 4215; www.avoca.ie; 11-13
Suffolk St; ⊙9.30am-6pm Mon-Wed & Sat, to
7pm Thu & Fri, 11am-6pm Sun; ▣all city centre)
Combining clothing, homewares, a base-
ment food hall and an excellent top-floor
cafe (Map p64; mains €9-16; ⊙9.30am-5.30pm
Mon-Wed & Sat, to 7pm Thu & Fri, 11am-6pm Sun),
Avoca promotes a stylish but homey brand

of modern Irish life – and is one of the best
places to find an original present. Many of
the garments are woven, knitted and natu-
rally dyed at its Wicklow factory. There's a
terrific kids' section.

Irish Design Shop Arts & Crafts
(Map p64; ☑01-679 8871; www.irishdesignshop.
com; 41 Drury St; ⊙10am-6pm Mon-Wed, Fri &
Sat, to 7pm Thu, 1-5pm Sun; ▣all city centre)
Beautiful, imaginatively crafted items – from
jewellery to kitchenware – carefully curated
by owners Clare Grennan and Laura Caffrey.
If you're looking for a stylish, Irish-made
memento or gift, you'll surely find it here.

Ulysses Rare Books Books
(Map p64; ☑01-671 8676; www.rarebooks.ie; 10
Duke St; ⊙9.30am-5.45pm Mon-Sat; ▣all city centre) Our favourite bookshop in the city stocks
a rich and remarkable collection of Irish-
interest books, with a particular emphasis on
20th-century literature and a large selection
of first editions, including rare ones by the
big guns: Joyce, Yeats, Beckett and Wilde.

Claddagh Records Music
(Map p64; ☑01-677 0262; www.claddagh
records.com; 2 Cecilia St; ⊙10am-6pm Mon-Sat,
noon-6pm Sun; ▣all city centre) An excellent
collection of good-quality traditional and
folk music is the mainstay at this centrally
located record shop. The profoundly
knowledgeable staff should be able to
locate even the most elusive recording

for you. There's also a decent selection of world music. There's another **branch** (Map p64; ☎01-888 3600; 5 Westmoreland St; ☺10am-6pm Mon-Sat, noon-6pm Sun; 🚌all city centre) on Westmoreland St; you can also shop online.

🍴 EATING

🍴 Grafton St & Around

Silk Road Café Middle Eastern €

(Map p64; Chester Beatty Library, Dublin Castle; mains €12; ☺10am-4.45pm Mon-Fri, 11am-4.45pm Sat & Sun May-Oct, Library closed Mon Nov-Apr; 🚌50, 51B, 77, 78A, 123) This vaguely Middle Eastern–North African–Mediterranean gem on the ground floor of the Chester Beatty Library (p46) is no ordinary museum cafe. Complementing house specialities including Greek moussaka and spinach lasagne are daily specials such as *djaj mehshi* (chicken stuffed with spices, rice, dried fruit, almonds and pine nuts). All dishes are halal and kosher.

Queen of Tarts Cafe €

(Map p64; ☎01-670 7499; www.queenoftarts. ie; 4 Cork Hill; mains €5-10; ☺8am-8pm Mon-Fri, 8.30am-8pm Sat, 9am-7pm Sun; 🚌all city centre) This cute little cake shop does a fine line in tarts, meringues, crumbles, cookies and brownies, not to mention a decent breakfast: the smoked bacon and leek potato cakes with eggs and cherry tomatoes are excellent. There's another, bigger, branch around the corner on **Cow's Lane** (Map p64; 3-4 Cow's Lane; mains €5-10; ☺8am-8pm Mon-Fri, 8.30am-8pm Sat, 9am 7pm Sun; 🚌all city centre).

Coburg Brasserie French €€

(Map p68; ☎01-602 8900; www.thecoburgdublin. com; Conrad International, Earlsfort Tce; mains €11-18; 🚌all city centre) The French-inspired cuisine at this revamped hotel brasserie puts the emphasis on shellfish: the all-day menu offers oysters, mussels and a range of 'casual' lobster dishes, from lobster rolls to lobster cocktail. The bouillabaisse is chock full of sea flavours, and you can also get a shrimp burger and a fine plate of Connemara whiskey-cured organic salmon. Top-notch.

Irish Design Shop

Top Five Dublin Restaurants

Restaurant Patrick Guilbaud

Chapter One

Shanahan's on the Green

Winding Stair (p75)

Fade Street Social

From left: Winding Stair (p75); Queen of Tarts (p71);
Restaurant Patrick Guillbaud

Fade Street Social   Modern Irish €€

(Map p64; ☏01-604 0066; www.fadestreet
social.com; 4-6 Fade St; mains €18-32, tapas
€5-12; ☺12.30-10.30pm Mon-Fri, 5-10.30pm Sat
& Sun; ☎; ▣all city centre) ✐ Two eateries
in one, courtesy of renowned chef Dylan
McGrath: at the front, the buzzy tapas
bar, which serves up gourmet bites from
a beautiful open kitchen. At the back, the
more muted restaurant specialises in Irish
cuts of meat – from veal to rabbit – served
with home-grown, organic vegetables.
There's a bar upstairs, too. Reservations
suggested.

Pig's Ear   Modern Irish €€

(Map p64; ☏01-670 3865; www.thepigsear.com;
4 Nassau St; mains €18-28; ☺noon-2.45pm &
5.30-10pm Mon-Sat; ▣all city centre) Looking
over the playing fields of Trinity College,
this fashionably formal restaurant is
spread over two floors and is renowned for
its exquisite and innovative Irish cuisine,
including dishes such as barbecued pork
belly, short rib of Irish beef and a superb
slow-cooked Lough Erne shepherd's pie.

Restaurant Patrick Guilbaud   French €€€

(Map p64; ☏01-676 4192; www.restaurantpatrick
guilbaud.ie; 21 Upper Merrion St; 2-/3-course set
lunch €50/60, dinner menu €90-185; ☺12.30-
2.30pm & 7.30-10.30pm Tue-Sat; ▣7, 46 from
city centre) Ireland's only Michelin two-star
is understandably considered the best in
the country by its devotees, who proclaim
Guillaume Lebrun's French haute cuisine
the most exalted expression of the culinary
arts. If you like formal dining, this is as good
as it gets: the lunch menu is an absolute
steal, at least in this stratosphere. Innovative and beautifully presented.

Shanahan's on the Green   Steak €€€

(Map p64; ☏01-407 0939; www.shanahans.ie; 119
St Stephen's Green W; mains €42-49; ☺6-10pm
Sat-Thu, noon-10pm Fri; ▣all city centre, ☒St
Stephen's Green) You could order seafood or a
plate of vegetables, but you'd be missing the
point of this supremely elegant steakhouse:
the finest cuts of juicy and tender Irish Angus
beef you'll find anywhere. The ambience is
upscale Americana – the bar downstairs is

LONELY PLANET/GETTY IMAGES ©

called the Oval Office and pride of place goes to a rocking chair owned by JFK.

Kilmainham & The Liberties

1837 Bar & Brasserie Brasserie €
(Map p68; ☎01-471 4602; www.guinness-store house.com; Guinness Storehouse, St James's Gate; mains €9-14; ☺noon-3pm; ☒21A, 51B, 78, 78A, 123 from Fleet St, ☒James's) This lunchtime brasserie serves up tasty dishes, from really fresh oysters to an insanely good Guinness burger, with skin-on fries and red-onion chutney. The drinks menu features a range of Guinness variants such as West Indian porter and Golden Ale. Highly recommended for lunch if you're visiting the museum.

Fumbally Cafe €
(Map p68; ☎01-529 8732; www.thefumbally.ie; Fumbally Lane; mains €5-9.50; ☺8am-5pm Tue-Fri, 10am-5pm Sat, plus 7-9.30pm Wed; ☒49, 54A from city centre) A bright, airy warehouse cafe that serves healthy breakfasts, salads and sandwiches – while the occasional guitarist strums away in the corner. Its Wednesday dinner (mains €16) is an organic, locally

sourced exploration of the cuisines of the world that includes a single dish (and its vegetarian variant) served in a communal dining experience; advance bookings suggested.

North of the Liffey

Oxmantown Cafe €
(Map p74; www.oxmantown.com; 16 Mary's Abbey, City Markets; sandwiches €5.50; ☺7.30am-4pm Mon-Fri; ☒Four Courts, Jervis) Delicious breakfasts and excellent sandwiches make this cafe one of the standout places for daytime eating on the north side of the Liffey. Locally baked bread, coffee supplied by Cloud Picker (Dublin's only microroastery) and meats sourced from Irish farms are the ingredients, but it's the way it's all put together that makes it so worthwhile.

Chapter One Modern Irish €€€
(Map p74; ☎01-873 2266; www.chapterone restaurant.com; 18 N Parnell Sq; 2-course lunch €32.50, 4-course dinner €75; ☺12.30-2pm Tue-Fri, 7.30-10.30pm Tue-Sat; ☒3, 10, 11, 13, 16, 19, 22 from city centre) Flawless haute cuisine and a

North of the Liffey

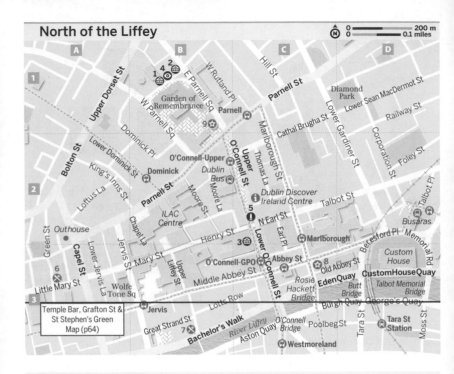

North of the Liffey

relaxed, welcoming atmosphere make this Michelin-starred restaurant in the basement of the Dublin Writers Museum our choice for best dinner experience in town. The food is French-inspired contemporary Irish, the menus change regularly and the service is top-notch. The three-course pre-theatre menu (€39.50) is great if you're going to the **Gate Theatre** (Map p74; ☎01-874 4045; www. gatetheatre.ie; 1 Cavendish Row; ⊗performances 7.30pm Mon-Sat, 2.30pm Wed; ☒all city centre) around the corner.

Fish Shop   Seafood €€
(Map p68; ☎01-430 8594; www.fish-shop.ie; 6 Queen St; 4-course/tasting menu €39/55; ⊗noon-2.30pm & 5-10pm Wed-Fri, 5-10pm Tue & Sat; ☒25, 25A, 66, 67 from city centre, ☒Smithfield) The menu changes daily at this tiny restaurant (it has only 16 seats) to reflect what's good and fresh, but you'll have to trust them: your only choice is a four-course or tasting menu. One day you might fancy line-caught mackerel with a green sauce, another day slip sole with caper butter. Maybe the best seafood restaurant in town.

Winding Stair   Modern Irish €€

(Map p74; ☑01 873 7320; www.winding-stair.com:
40 Lower Ormond Quay, 2-course lunch €22, mains
€22 28; ⏰noon 5pm & 5.30-10.30pm; ☐all city
centre) In a beautiful Georgian building that
once housed the city's most beloved bookshop – now the **Winding Stair Bookshop**
(Map p74; ☑01-872 6576; ⏰10am-6pm Mon-Wed
& Fri, to 7pm Thu & Sat, noon 6pm Sun) on the
ground floor – the Winding Stair's conversion
to elegant restaurant has been faultless. The
wonderful Irish menu (creamy fish pie, bacon
and organic cabbage, steamed mussels,
and Irish farmyard cheeses) coupled with an
excellent wine list makes for a memorable
meal.

🍸 DRINKING & NIGHTLIFE

🍺 Grafton St & Around

O'Donoghue's   Pub

(Map p64; www.odonoghues.ie; 15 Merrion Row;
⏰10.30am-11.30pm Mon-Thu, to 12.30am Fri & Sat,
noon-11pm Sun; ☐all city centre) The pub where
traditional music stalwarts The Dubliners
made their name in the 1960s still hosts live
music nightly, but the crowds would gather
anyway – for the excellent pints and superb
ambience in the old bar or the covered coach
yard next to it.

Grogan's Castle Lounge   Pub

(Map p64; www.groganspub.ie; 15 S William St;
⏰10.30am-11.30pm Mon-Thu, to 12.30am Fri &
Sat, 12.30-11pm Sun; ☐all city centre) Known
simply as Grogan's (after the original owner),
this city-centre institution has long been a
favourite haunt of Dublin's writers and paint-
ers, as well as others from the alternative
bohemian set, who enjoy fine Guinness while
they wait to be discovered.

Kehoe's   Pub

(Map p64; 9 S Anne St; ⏰10.30am-11.30pm Mon-
Thu, to 12.30am Fri & Sat, noon-11pm Sun; ☐all city
centre) This is the very exemplar of a traditional Dublin pub. The beautiful Victorian bar,
wonderful snug and side room have been
popular for Dubliners and visitors for generations, so much so that the publican's living
quarters upstairs have since been converted

into an extension – simply by taking out the
furniture and adding a bar.

Stag's Head   Pub

(Map p64; www.louisfitzgerald.com/stagshead;
1 Dame Ct; ⏰10.30am-1am Mon-Sat, to midnight
Sun; ☐all city centre) The Stag's Head was
built in 1770, remodelled in 1895 and
thankfully not changed a bit since then. It's
a superb pub: so picturesque that it often
appears in films and also featured in a post-
age-stamp series on Irish bars. A bloody
great pub, no doubt about it.

John Mulligan's   Pub

(Map p64; www.mulligans.io; 8 Poolbeg St;
⏰10.30am-11.30pm Mon-Thu, to 12.30am Fri
& Sat, noon-11pm Sun; ☐all city centre) This
brilliant old boozer is a cultural institution,
established in 1782 and in this location since
1854. A drink (or more) here is like attending
liquid services at a most sacred, secular
shrine. John F Kennedy paid his respects in
1945, when he joined the cast of regulars
that seems barely to have changed since.

🍺 Kilmainham & The Liberties

Old Royal Oak   Pub

(Map p68; 11 Kilmainham Lane; ⏰10.30am-
11.30pm Mon-Thu, to 12.30am Fri & Sat, noon-11pm
Sun; ☐68, 79 from city centre) Locals are fierce-
ly protective of this gorgeous traditional pub,
which opened in 1845 to serve the patrons
and staff of the Royal Hospital (now the Irish
Museum of Modern Art). The clientele has
changed, but everything else has remained
the same, which makes this one of the nicest
pubs in the city in which to enjoy a few pints.

Arthur's   Pub

(Map p68; ☑01-402 0914; www.arthurspub.
ie; 28 Thomas St; ⏰noon-11.30pm Mon-Thu,
11am-12.30am Fri & Sat, 11am-11pm Sun; ☐21A,
51D, 78, 78A, 123 from Fleet St, ☐James's) Given
its location, Arthur's could easily be a
cheesy tourist trap, and plenty of Guinness
Storehouse (p58) visitors do pass through
the doors tempted by another taste of
the black stuff. Instead it's a friendly, cosy
bar with a menu full of good comfort food.
Best visited in the winter so you get the

full benefit of the roaring fireplace and soft candlelight.

Brazen Head   Pub

(Map p68; ☑01-679 5186; www.brazenhead.com; 20 Lower Bridge St; ☺10am-midnight Mon-Thu, 10am-12.30am Fri & Sat, 11am-midnight Sun; ☐51B, 78A, 123 from city centre) Reputedly Dublin's oldest pub, the Brazen Head has been serving thirsty patrons since 1198 when it set up as a Norman tavern. It's a bit away from the city centre, and the clientele consists of foreign-language students, tourists and some grizzly auld locals.

🔘 North of the Liffey

Cobblestone   Pub

(Map p68; www.cobblestonepub.ie; N King St; ☺4.30-11.30pm Mon-Thu, to 12.30am Fri & Sat, 1.30-11.30pm Sun; ☐Smithfield) It advertises itself as a 'drinking pub with a music problem', which is an apt description for this Smithfield stalwart – although the trad music sessions that run throughout the week can hardly be described as problematic. Wednesday's Balaclava session (from 7.30pm) is for any musician who is learning an instrument, with musician Síomha Mulligan on hand to teach.

Walshe's   Pub

(Map p68; 6 Stoneybatter; ☺10.30am-11.30pm Mon-Thu, to 12.30am Fri & Sat, noon-11pm Sun; ☐25, 25A, 66, 67 from city centre, ☐Museum) If the snug is free, a drink in Walshe's is about as pure a traditional experience as you'll have in any pub in the city; if it isn't, you'll have to make do with the old-fashioned bar, where the friendly staff and brilliant clientele (a mix of locals and trendsetting imports) are a treat. A proper Dublin pub.

✪ ENTERTAINMENT

Believe it or not, there is life beyond the pub. There are comedy clubs and classical concerts, recitals and readings, marionettes and music – lots of music. The other great Dublin treat is the theatre, where you can enjoy a light-hearted musical alongside

the more serious stuff by Beckett, Yeats and O'Casey – not to mention a host of new talents.

O'Donoghue's   Traditional Music

(Map p64; ☑01-660 7194; www.odonoghues.ie; 15 Merrion Row; ☺from 7pm; ☐all city centre) There's traditional music nightly in the old bar of this famous boozer. Regular performers include local names such as Tom Foley, Joe McHugh, Joe Foley and Maria O'Connell.

Devitt's   Live Music

(Map p68; ☑01-475 3414; www.devittspub. ie; 78 Lower Camden St; ☺from 9pm Thu-Sat; ☐14, 15, 65, 83) Devitt's – aka the Cusack Stand – is one of the favourite places for the city's talented musicians to display their wares, with sessions as good as any you'll hear in the city centre. Highly recommended.

Whelan's   Live Music

(Map p68; ☑01-478 0766; www.whelanslive. com; 25 Wexford St; ☐16, 122 from city centre) Perhaps the city's most beloved live-music venue is this midsize room attached to a traditional bar. This is the singer-songwriter's spiritual home: when they're done pouring out the contents of their hearts on stage, you can find them in the bar along with their fans.

National Concert Hall   Live Music

(Map p68; ☑01-417 0000; www.nch.ie; Earlsfort Tce; ☐all city centre) Ireland's premier orchestral hall hosts a variety of concerts year-round, including a series of lunchtime concerts from 1.05pm to 2pm on Tuesdays from June to August.

Smock Alley Theatre   Theatre

(Map p64; ☑01-677 0014; www.smockalley. com; 6-7 Exchange St) One of the city's most diverse theatres is hidden in this beautifully restored 17th-century building. It boasts a diverse program of events (expect anything from opera to murder mystery nights, puppet shows and Shakespeare) and many events also come with a dinner option.

Smock Alley Theatre

Abbey Theatre
Theatre

(Map p74; ☑01-878 7222; www.abbeytheatre.
ie; Lower Abbey St; ☐all city centre, ☐Abbey)
Ireland's national theatre was founded by
WB Yeats in 1904 and was a central player
in the development of a consciously native cultural identity. In 2017 it appointed
Neil Murray and Graham McLaren of the
National Theatre of Scotland as its new
directors, and they have provided an exciting new program that fuses traditional
and contemporary fare.

 INFORMATION

Visit Dublin Centre (Map p64; www.visitdublin.
com; 25 Suffolk St; ☺9am-5.30pm Mon-Sat,
10.30am-3pm Sun; ☐all city centre) The main
tourist information centre, with free maps,
guides and itinerary planning, plus booking
services for accommodation, attractions and
events.

🛈 GETTING THERE & AWAY

AIR

Located 13km north of the city centre, **Dublin Airport** (p300) has two terminals: most international
flights (including most US flights) use Terminal
2; Ryanair and select others use Terminal 1. Both
terminals have the usual selection of pubs, restaurants, shops, ATMs and car-hire desks.

BOAT

The **Dublin Port Terminal** (☑01-855 2222; Alex-
andra Rd; ☐53 from Talbot St) is 3km northeast of
the city centre.

BUS

Dublin's central bus station, **Busáras** (Map p74;
☑01-836 6111; www.buseireann.ie; Store St,
☐Connolly) is just north of the river behind the
Custom House.

CAR & MOTORCYCLE

All the main rental agencies are represented
in Dublin. Book in advance for the best fares,

especially at weekends and during summer months, when demand is highest.

Avis Rent-a-Car (☎01-605 7500; www.avis.ie; 35 Old Kilmainham Rd; ⊙8.30am-5.45pm Mon-Fri, 8.30am-2.30pm Sat & Sun; ⊟23, 25, 25A, 26, 68, 69 from city centre)

Budget Rent-a-Car (☎01-837 9611; www.budget. ie; 151 Lower Drumcondra Rd; ⊙9am-6pm; ⊟41 from O'Connell St)

Europcar (☎01-812 2800; www.europcar.ie; 1 Mark St; ⊙8am-6pm Mon-Fri, 8.30am-3pm Sat & Sun; ⊟all city centre)

Hertz Rent-a-Car (☎01-709 3060; www.hertz. com; 151 South Circular Rd; ⊙8.30am-5.30pm Mon-Fri, 9am-4.30pm Sat, 9am-3.30pm Sun; ⊟9, 16, 77, 79 from city centre)

Thrifty (☎01-844 1944; www.thrifty.ie; 26 Lombard St E; ⊙8am-6pm Mon-Fri, to 3pm Sat & Sun; ⊟all city centre)

TRAIN

All trains in the Republic are run by **Irish Rail** (p304). Dublin has two main train stations: **Heuston Station** (☎01-836 5421; ☒Heuston), on the western side of town near the Liffey; and **Connolly Station** (☎01-836 3333; ☒Connolly, ☒Connolly Station), a short walk northeast of Busáras, behind the Custom House.

GETTING AROUND

PUBLIC TRANSPORT

BUS

The **Dublin Bus Office** (Map p74; ☎01-873 4222; www.dublinbus.ie; 59 Upper O'Connell St; ⊙8.30am-5.30pm Tue-Fri, to 2pm Sat, 9am-5.30pm Mon; ⊟all city centre) has free single-route timetables for all its services. Buses run from around 6am (some start at 5.30am) to about 11.30pm.

TRAIN

The **Dublin Area Rapid Transport** (DART; ☎01-836 6222; www.irishrail.ie) provides quick train access to the coast as far north as Howth (about 30 minutes) and as far south as Greystones in County Wicklow. There are services every 10 to 20 minutes, sometimes more frequently, from around 6.30am to midnight Monday to Saturday. Services are less frequent on Sunday.

TRAM

The Luas (www.luas.ie) light-rail system has two lines: the green line (running every five to 15 minutes) connects St Stephen's Green with Sandyford in south Dublin via Ranelagh and Dundrum; the red line (every 20 minutes) runs from the Point Village to Tallaght via the north quays and Heuston Station.

From 2018, a new cross-city line will connect the green and red lines with a route from St Stephen's Green through Dawson St and around Trinity College and over the river.

TAXI

Numerous taxi companies, such as **National Radio Cabs** (☎01-677 2222; www.nrc.ie), dispatch taxis by radio. You can also try mytaxi (www. mytaxi.com), a taxi app.

Where to Stay

Dublin is always bustling, so book your accommodation well in advance, especially for weekend visits.

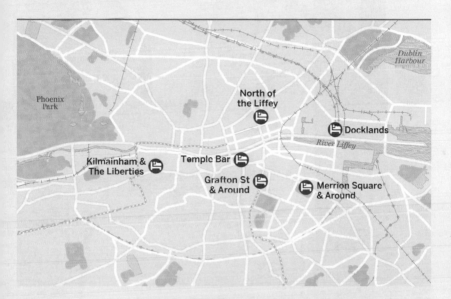

Neighbourhood	Atmosphere
Grafton St & Around	Close to sights, nightlife, etc; a good choice of midrange and top-end hotels. Not always good value for money and rooms tend to be smaller.
Merrion Square & Around	Lovely neighbourhood, elegant hotels and townhouse accommodation; some of the best restaurants in town. Not a lot of choice; virtually no budget accommodation.
Temple Bar	In the heart of the action, close to the party. Noisy and touristy; not especially good value for money.
Kilmainham & the Liberties	Close to the old city and the sights of west Dublin. No good accommodation; only a small selection of restaurants.
North of the Liffey	Good range of choices; within walking distance of sights and nightlife. Budget accommodation not always good quality.
Docklands	Excellent contemporary hotels with good service, including some top-end choices. Isolated in a quiet neighbourhood; reliant on taxis or public transport to get to city centre.
Southside	More bang for your buck; generally bigger rooms and properties with gardens. If not on the Luas line, bus transfers into town can take up valuable time.

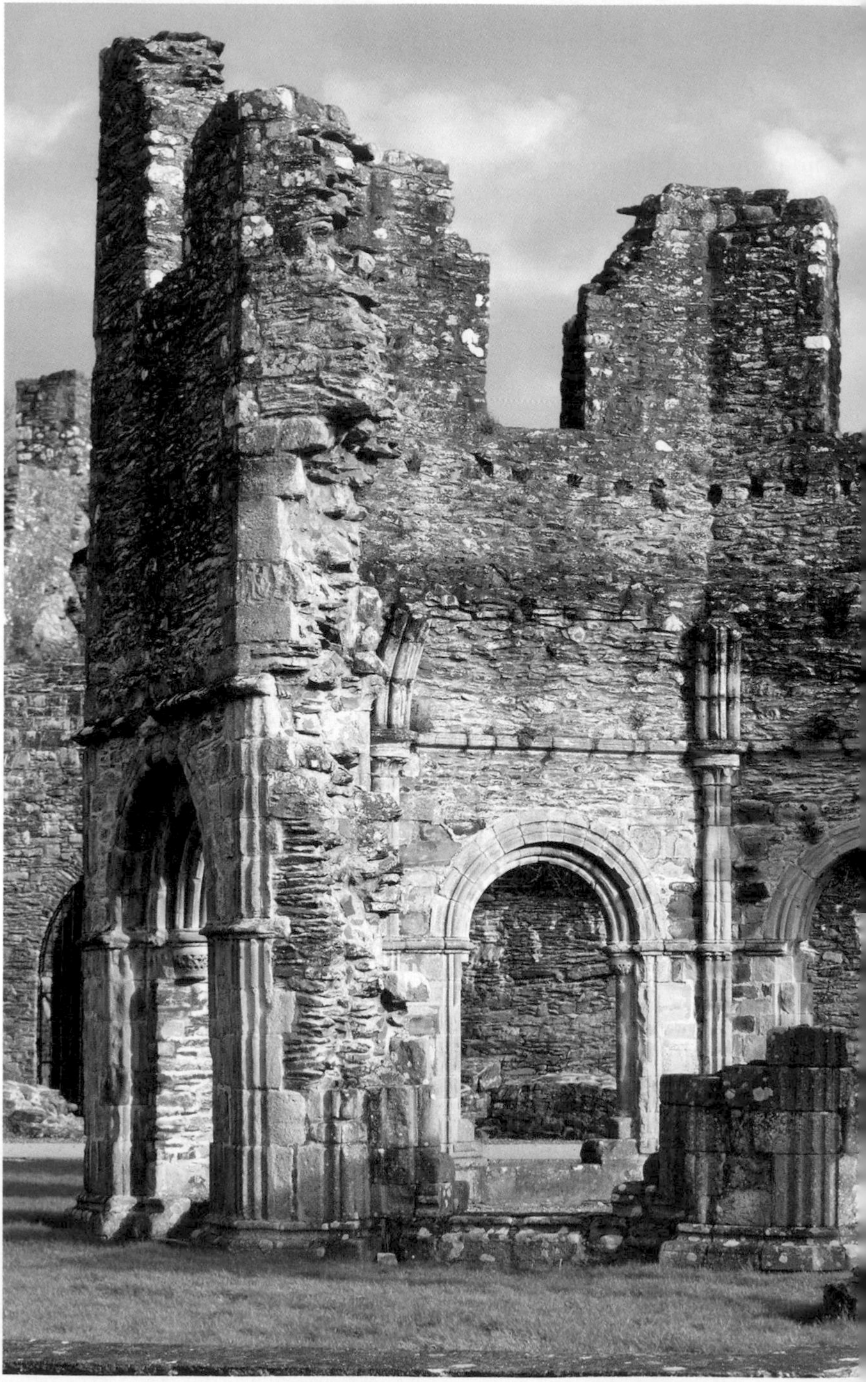

SPECTRUMBLUE/SHUTTERSTOCK ©

COUNTIES MEATH & LOUTH

Counties Meath & Louth at a Glance...

Meath's rich soil, laid down during the last ice age, drew settlers as early as 8000 BC. They worked their way up the banks of the River Boyne, transforming the landscape from forest to farmland. One of the five provinces of ancient Ireland, Meath was at the centre of Irish politics for centuries. Across the Boyne, Louth – Ireland's smallest county – was at the centre of ecclesiastical Ireland during the 5th and 6th centuries, with wealthy religious communities at the monastery at Monasterboice and the Cistercian abbey at Mellifont. There are numerous must-see attractions here, including many tangible reminders of Ireland's absorbing history.

Counties Meath & Louth in One Day

From Dublin, head to Brú na Bóinne and plan to spend most of the day there learning about the remarkable prehistoric passage tombs of **Newgrange** (p85), **Knowth** (p86) and **Dowth** (p86). Mid-afternoon visit the **Battle of the Boyne site** (p90) on the way to Drogheda, where you'll spend the night.

Counties Meath & Louth in Two Days

On day two, after a wander around the town, explore the fascinating ecclestiastical ruins of **Monasterboice** (p91) and **Old Mellifont Abbey** (p91), and in the afternoon, on your way back towards Dublin, visit the ancient capital of the High Kings of Ireland at the atmospheric **Hill of Tara** (p90).

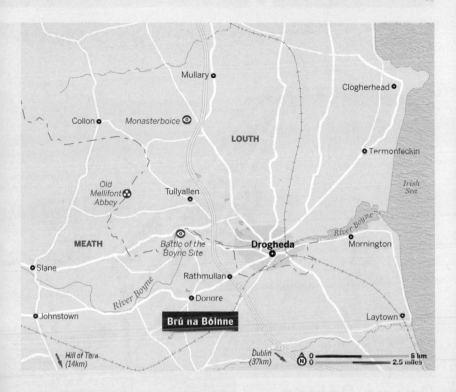

Arriving in Counties Meath & Louth

County Meath has numerous Bus Éireann (www.buseireann.ie) services, but to get off the beaten track your own wheels are best. Tour companies ply the main sights; most depart from Dublin.

Trains on the Dublin–Belfast line stop in Drogheda and Dundalk; the towns are also served by bus. Buses link Carlingford with Dundalk.

Sleeping

Most villages and towns throughout County Meath have good sleeping options. Beautiful manor houses dot the countryside.

While there are some B&Bs, hotels and hostels near Brú na Bóinne and Tara, Drogheda and Trim have a more comprehensive range of sleeping options and offer good transport links. Counties Louth and Meath can also be explored as a day trip from Dublin.

Display in the Brú na Bóinne visitor centre

©NATIONAL MONUMENTS SERVICE DEPT OF ARTS, HERITAGE AND THE GAELTACHT

Brú na Bóinne

The vast Neolithic necropolis of Brú na Bóinne is one of the most extraordinary sites in Europe. A thousand years older than Stonehenge, it's an evocative testament to the achievements of prehistoric humankind.

The complex of Brú na Bóinne (the Boyne Palace) was built to house the remains of those who were at the top of the social heap and its tombs were the largest artificial structures in Ireland until the construction of the Anglo-Norman castles 4000 years later. The area consists of many different sites; the three principal ones are Newgrange, Knowth and Dowth.

Over the centuries the tombs decayed, were covered by grass and trees, and were plundered by everybody from Vikings to Victorian treasure hunters, whose carved initials can be seen on the great stones of Newgrange. The countryside around the tombs is home to countless other ancient tumuli (burial mounds) and standing stones.

Great For...

☑ Don't Miss

The beautifully carved stone decoration in the passage entrance to Newgrange tomb.

Boyne Valley

ⒸNATIONAL MONUMENTS SERVICE DEPT OF ARTS, HERITAGE AND THE GAELTACHT

❶ Need to Know

Brú na Bóinne Visitor Centre (☏041-988 0300; www.heritageireland.ie; Donore; adult/child visitor centre €4/3, visitor centre & Newgrange €7/4, visitor centre & Knowth €6/4, all 3 sites €13/8; ⓢ9am-/pm Jun–mid-Sep, 9am-6.30pm May & mid-Sep–early Oct, 9.30am-5.30pm Feb-Apr & early Oct-early Nov, 9am-5pm early Nov-Jan)

✖ Take a Break

The cafe in the visitor centre serves excellent food, including extensive vegetarian options.

★ Top Tip

Tours are primarily outdoors so wear comfortable hiking shoes or boots and bring rain gear.

Newgrange

A startling 80m in diameter and 13m high, the white, round stone walls of **Newgrange** (www.newgrange.com; visitor centre & Newgrange €7/4; ⓢ9am-7pm Jun–mid-Sep, 9am-6.30pm May & mid-Sep–early Oct, 9.30am-5.30pm Feb-Apr & early Oct-early Nov, 9am-5pm early Nov-Jan), topped by a grass dome, look eerily futuristic. Underneath lies the finest Stone Age passage tomb in Ireland – one of the most remarkable prehistoric sites in Europe. Dating from around 3200 BC, it predates Egypt's pyramids by some six centuries.

The tomb's precise alignment with the sun at the time of the winter solstice suggests it was also designed to act as a calendar.

Newgrange Winter Solstice

At 8.20am on the winter solstice (between 18 and 23 December), the rising sun's rays shine through the roof-box above the entrance, creep slowly down the long passage and illuminate the tomb chamber for 17 minutes. There is little doubt that this is one of the country's most memorable, even mystical, experiences.

There's a simulated winter sunrise for every group taken into the mound. To be in with a chance of witnessing the real thing on one of six mornings around the solstice, enter the free lottery that's drawn in late September; 50 names are drawn and each winner is allowed to take one guest (be aware, however, that over 30,000 people apply each year). Fill out the form at the Brú na Bóinne Visitor Centre or email brunaboinne@opw.ie.

Knowth

Northwest of Newgrange, the burial mound of **Knowth** (visitor centre & Knowth €6/4; ⊘9am-7pm Jun–mid-Sep, 9am-6.30pm May & mid-Sep–early Oct, 9.30am-5.30pm Feb-Apr & early Oct-early Nov, 9am-5pm early Nov-Jan) was built around the same time. It has the greatest collection of passage-grave art ever uncovered in Western Europe. Early excavations cleared a passage leading to the central chamber, which at 34m, is much longer than the one at Newgrange. In 1968, a 40m passage was unearthed on the opposite side of the mound.

The site closes periodically for excavations; it is due to reopen after Easter 2018 when the latest round are complete.

Dowth

The circular mound at **Dowth** (⊘24hr) FREE is similar in size to Newgrange – about 63m in diameter – but is slightly taller at 14m high. Due to safety issues, Dowth's tombs are closed to visitors, though you can visit the mound (and its resident grazing sheep) from the L1607 road between Newgrange and Drogheda.

North of the tumulus are the ruins of **Dowth Castle** and **Dowth House**.

Visiting Brú na Bóinne

Advance planning will help you get the most out of your visit.

○ All visits to Brú na Bóinne start at the Brú na Bóinne Visitor Centre (p85) from where there's a shuttle bus to the tombs. If you turn up at either Newgrange or

Knowth western passage tomb

Knowth first, you'll be sent to the visitor centre, 4km from either site. Walking is discouraged, as the lanes are narrow and dangerous due to passing tour buses.

○ Allow plenty of time: an hour for the visitor centre alone, two hours to include a trip to Newgrange or Knowth, and half a day to see all three.

○ In summer, particularly at weekends, Brú na Bóinne gets very crowded; on peak days more than 2000 people can show up. As there are only 750 tour slots, you may not be guaranteed a visit to either of the passage tombs. Tickets are sold on a first-come, first-served basis (no advance booking). Arrive early in the morning or visit midweek and be prepared to wait. Alternatively, visiting as part of an organised tour, such as Mary Gibbons Tours, guarantees a spot.

Tours

Brú na Bóinne is one of the most popular tourist attractions in Ireland, and there are plenty of organised tours. Most depart from Dublin.

Tours are primarily outdoors with no shelter so bring rain gear, just in case.

Mary Gibbons Tours Tours
(☎086 355 1355; www.newgrangetours.com; tour incl entrance fees adult/child €40/35) Tours depart from numerous Dublin hotels, beginning at 9.30am Monday to Friday, 7.50am Saturday and Sunday, and take in the whole of the Boyne Valley including Newgrange and the Hill of Tara. The expert guides offer a fascinating insight into Celtic and pre-Celtic life in Ireland. No credit cards; pay cash on the bus.

---

❶ Where to Stay

While there are some B&Bs, hotels and hostels near Brú na Bóinne and Tara, Drogheda and Trim have a more comprehensive range of sleeping options.

FRANNIX/GETTY IMAGES ©

★ Daniel O'Connell

In August 1843 a crowd of 750,000 gathered at Tara to hear Daniel O'Connell, leader of the opposition to union with Great Britain, speak.

Brú na Bóinne

All visits start at the **❶visitor centre**, which has a terrific exhibit that includes a short context-setting film. From here, you board a shuttle bus that takes you to **❷Newgrange**, where you'll go past the **❸kerbstone** into the **❹main passage** and the **❺burial chamber**. If you're not a lucky lottery winner for the solstice, fear not – there's an artificial illumination ceremony that replicates it. If you're continuing on to tour **❻Knowth**, you'll need to go back to the visitor centre and get on another bus; otherwise, you can drive directly to **❼Dowth** and visit, but only from outside (the information panels will tell you what you're looking at).

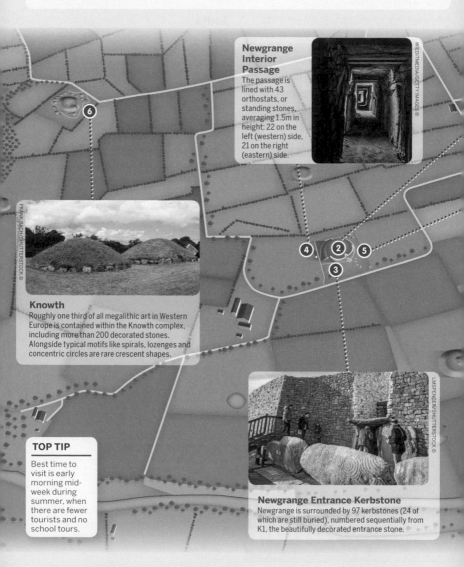

Newgrange Interior Passage

The passage is lined with 43 orthostats, or standing stones, averaging 1.5m in height: 22 on the left (western) side, 21 on the right (eastern) side.

Knowth

Roughly one third of all megalithic art in Western Europe is contained within the Knowth complex, including more than 200 decorated stones. Alongside typical motifs like spirals, lozenges and concentric circles are rare crescent shapes.

TOP TIP

Best time to visit is early morning midweek during summer, when there are fewer tourists and no school tours.

Newgrange Entrance Kerbstone

Newgrange is surrounded by 97 kerbstones (24 of which are still buried), numbered sequentially from K1, the beautifully decorated entrance stone.

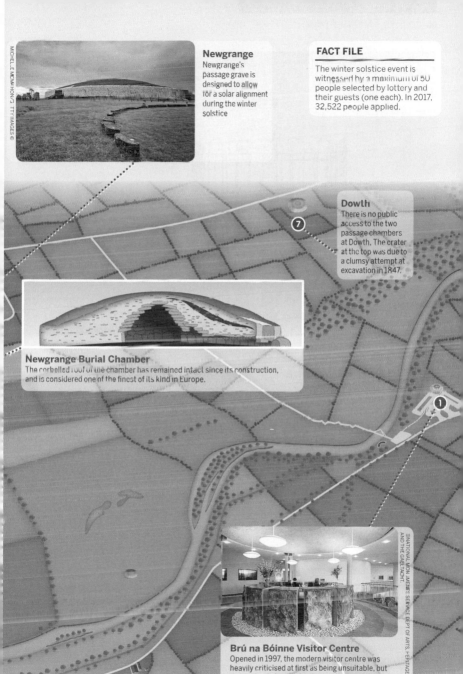

Newgrange
Newgrange's passage grave is designed to allow for a solar alignment during the winter solstice

FACT FILE

The winter solstice event is witnessed by a maximum of 50 people selected by lottery and their guests (one each). In 2017, 32,522 people applied.

Dowth
There is no public access to the two passage chambers at Dowth. The crater at the top was due to a clumsy attempt at excavation in 1847.

⑦

Newgrange Burial Chamber
The corbelled roof of the chamber has remained intact since its construction, and is considered one of the finest of its kind in Europe.

①

Brú na Bóinne Visitor Centre
Opened in 1997, the modern visitor centre was heavily criticised at first as being unsuitable, but then gained plaudits for the way it was integrated into the landscape.

Celtic cross at the Hill of Tara

Around Brú na Bóinne

Tara

The Hill of Tara is Ireland's most sacred stretch of turf, occupying a place at the heart of Irish history, legend and folklore. It was the home of the mystical druids, the priest-rulers of ancient Ireland, who practised their particular form of Celtic paganism under the watchful gaze of the all-powerful goddess Maeve (Medbh). Later it was the ceremonial capital of the high kings, all 142 of them, who ruled until the arrival of Christianity in the 5th century. It is also one of the most important ancient sites in Europe, with a Stone Age passage tomb and prehistoric burial mounds that date back some 5000 years.

Although little remains other than humps and mounds on the hill (named from ancient texts), its historic and folkloric significance is immense.

Battle of the Boyne

More than 60,000 soldiers of the armies of King James II and King William III fought in 1690 on this patch of farmland on the border of Counties Meath and Louth. William ultimately prevailed and James sailed off to France.

The **battle site** (www.battleoftheboyne. ie; Drybridge; adult/child €5/2; ◷9am-5pm May-Sep, to 4pm Oct-Apr) has an informative visitor centre and parkland walks. It's 6km west of Drogheda's town centre along Rathmullan Rd (follow the river). Buses run to/from Drogheda (€4.80, 25 minutes, two daily).

At the visitor centre you can watch a short film about the battle, see original and replica weaponry of the time and explore a laser battlefield model. Self-guided walks through the parkland and battle site allow time to ponder the events that saw Protestant interests remain in Ireland. Costumed reenactments take place in summer.

Drogheda & Around

Only 48km north of Dublin, Drogheda is a historic fortified town straddling the River Boyne. Stately old buildings, a handsome cathedral and a riveting museum provide plenty of cultural interest, while atmospheric pubs, fine restaurants, numerous sleeping options and good transport links make it a handy base for exploring the region.

A number of historic sites lie close to Drogheda, but you'll need your own transport to explore them.

◎ SIGHTS

Old Mellifont Abbey   Ruins

(☏041-982 6459; www.heritageireland.ie; Tullyallen; site admission free, visitor centre adult/student €5/3; ⊙site 24hr year round, visitor centre 10am-6pm Jun-Aug) In its Anglo-Norman prime, this abbey, 1.5km off the main Drogheda–Collon road (R168), was the Cistercians' first and most magnificent centre in Ireland. Highly evocative and well worth exploring, the ruins still reflect the site's former splendour.

Mellifont's most recognisable building and one of the country's finest examples of Cistercian architecture is the 13th-century lavabo, the monks' octagonal washing room.

Monasterboice   Historic Site

(⊙sunrise-sunset) FREE Crowing ravens lend an eerie atmosphere to Monasterboice, an intriguing monastic site down a leafy lane in sweeping farmland, which contains a cemetery, two ancient church ruins, one of the finest and tallest round towers in Ireland, and two of the most important high crosses.

Come early or late in the day to avoid the crowds. It's just off the M1 motorway, about 8km north of Drogheda.

✪ EATING & DRINKING

Kitchen   Mediterranean €€

(☏041-983 4630; 2 South Quay; mains lunch €13-17, dinner €17-25; ⊙11am-9pm Wed, 11am-10pm Thu-Sat, noon-9pm Sun; 🛜) Fronted by a sage-green facade, Drogheda's best restaurant is aptly named for its shiny open kitchen. Organic local produce is used along with worldly ingredients such as Cypriot halloumi and Serrano ham. Breads are made on-site and there's an excellent choice of wine by the glass. Don't miss the salted-caramel baked Alaska for dessert.

Grey Goose   Bar

(88 West St; ⊙10am-midnight Sun-Thu, to 2am Fri & Sat; 🛜) Drogheda's newest and hippest venue has a vast downstairs bar with herringbone floors, stained glass and leather sofas, and a grand piano in its upstairs cocktail lounge, the Birdcage, where a resident DJ spins cool '80s and '90s tunes on Saturdays. In addition to 23 Irish and international craft beers on tap, local spirits include Listoke gin and Slane whiskey.

➊ GETTING THERE & AWAY

BUS

The **bus station** (cnr Donore Rd & George's St) is on the south side of the river.

Bus Éireann (p302) regularly serves Drogheda from Dublin (€8.30, one hour, hourly) and Dundalk (€7.30, 30 minutes, hourly).

Matthews (☏042-937 8188; http://matthews.ie) also runs an hourly-or-better service to Dublin (€10) and Dundalk (€10).

TRAIN

The **train station** (www.irishrail.ie; off Dublin Rd) is just south of the river and east of the town centre. Drogheda is on the main Belfast–Dublin line (Dublin €11.80, 45 minutes; Belfast €14.50, 1½ hours) with hourly-or-better trains.

COUNTY
WICKLOW

County Wicklow at a Glance...

Just south of Dublin, County Wicklow (Cill Mhantáin) is the capital's favourite playground, a wild pleasure garden of coastline, woodland and daunting mountains through which runs the country's most popular walking trail. Stretching 127km from Dublin's southern suburbs to the rolling fields of County Carlow, the Wicklow Way leads walkers along disused military supply lines, old bog roads and forest trails. Along the way you can explore monastic ruins, handsome gardens and some magnificent 18th-century mansions.

County Wicklow in One Day

With only one day available, head straight to **Powerscourt Estate** (p96) and pass the morning walking around its glorious gardens. After lunch in the cafe at Powerscourt House, head south to **Glendalough** (p98) to explore its ancient monastic site before enjoying a late-afternoon walk along the shores of the scenic Upper Lake.

County Wicklow in Two Days

With two days you can be more relaxed. On day one, after visiting **Powerscourt Estate** (p96) and Enniskerry village, drive over to **Avoca Handweavers** (p105) at Kilmacanogue for lunch and shopping. On day two, visit **Glendalough** (p98) in the morning and devote the afternoon to one of Wicklow's famous gardens, such as **Mt Usher** (p105) or **Kilmacurragh Botanic Gardens** (p105).

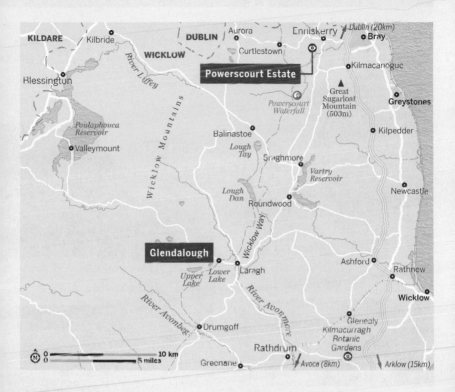

Arriving in County Wicklow

Enniskerry is 18km south of Dublin, just 3km west of the M11 along the R117. From here, getting to Powerscourt House on foot is not a problem (it's 500m from the town).

St Kevin's Bus (p101) runs twice daily from Dublin and Bray to Roundwood and Glendalough. Dublin Bus 65 runs regularly as far as Blessington.

Sleeping

As far as accommodation goes, County Wicklow has a bit of everything, from walkers' hostels and camping grounds to farmhouse B&Bs and luxurious country-house hotels. As it's a popular weekend escape for Dubliners, it's wise to book a bed in advance.

Enniskerry is the best base from which to explore Powerscourt, while both Enniskerry and Blessington are good options for visiting Glendalough.

Powerscourt House

Powerscourt Estate

Wicklow's most visited attraction is this magnificent 64-sq-km estate. At the heart of it is a 68-room Palladian mansion, but the real draw is the formal gardens and the stunning views that accompany them.

Great For...

☑ **Don't Miss**

The animal cemetery in the estate gardens, final resting place of the Wingfield pets and horses.

History

The estate has existed more or less since 1300, when the LePoer (later anglicised to Power) family built themselves a castle here. The property changed Anglo-Norman hands a few times before coming into the possession of Richard Wingfield, newly appointed Marshall of Ireland, in 1603. His descendants were to live here for the next 350 years. In 1730 the Georgian wunderkind Richard Cassels (or Castle) was given the job of building a 68-room Palladian-style mansion around the core of the old castle.

The Wingfields left during the 1950s, after which the house had a massive restoration. Then, on the eve of its opening to the public in 1974, a fire gutted the whole building. The estate was eventually bought by the Slazenger sporting-goods family who have overseen a second restoration as

Powerscourt Gardens

ERUMO_IL_SEGRETARIO/GETTY IMAGES ©

ⓘ Need to Know

01-204 6000; www.powerscourt.com; Enniskerry; house free, gardens adult/child €10/5; 9.30am-5.30pm Mar-Oct, to dusk Nov-Feb; P

✕ Take a Break

Enjoy lunch on the terrace at the cafe in Powerscourt House, with lovely views towards Great Sugarloaf mountain.

★ Top Tip

If you're driving, plan a picnic lunch at nearby Powerscourt Waterfall.

well as the addition of all the amenities the estate now has to offer, including the two golf courses and the fabulous hotel, now part of Marriott's Autograph collection.

The Gardens

The star of the show is the 20-hectare landscaped gardens, originally laid out in the 1740s but redesigned in the 19th century by gardener Daniel Robertson. Robertson was one of the foremost horticulturalists of his day and his passion for growing things was matched only by his love of booze: the story goes that by a certain point in the day he was too drunk to stand and so insisted on being wheeled around the estate in a barrow.

Perhaps this influenced his largely informal style, which resulted in a magnificent blend of landscaped gardens, sweeping terraces, statuary, ornamental lakes, secret hollows, rambling walks and walled enclosures replete with more than 200 types of trees and shrubs, all beneath the stunning natural backdrop of the Great Sugarloaf mountain to the southeast. Tickets come with a map laying out 40-minute and hour-long walks around the gardens.

The Mansion

The house itself is every bit as grand, but the ongoing renovation means there's not much to see beyond the bustle of the ground-floor Avoca cafe and craft shop. The sole exception is the **Museum of Childhood** (Tara's Palace; 01-274 8090; www.childhoodmuseum.org; Powerscourt Estate; adult/child/family €5/3/12; 10am-5pm Mon-Sat, noon-5pm Sun; P), full of period miniature dolls and dolls' houses, including Tara's Palace, a 22-room house designed to one-twelfth scale and inspired by the Palladian piles of Castletown House, Leinster House and Carton House. Each of the rooms is decorated in exquisite, hand-crafted miniatures.

Ruins of the Cathedral of St Peter and St Paul (p100)

Glendalough

Glendalough is one of the most beautiful corners of the whole country and the epitome of the kind of rugged, romantic Ireland that probably drew you to the island in the first place.

Great For...

Don't Miss

The 33m-tall, 1000-year-old Round Tower at the heart of the site.

History

In AD 498 a young monk named Kevin arrived in Glendalough (Gleann dá Loch, 'Valley of the Two Lakes') looking for somewhere to kick back, meditate and be at one with nature. He pitched up at what had been a Bronze Age tomb on the southern side of the Upper Lake and for the next seven years slept on stones, wore animal skins, maintained a near-starvation diet and – according to the legend – became bosom buddies with the birds and animals. Kevin's ecofriendly lifestyle soon attracted a bunch of disciples, all seemingly unaware of the irony that they were flocking to hang out with a hermit who wanted to live as far away from other people as possible. Over the next couple of centuries his one-man operation mushroomed into a proper settlement and by the 9th century Glendalough rivalled Clonmac-

Round Tower (p100)

VINCENT MACNAMARA/SHUTTERSTOCK ©

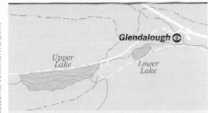

Glendalough ⊙

Upper Lake

Lower Lake

❶ Need to Know

www.glendalough.ie; 25km south of Dublin; ⊙24hr; ℗; 🚌St Kevin's Bus) `FREE`

✕ Take a Break

Wicklow Heather (📞0404-45157; www. wicklowheather.ie; Glendalough Rd, Laragh; mains €13-29; ⊙8am-9.30pm Mon-Thu, to 10pm Fri & Sat, to 9pm Sun, ℗🖫) is the best place for anything substantial.

★ Top Tip

Take a look around the **visitor centre** (📞0404-45352; www.heritageireland.ie; adult/child €5/3; ⊙9.30am-6pm mid-Mar–mid-Oct, to 5pm mid-Oct–mid-Mar) to get a feel for the history before touring the monastic site itself

noise as the island's premier monastic city. Thousands of students studied and lived in a thriving community that was spread over a considerable area.

Inevitably, Glendalough's success made it a key target for Viking raiders, who sacked the monastery at least four times between 775 and 1071. The final blow came in 1398, when English forces from Dublin almost destroyed it. Efforts were made to rebuild and some life lingered on here as late as the 17th century when, under renewed repression, the monastery finally died.

Upper Lake

The original site of St Kevin's settlement, **Teampall na Skellig** is at the base of the cliffs towering over the southern side of the Upper Lake and is accessible only by boat; unfortunately, there's no boat service to the

site and you'll have to settle for looking at it across the lake. The terraced shelf has the reconstructed ruins of a church and early graveyard. Rough wattle huts once stood on the raised ground nearby. Scattered around are some early grave slabs and simple stone crosses.

Just east of here and 10m above the lake waters is the 2m-deep artificial cave called **St Kevin's Bed**, said to be where Kevin lived. The earliest human habitation of the cave was long before St Kevin's era – there's evidence that people lived in the valley for thousands of years before the monks arrived. In the green area just south of the car park is a large circular wall thought to be the remains of an early Christian **stone fort** *(caher)*.

Follow the lakeshore path southwest of the car park until you come to the considerable remains of **Reefert Church** above the tiny River Poulanass. It's a small, plain, 11th-century Romanesque nave-and-chancel church with some reassembled arches and walls. Traditionally, Reefert (literally 'Royal Burial Place') was the burial site of the chiefs of the local O'Toole family. The surrounding graveyard contains a number of rough stone crosses and slabs, most made of mica schist.

Climb the steps at the back of the churchyard and follow the path to the west and you'll find, at the top of a rise overlooking the lake, the scant remains of **St Kevin's Cell**, a small beehive hut.

Lower Lake

While the Upper Lake has the best scenery, the most fascinating buildings lie in the lower part of the valley east of the Lower Lake, huddled together in the heart of the ancient **monastic site**.

Just round the bend from the Glendalough Hotel is the stone arch of the **monastery gatehouse**, the only surviving example of a monastic entranceway in the country. Just inside the entrance is a large slab with an incised cross.

Beyond that lies a **graveyard**, which is still in use. The 10th-century **Round Tower** is 33m tall and 16m in circumference at the base. The upper storeys and conical roof were reconstructed in 1876. Near the tower, to the southeast, is the **Cathedral of St Peter and St Paul** with a 10th-century nave. The chancel and sacristy date from the 12th century.

At the centre of the graveyard to the south of the round tower is the **Priest's House**. This odd building dates from 1170 but has been heavily reconstructed. It may have been the location of shrines of St Kevin. Later, during penal times, it became

Upper and Lower lakes

a burial site for local priests – hence the name. The 10th-century **St Mary's Church**, 140m southwest of the round tower, probably originally stood outside the walls of the monastery and belonged to local nuns. It has a lovely western doorway. A little to the east are the scant remains of **St Kieran's Church**, the smallest at Glendalough.

Glendalough's trademark is **St Kevin's Kitchen** or **Church** at the southern edge of the enclosure. This church, with a miniature round tower like belfry, protruding sacristy and steep stone roof, is a masterpiece. The oldest parts of the building date from

the 11th century – the structure has been remodelled since but it's still a classic early Irish church.

At the junction with Green Rd as you cross the river just south of these two churches is the **Deer Stone** in the middle of a group of rocks. Legend claims that when St Kevin needed milk for two orphaned babies, a doe stood here waiting to be milked. The stone is actually a *bullaun* (a stone used as a mortar for grinding medicines or food)

The road east leads to **St Saviour's Church** with its detailed Romanesque carvings. To the west, a nice woodland trail leads up the valley past the Lower Lake to the Upper Lake.

☑ Don't Miss

If you have time, don't miss the walk from the monastic site along the south side of the Lower Lake to the Upper Lake.

CHRISTINA MEIMA/SHUTTERSTOCK ©

Tours

Wild Wicklow Tour (☑01-280 1899; www.wildwicklow.ie; adult €28, student/child €25; ⊙departs 9am) run award-winning bus tours of Glendalough, Avoca and the Sally Gap that never fail to generate rave reviews for atmosphere and all-round fun. The first pickup is at the Shelbourne Hotel and then the **tourist office** (14 Upper O'Connell St; ⊙9am-5pm Mon-Sat; ▣all city centre), but there are a variety of pick-up points throughout Dublin; check the point nearest you when booking. The tour returns to Dublin about 5.30pm.

Getting to Glendalough

St Kevin's Bus (☑01-281 8119; www.glendaloughbus.com) departs from the bus stop on St Stephen's Green North in Dublin at 11.30am and 6pm daily (one way/return €13/20, 1½ hours); from March to October the evening bus leaves at 7pm on Saturday and Sunday. It also stops at the Town Hall in Bray (one way/return €9/15, 40 mins). Departures from Glendalough are at 7.15am and 4.30pm weekdays, and 9.45am and 5.40pm on weekends. Buy your ticket on the bus.

✖ Take A Break

If the weather's good, pack a picnic basket and head for the gravel beach at the east end of the Upper Lake for lunch with a view.

Glendalough

A WALKING TOUR

A visit to Glendalough is a trip through ancient history and a refreshing hike in the hills. The ancient monastic settlement founded by St Kevin in the 5th century grew to be quite powerful by the 9th century, but it started falling into ruin from 1398 onwards. Still, you won't find more evocative clumps of stones anywhere.

Start at the ❶ **Main Gateway** to the monastic city, where you will find a cluster of important ruins, including the (nearly perfect) 10th-century ❷ **Round Tower**, the ❸ **cathedral** dedicated to Sts Peter and Paul, and ❹ **St Kevin's Kitchen**, which is really a church. Cross the stream past the famous ❺ **Deer Stone**, where Kevin was supposed to have milked a doe, and turn west along the path. It's a 1.5km walk to the ❻ **Upper Lake**. On the lake's southern shore is another cluster of sites, including the ❼ **Reefert Church**, a plain 11th-century Romanesque church where the powerful O'Toole family buried their kin, and ❽ **St Kevin's Cell**, the remains of a beehive hut where Kevin is said to have lived.

ST KEVIN

St Kevin came to the valley as a young monk in AD 498, in search of a peaceful retreat. He was reportedly led by an angel to a Bronze Age tomb now known as St Kevin's Bed. For seven years he slept on stones, wore animal skins, survived on nettles and herbs and – according to legend – developed an affinity with the birds and animals. One legend has it that, when Kevin needed milk for two orphaned babies, a doe stood waiting at the Deer Stone to be milked.

Kevin soon attracted a group of disciples and the monastic settlement grew, until by the 9th century Glendalough rivalled Clonmacnoise as Ireland's premier monastic city. According to legend, Kevin lived to the age of 120. He was canonised in 1903.

OLOS/SHUTTERSTOCK ©

Round Tower
Glendalough's most famous landmark is the 33m-high Round Tower, which is exactly as it was when it was built a thousand years ago except for the roof; this was replaced in 1876 after a lightning strike.

Deer Stone
The spot where St Kevin is said to have truly become one with the animals is really just a large mortar called a *bullaun*, used for grinding food and medicine.

St Kevin's Kitchen
This small church is unusual in that it has a round tower sticking out of the roof – it looks like a chimney, hence the church's nickname.

SIR FRANCIS CANKER PHOTOGRAPHY/GETTY IMAGES ©

St Kevin's Cell
This beehive hut is reputedly where St Kevin would go for prayer and meditation; not to be confused with St Kevin's Bed, a cave where he used to sleep.

Reefert Church
Its name derives from the Irish *righ fearta*, which means 'burial place of the kings'. Seven princes of the powerful O'Toole family are buried in this simple structure.

Upper Lake
The site of St Kevin's original settlement is on the banks of the Upper Lake, one of the two lakes that give Glendalough its name – the 'Valley of the Lakes'.

(8)

(7)

(6)

(2)

(3)

(1)

INFORMATION
At the eastern end of the Upper Lake is the National Park Information Point, which has leaflets and maps on the site, local walks etc. The grassy spot in front of the office is a popular picnic spot in summer.

NORTH

Cathedral of Sts Peter & Paul
The largest of Glendalough's seven churches, the cathedral was built gradually between the 10th and 13th centuries. The earliest part is the nave, where you can still see the *antae* (slightly projecting column at the end of the wall) used for supporting a wooden roof.

Main Gateway
The only surviving entrance to the ecclesiastical settlement is a double arch; notice that the inner arch rises higher than the outer one in order to compensate for the upward slope of the causeway.

Enniskerry

At the top of the '21 Bends', as the steep and winding R117 road from Bray is known, the handsome village of Enniskerry is home to upmarket shops and the kind of all-organic gourmet cafes that would treat you as a criminal if you admitted to eating battery eggs. Such self-regard is a far cry from the village's origins, when Richard Wingfield, Viscount of nearby Powerscourt, commissioned a row of terraced cottages for his labourers in 1760. These days, you'd need to have laboured pretty successfully to get your hands on one of them.

◉ SIGHTS

Powerscourt Waterfall   Waterfall
(www.powerscourt.com/waterfall; Powerscourt Estate; adult/child €6/3.50; ⊗9.30am-7pm May-Aug, 10.30am-5.30pm Mar-Apr, Sep & Oct, to 4.30pm Nov-Feb; P) On the southern edge of Powerscourt Estate, 6km south of Powerscourt House, is this picturesque waterfall. At 121m it's the highest in Ire-land (though it's a cascade, rather than a single drop) and is at its most impressive after heavy rain. The waterfall is signposted from the main estate entrance; walking is not recommended, because the route lies on narrow roads with no footpath.

A nature trail has been laid out around the base of the waterfall, taking you past giant redwoods, ancient oaks, beech, birch and rowan trees. There are plenty of birds in the vicinity, including the chaffinch, cuckoo, chiffchaff, raven and willow warbler.

Great Sugarloaf   Hill
At 503m it's nowhere near Wicklow's highest summit, but the Great Sugarloaf is one of the most distinctive hills in Ireland, its conical peak visible for many kilometres around. The mountain towers over the small village of Kilmacanogue, on the N11 about 35km south of Dublin, and can be climbed from a car park on the L1031 minor road (off the R755 road, 7.5km south of Enniskerry). It's a steep but straightforward hike (one hour return trip).

Powerscourt Waterfall

ERIK BOUMA/SHUTTERSTOCK ©

TOURS

DoDublin Bus Tour
Bus

(www.dodublin.ie; adult/child €21.60/9.60; ☺10.30am daily Apr-Oct) Departing at 10.30am from the Dublin Bus office at 59 Upper O'Connell St in Dublin, this tour takes in both Glendalough and Powerscourt, returning to Dublin at 5pm.

SHOPPING

Avoca Handweavers
Arts & Crafts

(☑01 286 7466; www.avoca.ie; Main St, Kilmacanogue; 9am-6pm Mon-Fri, 9.30am-6pm Sat & Sun; 🛜👶) Avoca is one hell of an operation, with seven branches nationwide and a widespread reputation for adding elegance and style to traditional rural handicrafts. Operational HQ is set in a 19th-century arboretum 5km southeast of Enniskerry, and the bustling shop crammed with knitwear, textiles, ceramics, toys, homewares and gourmet foodstuffs will leave you in no doubt as to the company's incredible success.

The attached **cafe** (mains €7 to €15) is excellent and you can bring a little of it home with you by purchasing one (or all) of the Avoca cookbooks.

✴ EATING

Kennedy's
Cafe €

(www.kennedysofenniskerry.com; Church Hill; mains €5-12; ☺8.30am-5pm; 🛜👶) A lovely cafe with old-fashioned furniture in cool pastel shades, this is the place to get excellent breakfasts (it does great poached eggs on sourdough toast) and homemade soups and sandwiches. It also sells delicious artisan bread made by the Bretzel Bakery in Dublin.

Johnnie Fox's
Seafood €€

(☑01-295 5647; www.jfp.ie; Glencullen; mains €11-30; ☺food served 12.30-9.30pm; 🅿🛜👶) Busloads of tourists fill this place nightly throughout the summer, mostly for the

Wicklow Gardens

Kilmacurragh Botanic Gardens

(☑0404-48844; www.botanicgardens.ie; Kilbride; ☺9am-6pm mid-Feb–Oct, to 4.30pm Nov–mid Feb) FREE Surrounding the ruins of an 18th-century mansion are these ornamental gardens originally laid out in 1712 and replanted in the 19th century to reflect the wilder, antiformal style of William Robinson (1838–1935); particularly notable are the South American conifers, the colourful rhododendrons and the avenue of yews. The gardens are 3km east of Rathdrum; get directions from the website.

Mt Usher Gardens (☑0404-40205; www.mountushergardens.ie; Ashford; adult/child €7.50/3.50; ☺10am-6pm) Wicklow's nickname, 'the Garden of Ireland', is justified by green idylls such as the 8-hectare Mt Usher Gardens, about 10km south of Greystones on the N11. Trees, shrubs and herbaceous plants from around the world are laid out in Robinsonian style rather than in the formalist manner of preceding gardens.

Mt Usher Gardens
OSHER AVZIROV/SHUTTERSTOCK ©

knees up, faux-Irish Hooley Show of music and dancing. But there's nothing contrived about the seafood, which is so damn good we'd happily sit through yet another chorus of 'Danny Boy' and even consider joining in the jig. The pub is 3km northwest of Enniskerry.

Ireland's Ancient East

Capitalising on the success of the Wild Atlantic Way, the Irish tourist board's latest promotional venture is **Ireland's Ancient East** (www.irelandsancient east.com). You'll see new road signs with the Ancient East logo dotted all over the country, pointing the way to various sights.

However, this is not a driving route, like the Wild Atlantic Way, but more of a branding and signposting exercise. As well as taking in big-name attractions such as Newgrange (p85), Glendalough (p98) and the Rock of Cashel (p256), the campaign encourages visitors to visit central and eastern Ireland's lesser-known historical attractions.

Hundreds of sights spread over 17 counties have been grouped into stories and themes. The website (and smartphone app) allows you to explore each theme (such as Sacred Ireland; Castles and Conquests; and Vikings) along with related background stories, and then click through to travel itineraries that you can customise and download.

Glendalough (p98)
PETER ZELEI/GETTY IMAGES ©

❶ GETTING THERE & AWAY

Bus Éireann (☑01-836 6111; www.buseireann. ie) No 133 from Dublin to Wicklow town stops in Kilmacanogue (one way/return €4.90/8.30, 45 minutes, 10 daily).

Vale of Avoca

One of the most scenic spots in the county is the Vale of Avoca, a darkly wooded valley that begins where the Rivers Avonbeg and Avonmore come together to form the River Avoca. Bearing the literal name the Meeting of the Waters, this watery junction was made famous by Thomas Moore's 1808 poem of the same name.

Tiny Avoca (Abhóca) village is a pleasant enough spot that's best known as the birthplace of the superstar of all Irish cottage industries, Avoca Handweavers. Ask at the **tourist office** for details of nearby walks.

❻ SHOPPING

Avoca Handweavers Arts & Crafts
(☑0402-35105; www.avoca.ie; Main St; ⊙shop 9.30am-6pm May-Sep, to 5.30pm Oct-Apr) Ireland's oldest working mill is the birthplace of Avoca Handweavers, a company that is now famous across Ireland and the world. The mill (open from 10am to 4.30pm) has been turning out woollens and other fabrics since 1723, and a lot of Avoca's much-admired line is produced here and sold in the neighbouring shop.

You are free to wander around the weaving sheds and chat to the weavers, or have lunch in the excellent cafe. Arrive early or late to avoid coach tour groups.

❼ DRINKING & NIGHTLIFE

Meetings Pub
(☑0402-35226; www.themeetings.ie; Meeting of the Waters; ⊙noon-11pm; ☎) The meeting of the Avonmore and Avonbeg rivers is marked by this excellent pub, which has music at weekends year-round. There's also a cafe and crafts gallery with a lovely terrace overlooking the river, Lily's Restaurant (open Friday to Sunday) and a choice of sleek modern guest bedrooms (doubles from €95).

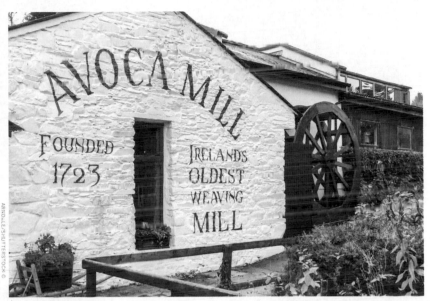

Avoca Handweavers

🛈 INFORMATION

If you need local info, the **tourist office** (📞0402-35022; Old Courthouse; 🕙10am-5pm Mon-Sat) is in a small cottage called The Courthouse, Avoca.

🛈 GETTING THERE & AWAY

Bus Éireann (📞01-836 6111; www.buseireann. ie) service 133 runs hourly from Dublin (Georges Quay) to Wicklow town, with two buses a day continuing to Avoca (€11, two hours), with stops at Rathdrum and the Meeting of the Waters.

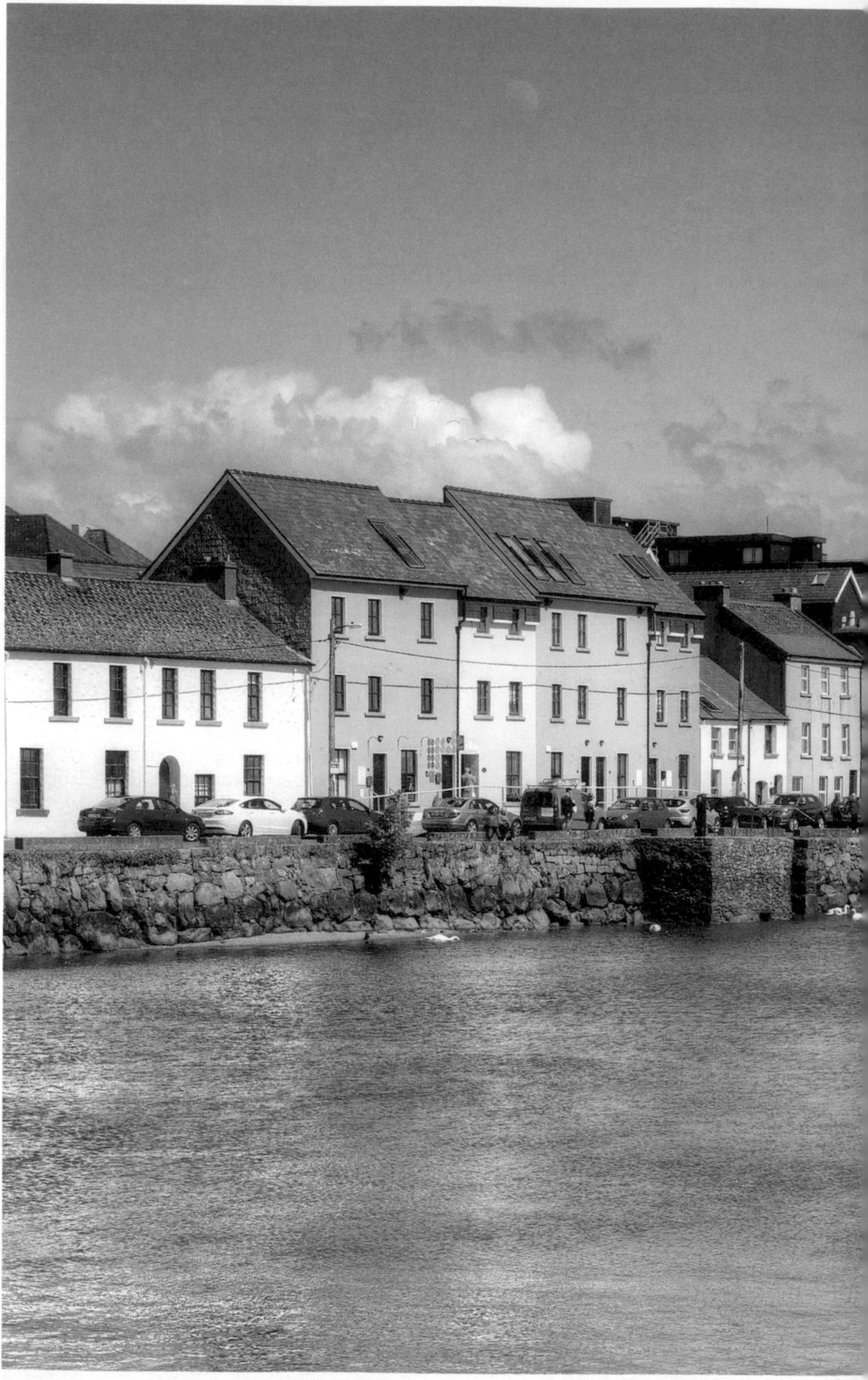

STLJB/SHUTTERSTOCK ©

COUNTY GALWAY

County Galway at a Glance...

County Galway's exuberant namesake city – the only major urban centre on the Wild Atlantic Way – is a swirl of colourful shop-lined streets filled with buskers and performance artists, enticing old pubs that hum with trad music sessions, and a sophisticated food scene.

Some of Ireland's most picturesque scenery fans out from Galway's city limits, particularly along the breathtaking Connemara Peninsula. Tiny roads wander along its coastline studded with islands, dazzling white sandy beaches and intriguing villages, while its interior shelters heath-strewn boglands, glassy lakes, looming mountains and isolated valleys.

County Galway in Two Days

Day one is for Galway city – be sure to visit the **City Museum** (p119), and fit in lunch at **Ard Bia** (p120) cafe. If it's the weekend, **Galway Market** (p119) is a must. In the evening, gird your loins for a crawl around Galway's lively pubs and trad music sessions. On day two take a cruise to **Lough Corrib** (p120).

County Galway in Four Days

On day three follow our **Connemara coastal drive** (p112) and continue to the attractive village of **Clifden** where you'll spend the night; prebook a table for dinner at **Mitchell's** (p124). On day four head back to Galway city via **Kylemore Abbey** (p125) and the wild bogs of **Connemara National Park** (p125).

Arriving in County Galway

A car is the best option for exploring County Galway. If using public transport, base yourself in Galway city and take guided bus tours to the surrounding attractions.

There are up to nine fast, comfortable trains daily between Dublin's Heuston Station and Galway city (from €35, 2¼ hours). Citylink coaches run between Galway and Killarney twice a day (€30, three hours).

Sleeping

It's possible to explore the entire county on day trips from Galway city, which has a wealth of options in all categories (book accommodation well in advance at peak times), but some wonderful hostels, B&Bs, inns and hotels county-wide allow more time for exploration. Properties in rural areas often close outside high season – check ahead.

Connemara Coastal Drive

With its shimmering black lakes, pale mountains, lonely valleys and more than the occasional rainbow, Connemara is one of the most gorgeous corners of Ireland. The lack of English signposting can be confusing at times, so a good road map is needed.

Start Barna Woods
Distance 90km
Duration Five to seven hours

6 Carna is a small fishing village, with pleasant walks north to Moyrus and out to the wild headlands at Mace Head.

5 Kilkieran Bay is an intricate system of tidal marshes, bogs and tidal basins that contains an amazing diversity of wildlife.

3 The scenery becomes more dramatic west of Spiddal. **Carraroe** has fine beaches, including the Coral Strand, which is composed entirely of shell and coral fragments.

Classic Photo: Patrick Pearse's Cottage

4 Patrick Pearse's Cottage
(Teach an Phiarsaigh; www.heritage
ireland.ie; R340, Ros Muc; adult/child
€4/2; ⊙9.30am-6pm Easter-Sep,
10am-4pm Oct-Easter) was once the
home of the man who led the Easter
Rising with James Connolly in 1916.

Take a Break...
Relax with coffee and cake at the
Builín Blasta (https://builinblasta.
com; dishes €4.50-14; ⊙10am-5pm
Mon-Fri, from 11am Sat & Sun) **cafe
near Spiddal.**

1 The dense, deep green forest of
Barna Woods contains the last
natural growing oaks in Ireland's
west.

2 Look for the Ceardlann Spiddal
Craft & Design Studios in the refreshingly untouched little village
of **Spiddal**, and enjoy a cake at
Builín Blasta.

0 — 10 km
0 — 5 miles

Clonbur
Cross
Shrule
Glenhaun
Headford
Galway
Salthill
Inverin
Spiddal
Barna
Galway Bay
New Quay

TIM GRAHAM/GETTY IMAGES © S PAUL SHELS/SHUTTERSTOCK ©

Pub Crawl in Galway City

Galway's pub selection is second to none. The city is awash with traditional pubs offering live music, along with stylish wine and cocktail bars, which are thronged with revellers, especially on weekends.

Great For...

☑ **Don't Miss**

Taking in a live *céilidh* (trad music and dancing session) at the crowded traditional Irish pub, Tig Cóilí (p115).

Tigh Neachtain   Pub

(www.tighneachtain.com; 17 Upper Cross St; ⊙11.30am–midnight Mon-Thu, 11.30am–1am Fri, 10.30am–1am Sat, 12.30–11.30pm Sun) Painted a bright cornflower blue, this 19th-century corner pub – known simply as Neáchtain's (*nock*-tans) or Naughtons – has a wraparound terrace for watching Galway's passing parade, and a timber-lined interior with a roaring open fire, snugs and atmosphere to spare. Along with perfectly pulled pints of Guinness and 130-plus whiskeys, it has its own range of beers brewed by Galway Hooker.

O'Connor's   Pub

(⌨091-523 468; www.oconnorsbar.com; Upper Salthill Rd, Salthill; ⊙7.30pm–late) Antiques fill every nook, cranny, wall and ceiling space of this 1942-established pub: clocks, crockery, farming implements, gaslights, sewing

ⓘ Need to Know

Most of Galway's pubs have live music at least a couple of nights a week, whether in an informal trad session or a headline act.

✕ Take a Break

Stop off for top-notch fish and chips at **McDonagh's** (📞091-565 001; www. mcdonaghs.net; 22 Quay St; cafe & takeaway mains €6-14.50, restaurant mains €13.50-26; ⊙cafe & takeaway noon-11pm Mon-Sat, 2-9pm Sun, restaurant 5-10pm Mon-Sat).

★ Top Tip

Look out for craft beers by local success story Galway Hooker (www. galwayhooker.ie), named for the iconic local fishing boats, on tap around town.

day draw the crowds to this authentic fire-engine-red pub just off High St. Decorated with photos of those who have played here, it's where musicians go to get drunk or drunks go to become musicians...or something like that. A gem.

machines, fishing equipment, a stag's head and an almost life-size statue of John Wayne from *The Quiet Man*. Learn about them – and Irish history – on storyteller Brian Nolan's free Fireside Tour, aka the 'shortest walking tour of Ireland'.

Crane Bar   Pub

(www.thecranebar.com; 2 Sea Rd; ⊙10.30am-11.30pm Mon-Fri, 10.30am-12.30am Sat, 12.30pm-11pm Sun) West of the Corrib, this atmospheric, always crammed two-storey pub is the best spot in Galway to catch an informal *céilidh* (traditional music and dancing session). Music on both levels starts at 9.30pm.

Tig Cóilí   Pub

(www.tigcoiligalway.com; Mainguard St; ⊙10.30am-11.30pm Mon-Thu, 10.30am-12.30am Fri & Sat, 12.30pm-11pm Sun) Two live *céilidh* a

Róisín Dubh   Pub

(www.roisindubh.net; 9 Upper Dominick St; ⊙5pm-2am Sun-Thu, to 2.30am Fri & Sat) From the rooftop terrace you can see sweeping views of Galway; inside, emerging acts play here before they hit the big time. It's *the* place to hear bands but comedy's also on the menu.

Monroe's Tavern   Pub

(www.monroes.ie; Upper Dominick St; ⊙10am-11.30pm Sun-Thu, to 1am Fri & Sat) Often photographed for its classic black-and-white facade, Monroe's delivers traditional music and ballads, plus it remains the only pub in the city with regular Irish dancing. Live music every night.

Clonmacnoise

Gloriously situated overlooking the River Shannon, Clonmacnoise is one of Ireland's most important ancient monastic cities. Although it's located in neighbouring County Offaly, it's easily visited from Galway city.

Great For...

☑ **Don't Miss**

The Cross of the Scriptures, one of Ireland's finest carved stone high crosses.

When St Ciarán founded a monastery here in AD 548, it was the most important crossroads in the country, the intersection of the north–south River Shannon, and the east–west Esker Riada (Highway of the Kings).

The giant ecclesiastical city had a humble beginning and Ciarán died just seven months after building his first church. Over the years, however, Clonmacnoise grew to become an unrivalled bastion of Irish religion, literature and art and attracted a large lay population. Between the 7th and 12th centuries, monks from all over Europe came to study and pray here, helping to earn Ireland the title of the 'land of saints and scholars'.

The site is enclosed in a walled field and contains several early churches, high crosses, round towers and graves in astonishingly good condition. The surrounding marshy area is known as the Shannon Callows, home

Celtic cross

MICHAEL MANTKE/SHUTTERSTOCK ©

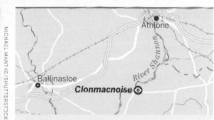

ⓘ Need to Know

www.heritageireland.ie; adult/child €8/4;
🕘9am-6.30pm Jun-Aug, 10am-6pm mid-
Mar-May, Sep & Oct, 10am-5.30pm Nov-
mid-Mar; P

✕ Take A Break

There's a coffee shop at the visitor centre, but no other source of refreshment
nearby.

★ Top Tip

If you plan to visit more than three
or four Heritage Ireland sites, save
money with an OPW (Office of Public
Works) Heritage Card (€25). You can
buy it at OPW sites or Dublin Tourism
offices.

to many wild plants and one of the last refug-
es of the seriously endangered corncrake (a
pastel-coloured relative of the coot).

Most of what you can see today dates
from the 10th to 12th centuries. The
monks would have lived in small huts
surrounding the monastery. The site was
burned and pillaged on numerous occasions by both the Vikings and the Irish.
After the 12th century it fell into decline,
and by the 15th century was home solely
to an impoverished bishop. In 1552 the
English garrison from Athlone reduced the
site to a ruin.

Visitor Centre

Three connected conical huts, echoing the
design of early monastic dwellings, house
the **visitors centre museum** (☎090-967
4195; adult/child €8/4; last admission 1hr before

closing). A 20-minute audiovisual show provides an excellent introduction to the site

The exhibition area contains the original
high crosses (replicas have been put in their
former locations outside) and various artefacts uncovered during excavation, including
silver pins, beaded glass and an Ogham
stone (a stone carved with carved with runic
inscriptions; the earliest form of writing in
Ireland).

Cathedral

The largest building at Clonmacnoise,
the **cathedral** was originally built in AD
909, but was significantly altered and
remodelled over the centuries. Its most interesting feature is the intricate 15th-cen-
tury Gothic doorway with carvings of Sts
Francis, Patrick and Dominic. A whisper
carries from one side of the door to the
other and this feature was supposedly
used by lepers to confess their sins without infecting the priests.

Galway City

Arty, bohemian Galway (Gaillimh) is one of Ireland's most engaging cities. Brightly painted pubs heave with live music, while restaurants and cafes offer front-row seats for observing buskers and street theatre. Remnants of the medieval town walls lie between shops selling handcrafted Claddagh rings, books and musical instruments, bridges arch over the salmon-stuffed River Corrib, and a long promenade leads to the seaside suburb of Salthill, on Galway Bay, the source of the area's famous oysters.

While it's steeped in history, the city buzzes with a contemporary vibe, thanks in part

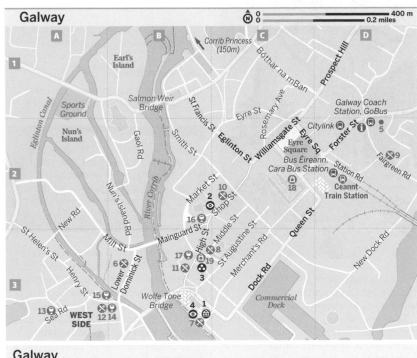

Galway

to students, who make up a quarter of the population. Its energy and creativity have seen it designated the European Capital of Culture in 2020.

◎ SIGHTS

Galway City Museum   Museum
(www.galwaycitymuseum.ie; Spanish Parade House, Merchant's Rd; ◎10am-5pm Tue-Sat year-round, noon-5pm Sun Easter-Sep) **FREE**
Exhibits at this modern museum covering the city's history from 1800 to 1950 include an iconic Galway hooker fishing boat, a collection of *currachs* (boats made of a framework of laths covered with tarred canvas) and sections covering Galway and the Great War and the city's cinematic connections.

Spanish Arch   Historic Site
The Spanish Arch is thought to be an extension of Galway's medieval city walls, designed to protect ships moored at the nearby quay while they unloaded goods from Spain, although it was partially destroyed by the tsunami that followed the 1755 Lisbon earthquake. Today it reverberates with buskers and drummers, and the lawns and riverside form a gathering place for locals and visitors on sunny days, as kayakers negotiate the tidal rapids of the River Corrib.

Galway Market   Market
(www.galwaymarket.com; Church Lane; ◎8am-6pm Sat, noon-6pm Sun) Galway's bohemian spirit comes alive at its street market, which has set up in this spot for centuries. Saturdays are the standout for food, when farmers sell fresh produce alongside stalls selling arts and crafts, and cooking up ready-to-eat dishes. Additional markets take place from noon to 6pm on bank holidays, Fridays in July and August and every day during the Galway International Arts Festival. Buskers add to the festive atmosphere.

Hall of the
Red Earl   Archaeological Site
(www.galwaycivictrust.ie; Druid Lane; ◎9.30am-5pm Mon-Fri year-round, 10am-1pm Sat May-Sep) **FREE** In the 13th century when the de Burgo

  Top Galway Festivals

Galway's packed calendar of festivals turns the city and surrounding communities into what feels like one nonstop party – streets overflow with revellers, and pubs and restaurants often extend their opening hours.

Galway Food Festival (www.galwayfoodfestival.com; ◎Easter) The area's sublime food and drink are celebrated for five days with food and foraging tours, talks, cookery demonstrations and a market.

Cúirt International Festival of Literature (www.cuirt.ie; ◎late Apr) Top-name authors converge on Galway for one of Ireland's premier literary festivals, featuring poetry slams, theatrical performances and readings.

Galway Film Fleadh (www.galwayfilmfleadh.com; ◎early Jul) Early July sees the six-day Galway Film Fleadh set screens alight with new, edgy works.

Galway International Arts Festival (www.giaf.ie; ◎mid-late Jul) Catch performances and exhibits by top drama groups, musicians and bands, comedians, artists and much more during this two-week extravaganza.

Galway International Oyster & Seafood Festival (www.galwayoysterfest. com; ◎late Sep) Going strong since 1954, the world's oldest oyster festival draws thousands of visitors. Events include the National and World Oyster Opening Championships, live music, a masquerade carnival and family activities.

Galway International Arts Festival
JOSE IGNACIO RETAMAL/SHUTTERSTOCK ©

family ruled Galway, Richard – the Red Earl – erected a large hall as a seat of power, where locals would arrive to curry favour. After the 14 tribes took over, the hall fell into ruin, and was lost until 1997 when expansion of the city's Custom House uncovered its foundations, along with over 11,000 artefacts including clay pipes and gold cuff links. The Custom House was built on stilts overhead, leaving the old foundations open.

TOURS

Corrib Princess   Cruise
(☎091-563 846; www.corribprincess.ie; Woodquay; adult/child €16/7; ☺May-Sep) Cruises aboard an open-topped 157-seat boat pass historic landmarks along the River Corrib en route to the Republic's largest lake, Lough Corrib, taking 90 minutes all up. There are two or three departures per day, leaving from Woodquay, just beyond the Salmon Weir Bridge.

Galway Food Tours   Food & Drink
(☎086 733 2885; www.galwayfoodtours.com; €35; ☺by appointment) These two-hour tours delve into Galway's food scene,

taking in gourmet food shops and dining hot spots, with tastings including local cheeses, artisan breads and Galway Bay oysters. Further afield, other tours include a six-hour pub tour of Galway and Connemara (€80). There's an additional booking fee of €2. Tours depart from **McCambridge's** (www.mccambridges.com; 38/39 Shop St; dishes €5-14; ☺cafe 8.30am-5.30pm Mon-Wed, 8.30am-9pm Thu-Sat, 9.30am-6pm Sun, deli 8am-7pm Mon-Wed, 8am-9pm Thu-Sat, 9.30am-6pm Sun).

EATING

**Ard Bia at
Nimmo's**   Modern Irish €€
(☎091-561 114; www.ardbia.com; Spanish Arch, Longwalk; cafe dishes €6-12, dinner mains €20-28; ☺cafe 10am-3.30pm Mon-Fri, to 3pm Sat & Sun, restaurant 6-9pm; ☯) ✐ Inside the 18th-century Custom House near the Spanish Arch (p119), Ard Bia ('High Food' in Irish) is decorated with works by local artists and upcycled vintage furniture. Organic produce (some foraged) features on the seasonal menus of both the up-

---

Top Five Galway Restaurants

Loam (p121)

Ard Bia at Nimmo's (p120)

Aniar (p121)

O'Dowd's (p124)

Mitchell's (p124)

From left: Spanish Arch (p119); Galway oysters; Ard Bia at Nimmo's

stairs restaurant (adjoining a wine bar), and the street-level cafe serving fantastic brunches followed by lunch dishes such as tomato and fennel chowder.

Oscar's
Seafood €€

(☎091-582 180; www.oscarsseafoodbistro.com; Upper Dominick St; mains €15.50-25.50; ⊗6-9.30pm Mon-Sat) The menu changes daily at this outstanding seafood restaurant but might include monkfish poached in saffron and white wine served with cockles, seaweed-steamed Galway Bay lobster with garlic-lemon butter, or lemon sole with samphire. From Monday to Thursday before 7pm, its two course early-bird menu (€18.50) is a steal.

Cava Bodega
Tapas €€

(☎091-539 884; www.cavarestaurant.ie; 1 Middle St; tapas €4-16, paella €15; ⊗5-10pm Mon-Wed, 5-10.30pm Thu, 4-11pm Fri, noon-11.30pm Sat, noon-9.30pm Sun; ⊿) Over 50 regional Spanish tapas dishes are given a gourmet twist by star chef JP McMahon, whose other ventures include Michelin-starred Aniar. Showstoppers include salt cod with seaweed jam, black-olive fig

cake, quail eggs with chorizo oil, and pine nut-crusted beetroot, along with over 100 Spanish wines. On Friday and Saturday, the Bodega's bar stays open late.

Loam
Gastronomy €€€

(☎091-569 727; https://loamgalway.com; 2-/3-course menus €40/50, 7-course menu €70, with wine pairings €105; ⊗6-11pm Tue-Sat) ⊘ Enda McEvoy is one of the most groundbreaking chefs in Ireland today (with a Michelin star to prove it), producing inspired flavour combinations from home-grown, locally sourced or foraged ingredients: dried hay, fresh moss, edible flowers, wild oats, forest gooseberries, Salthill sea vegetables and hand-cut peat (which McEvoy uses in his extraordinary peat-smoked ice cream).

Aniar
Modern Irish €€€

(☎091-535 947; http://aniarrestaurant.ie; 53 Lower Dominick St; lunch menu €55, dinner menus €70-115, with wine pairings €105-180; ⊗6-9.30pm Tue-Thu, 5.30-9.30pm Fri, noon-2pm & 5.30-9.30pm Sat) ⊘ Terroir specialist Aniar is passionate about the flavours and food producers of Galway and West

 Spoken Irish

One of the most important Gaeltacht (Irish-speaking) areas in Ireland begins around Spiddal just east of Connemara and stretches west to Cashel and north into County Mayo.

That the Irish language is enjoying a renaissance around the country can be credited in part to media outlets based in Connemara and Galway. Ireland's national Irish-language radio station Radio na Gaeltachta (www.rte.ie/rnag) and its Irish-language TV station, TG4 (www.tg4.ie), sprang up in the 1990s and continue to thrive.

Connemara
PETR BREZINA/SHUTTERSTOCK ©

Ireland. Owner/chef JP McMahon's multi-course tasting menus have earned him a Michelin star, yet the casual spring-green dining space remains refreshingly down to earth. The wine list favours small producers. Reserve at least a couple of weeks in advance.

 DRINKING & NIGHTLIFE

Galway's nightlife is a blast; see Pub Crawl in Galway City (p114) for a top night out.

 INFORMATION

Galway's large, efficient **tourist office** (☏091-537 700; www.discoverireland.ie; Forster St; ☺9am-5pm Mon-Sat) can help arrange tours and has reams of information on the city and region.

 GETTING THERE & AWAY

BUS

Bus Éireann (www.buseireann.ie; Cara Bus Station, Station Rd) operates daily services to all major cities in the Republic and the North from **Cara Bus Station** (☏091-562 000; Station Rd), near the train station. There's an hourly service to Dublin (€15.70, 3¾ hours). Other services fan out across the region.

Citylink (www.citylink.ie; ticket office 17 Forster St; ☺office 9am-6pm; 🖥) services depart from **Galway Coach Station** (New Coach Station; Fairgreen Rd), near the tourist office. Destinations include Clifden, Cork and Dublin.

GoBus (www.gobus.ie; Galway Coach Station; 🖥) has frequent services between Galway Coach Station and Dublin (3½ hours) and Dublin Airport (three hours). Fares start at €18.

TRAIN

From the **train station** (www.irishrail.ie), just off Eyre Sq, there are up to 10 direct trains daily to/from Dublin's Heuston Station (from €18, 2¼ hours), and five daily to Ennis (€10, 1¼ hours). Connections with other train routes can be made at Athlone (from €18, one hour).

Connemara

The name Connemara (Conamara) translates as 'Inlets of the Sea' and the roads along the peninsula's filigreed coast bear this out as they wind around the small bays and coves of this breathtaking stretch of the Wild Atlantic Way.

Connemara's starkly beautiful interior, traversed by the N59, is a kaleidoscope of rusty bogs, lonely valleys and shimmering black lakes. At its heart are the Maumturk Mountains and the pewter-tinged quartzite peaks of the Twelve Bens mountain range, with a network of hiking and biking trails.

 INFORMATION

Galway's **tourist office** has lots of information on the area. Online, Connemara Tourism (www.connemara.ie) and Go Connemara (www.goconnemara.com) have region-wide info and links.

ℹ️ GETTING THERE & AROUND

BUS

Bus Éireann (www.buseireann.ie) serves most of Connemara. Services can be sporadic, and some operate May to September only, or July and August only.

Citylink (www.citylink.ie) has several buses a day linking Galway city with Clifden via Oughterard and on to Cleggan and Letterfrack.

For stop offs between towns, you might be able to arrange a drop-off with the driver.

CAR

Your own wheels are the best way to get off this scenic region's beaten track. Watch out for the narrow roads' stone walls and meandering Connemara sheep.

Oughterard & Around

The charmingly down-to-earth village of Oughterard (Uachtar Árd) sits on the shore of the Republic's biggest lake, Lough Corrib. Over 48km long and covering some 200 sq km, the lake virtually cuts off western Galway from the rest of the country and encompasses more than 360 islands.

◎ SIGHTS & ACTIVITIES

Aughnanure Castle   Castle
(www.heritageireland.ie; off N59; adult/child €5/3; ⏰9.30am-6pm Mar-late Oct) Built around 1500, this superbly preserved fortress signposted 4.2km east of Oughterard was home to the 'Fighting O'Flahertys', who controlled the region for hundreds of years after they fought off the Normans. The six-storey **tower house** stands on a rocky outcrop overlooking Lough Corrib and has been extensively restored.

Surrounding the castle are the remains of an unusual double *bawn* (area surrounded by walls outside the main castle); there's also the remains of the Banqueting Hall and a small, now isolated **watchtower**, with a conical roof. The River Drimneen once enclosed the castle on three sides, while today the river washes through a number of natural caverns and caves beneath the castle.

Inchagoill

The largest island on Lough Corrib, Inchagoill lies about 2km offshore from the lake's edge 4.5km north of Oughterard. The island is a lonely place dotted with ancient remains. **Corrib Cruises** runs day cruises. Alternatively rent your own boat from **Molloy's Boats** (📞091-866 954; Baurisheen; motor/rowing boat per day €65/35, motor boat with guide €140; ⏰by appointment).

Inchagoill's most fascinating sight is **Lia Luguaedon Mac Menueh** (Stone of Luguaedon, Son of Menueh), an obelisk which identifies a burial site. It stands about 75cm tall, near the Saints' Church.

It's claimed that the Latin writing on the stone is the second-oldest Christian inscription in Europe, after those in the catacombs in Rome.

The prettiest church is the Romanesque **Teampall na Naoimh** (Saints' Church), probably built in the 9th or 10th century, with carvings around its arched doorway. **Teampall Phádraig** (St Patrick's Church) is a small oratory of a very early design, with some later additions.

Church ruins, Inchagoill
REMIZOV/SHUTTERSTOCK ©

Corrib Cruises   Cruise
(📞087 994 6380; www.corribcruises.com; Oughterard Pier; adult/child €28/14; ⏰noon Wed-Mon Jul & Aug) Cruises from Oughterard run to **Inchagoill** island and Ashford Castle near Cong, County Mayo and back, taking a total of six hours. Check the website for seasonal sailing schedules.

GETTING THERE & AWAY

Bus Éireann (www.buseireann.ie) runs up to eight times daily to/from Galway city (€8.30, 40 minutes) and Clifden (€15.50, two hours) via Roundstone (€15.50, 1½ hours).

Citylink (www.citylink.ie) has five services daily to/from Galway (€9, 40 minutes) and Clifden (€13, 50 minutes) via the quicker N59.

Roundstone

Clustered around a boat-filled harbour, picture-perfect Roundstone (Cloch na Rón) is the kind of Irish village you hoped to find. Colourful terrace houses and inviting pubs overlook the shimmering recess of Bertraghboy Bay, which is home to dramatic tidal flows, lobster trawlers and traditional *currach* boats with tarred canvas bottoms stretched over wicker frames.

EATING

O'Dowd's Seafood €€
(☏095-35809; www.odowdsseafoodbar.com; Main St; mains restaurant €13-22, bar €13-15; ⊙restaurant 5-9.30pm, bar menu 10am-9.30pm; 🕾) ✦ Roundstone lobster, Aran Islands hake, plaice and sea bass, local crab and mackerel smoked in-house are sourced off the old stone dock directly opposite this wonderfully authentic old pub and restaurant, while produce comes from its garden. Bountiful seafood platters cost €29. There's a great list of Irish craft beers and ciders. Its neighbouring summertime **cafe** (dishes €5.50-11.50; ⊙9am-6pm Mar-Oct; 🕾) serves breakfast and lunch.

Top Five Historic Sites

Clifden & Around

A definitive stop on the Wild Atlantic Way, Connemara's 'capital', Clifden (An Clochán, meaning 'stepping stones'), is an appealing Victorian-era town presiding over the head of the narrow bay where the River Owenglin tumbles into the sea.

ACTIVITIES

Sky Road Scenic Drive
Signposted west of Clifden's Market Sq, this aptly named 15km driving and cycling route traces a dizzying loop out to the township of Kingston and back to Clifden, taking in rugged, stunningly beautiful coastal scenery en route. Set out clockwise from the southern side for the best views, which peak at sunset. There are several viewpoints en route where you can park.

EATING

Mitchell's Seafood €€
(☏095-21867; www.mitchellsrestaurantclifden.com; Market St; mains lunch €10.50-15, dinner €18-28, seafood platter €24; ⊙noon-10pm) Seafood from the surrounding waters takes centre stage at this elegant spot, from lunchtime sandwiches such as smoked mackerel and velvety chowder through to its standout Connemara platter (available at both lunch and dinner), piled high with Rossaveal prawns, Oranmore oysters, Connemara smoked salmon and Dunloughan crab. Strong wine list. Book ahead in the evenings.

Letterfrack & Around

Founded by Quakers in the mid-19th century, Letterfrack (Leitir Fraic) is a crossroads with a few pubs and B&Bs. But the forested setting and nearby coast are a magnet for outdoors adventure seekers. A 4km walk to the peak of **Tully Mountain** (356m) takes 40 minutes and offers uplifting ocean views.

⊙ SIGHTS

Connemara National Park   Park

(www.connemaranationalpark.ie; off N59;
⊙24hr) FREE Immediately southeast of Letterfrack, Connemara National Park spans
2957 dramatic hectares of bog, mountains,
heath and woodlands.

The park encloses a number of the
Twelve Bens, including Bencullagh, Ben-
brack and Benbaun. The heart of the park is
Gleann Mór (Big Glen), through which the
River Polladirk flows. There's fine walking up
the glen and over the surrounding mountains along with short self-guided walks

Guided nature walks (www.connemara
nationalpark.ie, ⊙11am Wed & Fri early Jul-Aug)
led by park rangers depart from the **visitor
centre** (www.connemaranationalpark.ie; off N59;
⊙9am-5.30pm Mar-Oct).

Kylemore Abbey   Historic Building

(www.kylemoreabbey.com; off N59, adult/child
€13/free; ⊙9am-7pm Jul & Aug, 9.30am-5.30pm
Sep & Oct, 9am-6pm Apr-Jun, 10am-4.30pm
Nov-Mar) Photogenically perched on the
shores of Pollacapall Lough, 4.3km east of
Letterfrack, this crenellated 19th-century
neo-Gothic fantasy was built for a wealthy
English businessman, Mitchell Henry, who
spent his honeymoon in Connemara. Only
ground-floor rooms are open to visitors, but
you can wander down the lake to the **Gothic
church**, and admission includes entry to
the extravagant **Victorian walled gardens**,
around a 20-minute walk away (linked by a
free shuttle bus from April to October).

👍 Claddagh Rings

The fishing village of Claddagh has long
been subsumed into Galway's city centre,
but its namesake rings survive as a time-
less reminder.

Popular with people of Irish descent
everywhere, the rings depict a heart
(symbolising love) between two out-
stretched hands (friendship), topped by
a crown (loyalty). Jewellery shops selling
Claddagh rings include Ireland's oldest,
Thomas Dillon's Claddagh Gold (www.
claddaghring.ie; 1 Quay St; ⊙10am-5.30pm
Mon-Sat, 12-5pm Sun).

GRACEPHOTO/SHUTTERSTOCK ©

ℹ GETTING THERE & AWAY

Citylink (www.citylink.ie) buses serve Letterfrack from Galway (€15, two hours, three daily)
and continue to Clifden (€5, 20 minutes).

ARAN ISLANDS

Aran Islands at a Glance...

Easily visible from the coast of counties Galway and Clare along the Wild Atlantic Way, the rocky, wind-buffeted Aran Islands have a desolate beauty that draws countless day trippers. Visitors who stay longer may feel that they're far further removed from the Irish mainland than the 45-minute ferry ride or 10-minute flight would suggest.

An extension of the limestone escarpment that forms the Burren in Clare, the islands have shallow topsoil scattered with wildflowers, grass where livestock grazes and jagged cliffs pounded by surf. Ancient forts here are some of the oldest archaeological remains in Ireland.

Aran Islands in One Day

It's pretty much impossible to visit more than one island per day, so if you have only one day plump for **Inishmore** (p132) and explore the spectacular prehistoric fort of **Dun Aengus** (p130), and its smaller cousins **Dún Eochla** (p130) and **Dún Eoghanachta** (p131). If time allows, sit down to a cosy pub lunch at **Tí Joe Watty's Bar** (p132).

Aran Islands in Two Days

With two days, you have the choice of relaxing overnight on Inishmore and taking in a trad music session at **Tí Joe Watty's Bar** (p132), or heading back to the mainland, spending the night there, and using day two for a trip to **Inisheer** (p134) to see **O'Brien's Castle** (p134) and a Father Ted photo-op at the wreck of the **Plassy** (p134).

Arriving in the Aran Islands

Air Flights depart from Connemara regional airport, about 35km west of Galway. **Aer Arann Islands** offers flights to each of the islands several times daily (10 minutes, €49 return, hourly in summer).

Boat Aran Island Ferries leave from Rossaveal, 40km west of Galway City. Buses from Queen St in Galway (adult/child €//4) connect with the sailings. From March to October there are also ferries from **Doolin** (p151).

Sleeping

After the last day trippers have left in summer, the islands assume a lovely serenity. All three islands have B&Bs and pub accommodation, and Inishmore and Inishmaan have inns. Inishmore has a great camping and glamping site and a hostel; there's also a hostel on Inisheer. Advance bookings in summer and during festivals are essential. Some places only accept cash. Closures are common during winter.

ECOVENTURESTRAVEL/SHUTTERSTOCK ©

Dun Aengus

Three spectacular prehistoric forts stand guard over Inishmore, each believed to be around 2000 years old. Chief among them is Dun Aengus, with three massive drystone walls that run right up to sheer drops to the ocean below.

Great For...

☑ Don't Miss

The stunning view along the cliff tops to the west of Dun Aengus.

The fort is protected by remarkable *chevaux de frise*, fearsome and densely packed defensive limestone spikes. A small visitor centre has displays that put everything in context and a slightly strenuous 900m walkway wanders uphill to the fort itself. Dun Aengus is around 7km west of Kilronan.

Powerful swells pound the 60m-high cliff face. A complete lack of railings or other modern additions that would spoil this incredible site means that you can not only go right up to the cliff's edge but also potentially fall to your doom below, so take care.

Nearby Historic Sites

Between Kilronan and Dun Aengus you'll find the small, perfectly circular fort **Dún**

Tourists on Dún Aengus cliffs

S'EFANC_VALERI/SHUTTERSTOCK ©

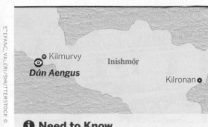

❶ Need to Know

Dún Aonghasa; www.heritageireland.ie;
site adult/child €5/3, visitor centre €2/1;
🕙9.30am-6pm Apr-Oct, to 4pm Nov-Mar

✖ Take a Break

Refuel with a slap-up meal of fish and
chips at Tí Joe Watty's Bar (p132).

★ Top Tip

Hiring a bike makes it easier to
explore the myriad sites around the
island.

Eochla FREE, which makes for a good walk
from the main road.

The ruins of numerous stone churches
identify the island's monastic history. The
small **Teampall Chiaráin** (Church of St Kieran), with a high cross in the churchyard,
is near Kilronan.

West of Kilmurvey is the perfect
Clochán na Carraige, an early Christian stone hut that stands 2.5m tall, and
various small early Christian ruins known
rather inaccurately as the **Na Seacht
dTeampaill** (Seven Churches), comprising a couple of ruined churches, monastic
houses and some fragments of a high
cross from the 8th or 9th century. To the
south of the ruins is **Dún Eoghanachta**
FREE, another circular fort.

Along the low-lying northern coast,
the sheltered little bay of **Port Chorrúch**
is home to up to 50 grey seals, who sun
themselves and feed in the shallows.
Further on, **Kilmurvey Beach** gets an EU
Blue Flag for its clean white-sand beach.
In the southeast, near Cill Éinne Bay, is
the early Christian **Teampall Bheanáin**
(Church of St Benen). Near the airport are
the sunken remains of a church; the spot
is said to have been the site of **St Enda's
Monastery** in the 5th century, though
what's visible dates from the 8th century
onwards.

Dún Dúchathair FREE (the Black Fort)
is an ancient fort dramatically perched on
a south-facing cliff top promontory to the
southwest of Kilronan.

Shopping on Inishmore

Kilmurvey Craft Village (Kilmurvey; ⊙hours vary) Hand-knitted woollens, carved stonework and jewellery incorporating Celtic designs are among the local arts and crafts sold at this charming collection of traditional thatched cottages near Dun Aengus (p130).

Man of Aran Gift Shop (http://mano-faran.eu; Kilronan; film per adult/child €5/3; ⊙9am-8pm; 🛜) At Kilronan's main crossroads, this eclectic shop stocks souvenirs from T-shirts to stained glass and Celtic-design jewellery, and screens the iconic film *Man of Aran* five times daily in its tiny 24-seat theatre. It also has wi-fi (free with purchase) and a fine little coffee bar serving Italian brews.

Kilmurvey Craft Village
MARIA_JANUS/SHUTTERSTOCK ©

Inishmore

Most visitors who venture out to the Aran Islands don't make it beyond the largest and closest island to Galway, Inishmore (Inis Mór), and its spectacular prehistoric stone fort, Dun Aengus (p130), perched on the island's towering cliffs.

Inishmore is 14.5km long and 4km at its widest stretch. Boats arrive and depart from Inishmore's main settlement, **Kilronan** (Cill Rónáin), on the eastern side of the island. The arid landscape to its west is dominated by stone walls, boulders, scattered buildings and the odd patch of deep-green grass and potato plants.

Today, tourism turns the wheels of the island's economy: from May to September tour vans greet each ferry and flight, offering a ride around the sights.

⊗ EATING & DRINKING

Bayview Restaurant International €€

(📱086 792 9925; www.bayviewrestaurantinish-more.com; mains lunch €10-15, dinner €19-40; ⊙noon-9pm; 🛜🍴) Inside a landmark sunset-pink building 200m west of the pier, Bayview's dining room showcases local art. Lunch features classics such as Guinness beef stew, while dinner ups the ante with whole lobster, chargrilled steaks and amazing desserts such as grilled pineapple marinated in cinnamon and ginger and served with vanilla-bean ice cream and ginger coulis. Kids are well catered for.

Pier House Irish €€

(📱099-61417; www.pierhousearan.com; Kilronan; mains €14.50-27; ⊙noon-5pm & 6-10pm May-Sep; 🛜🍴) Watch the ferries come and go from the terrace of this restaurant downstairs from the guesthouse of the same name, or keep warm by the open fire. Seafood is a speciality – crab, oysters, lobster, smoked salmon and mackerel, prawns and a fish of the day – along with land-based dishes like Irish beef Wellington. Kids' menu available.

Tí Joe Watty's Bar Pub

(www.joewattys.ie; Kilronan; ⊙noon-midnight Sun-Thu, 11.30am-12.30am Fri & Sat Apr-Oct, 4pm-midnight Mon-Fri, noon-midnight Sat & Sun Nov-Mar) Warmed by peat fires, the island's oldest and most popular pub has trad sessions every night in summer from 9pm and weekends the rest of the year. Darts night on Wednesday is a local fixture. There's a large beer garden and an extensive list of Irish gins, craft beers and whiskeys.

Its seafood-focused menu (mains €10 to €16.50) is excellent; book for dinner in summer.

INFORMATION

The **tourist office** (☏099-61263; www.aranislands.ie; Kilronan; ☉10am-5pm) is on the waterfront 50m northwest of the ferry pier in Kilronan.

GETTING AROUND

From May to September, minibuses offer 2½-hour tours of the island (€10) to ad hoc groups. The drive – with commentary – between Kilronan and **Dun Aengus** (p130) takes about 45 minutes each way. You can also negotiate for private and customised tours.

To see the island at a gentler pace, pony traps with a driver are available from May to September for trips between Kilronan and Dun Aengus; the return journey costs between €50 and €100 for up to four people.

Many places to stay have bicycles for use or rent; alternatively **Aran Bike Hire** (☏099-61132; www.aranislandsbikehire.com; Inishmore Pier; mountain & road bike rental per day €10, electric bikes from €30, deposit €20-30; ☉Apr-Oct) rents out road, mountain and electric bikes, which it delivers to your accommodation anywhere on the island.

Inishmaan

The least-visited of the islands, with the smallest population, Inishmaan (Inis Meáin) is a rocky respite, roughly 5km long by 3km wide. Early Christian monks seeking solitude were drawn to Inishmaan, as was the author JM Synge (1871–1909), who spent five summers here over a century ago.

The 300-year-old thatched cottage of **Teach Synge** (☏099-73036; €3; ☉by appointment Apr-mid–Sep), now a small museum, is where Synge spent his summers between 1898 and 1902.

At the desolate western end of the island, **Synge's Chair** is a viewpoint at the edge of a sheer limestone cliff with the surf from Gregory's Sound booming below. The cliff ledge is often sheltered from the wind; do as Synge did and find a stone perch to take it all in.

Quintessential stone walls of the Aran Islands

TRAVELMOOS/SHUTTERSTOCK ©

From left: O'Brien's Castle; Donkey on Inishmore (p132); *Plassy* shipwreck

Inisheer

Inisheer (Inis Oírr), the smallest of the Aran Islands at roughly 4km wide by 2km long, has a palpable sense of enchantment, enhanced by the island's wildflower-strewn landscapes, deep-rooted mythology and enduring traditional culture.

⊙ SIGHTS

Tobar Éinne   Historic Site

(Well of Enda) Locals still carry out a pilgrimage known as the Turas to the Well of Enda, a bubbling spring in a remote rocky expanse in the southwest. The ceremony involves, over the course of three consecutive Sundays, picking up seven stones from the ground nearby and walking around the small well seven times, putting one stone down each time, while saying the rosary until an elusive eel appears from the well's watery depths.

If, during this ritual, you're lucky enough to see the eel, it's said your tongue will be bestowed with healing powers, enabling you to literally lick wounds.

O'Brien's Castle   Historic Building

(Caisleán Uí Bhriain) FREE Built in 1585 on the island's highest point, this tower house was constructed within the remains of a ring fort called Dún Formna, dating from as early as the 1st century AD. The 100m climb rewards with a sweeping panorama across clover-covered fields to the beach and harbour. The views are especially dramatic at sunset. You're free to walk around the ruins.

Plassy   Shipwreck

A steam trawler launched in 1940, the *Plassy* was thrown onto the rocks on 8 March 1960 and driven onto the island a couple of weeks later after another storm. Its cargo of whiskey was never recovered but miraculously, all on board were saved. Tigh Ned (p135) pub has a collection of photographs and documents detailing the rescue. An aerial shot of the wreck was used in the opening sequence of the cult TV series *Father Ted*.

TINYAJ/GETTY IMAGES ©

⊗ EATING

Teach an Tae   Cafe €

(☎099-75092; http://cafearan.ie; dishes €3.50-
9.50; ⊗11am-5pm May-early Nov) ☞ Wild island
raspberries and blackberries, home-grown
salad ingredients, eggs from the cafe's
chickens and apples from its orchard of
30 heritage trees are used in dishes here.
Sweet treats include rhubarb-and-apple pie
and scones with homemade jam; for something savoury try the grilled pollack with
herbed couscous and sorrel, or the Aran
Islands' goat's cheese tart. Cash only.

Tigh Ned   Pub Food €

(☎099-75004; http://tighned.com; dishes
€7-10.50; ⊗kitchen noon-4pm Apr-Oct, bar
10am-midnight Apr-Oct) Here since 1897, Tigh
Ned is a welcoming, unpretentious place
with inexpensive lunchtime fare (sandwiches, cottage pie, fish and chips), along with
craft beers, whiskey and Guinness. Tables
in the garden have harbour views. Lively
traditional music plays on weekends from
June to August.

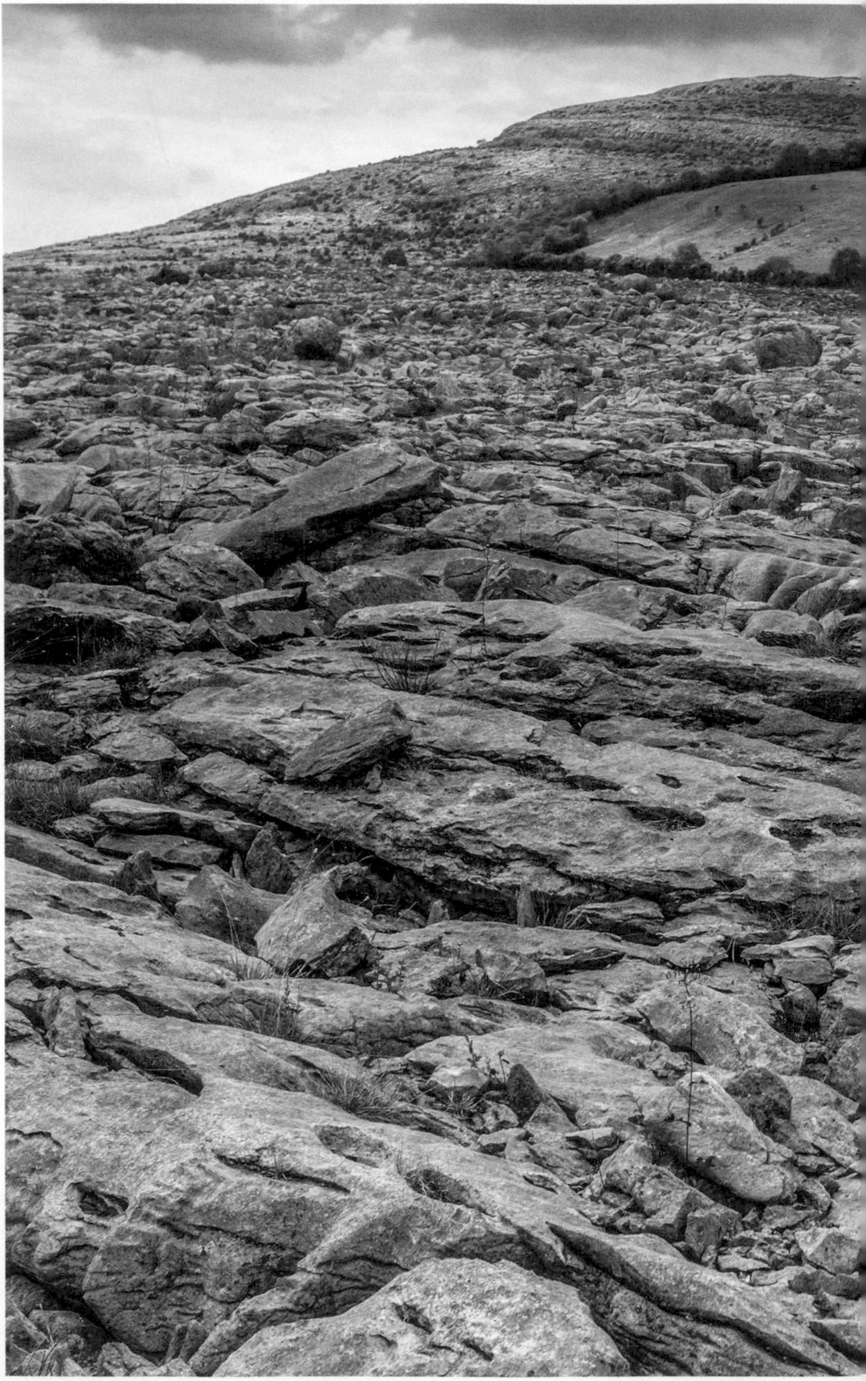

COUNTY CLARE

County Clare at a Glance...

Along the Wild Atlantic Way, the ocean relentlessly pounds Clare's coastline eroding rock into fantastic formations, and fashioning sheer cliffs including those at the iconic Cliffs of Moher and at ends-of-the-earth Loop Head. Along the coast, the waves are a magnet for surfers, and surf schools set up on many of Clare's beaches in summer.

If the land is hard, Clare's soul certainly isn't: traditional Irish culture and music flourish here. And it's not just a show for tourists, either. In larger towns and even the tiniest of villages you'll find pubs with trad music sessions year-round.

County Clare in One Day

Explore the town of **Ennis** (p144), taking in **Ennis Friary** (p144) and a hearty pub lunch in **Nora Culligans** (p144), then head west with camera in hand to view the magnificent **Cliffs of Moher** (p141). Plan to spend the night in nearby Doolin so you can see the sunset from the cliffs and take in a **trad music session** (p142) in one of its pubs.

County Clare in Two Days

Day two depends on which direction you're heading. If it's south towards Kerry, visit **Loop Head** (p147) for more spectacular coastal scenery before taking the ferry across the Shannon to Tarbert and the road to Dingle. If it's north towards Galway, book a day's **guided walk** (p150) exploring the beguiling limestone landscapes of the **Burren** (p148).

Arriving in County Clare

Exploring County Clare by public transport is difficult and time-consuming. If you don't have a car, it's best to base yourself in Galway city, and visit the Cliffs of Moher and Doolin as part of a guided coach tour such as **Burren Wild Tours** (p150).

Sleeping

Ennis makes a central base for exploring Clare but you'll find camping grounds, hostels, B&Bs, pubs and hotels throughout the county, notably in and around Doolin and Lahinch. Many places only open from around Easter to October and fill quickly at weekends and during school holidays, when you'll need to book ahead.

PATRYK KOSMIDER/SHUTTERSTOCK ©

Cliffs of Moher

In good visibility, the Cliffs of Moher are staggeringly beautiful. Views stretch to the Aran Islands and the hills of Connemara. Sunsets here see the sky turn a kaleidoscope of amber, rose-pink and deep garnet-red.

Great For...

☑ **Don't Miss**

The view west along the cliffs around sunset, when the scenery is at its most spectacular.

The entirely vertical cliffs rise to a height of 203m, their edge falling away abruptly into the constantly churning sea. A series of heads, the dark limestone seems to march in a rigid formation that amazes, no matter how many times you look. On a clear day you'll channel Barbra Streisand as you can see forever; the Aran Islands stand etched on the waters of Galway Bay, and beyond lie the hills of Connemara in western Galway.

Its fame guarantees a steady stream of visitors that can surge to a swell almost as impressive as the raging ocean below, but the tireless Atlantic winds can drown out the chatter and you can shrug off the crowds, even though busloads arrive in summer. A vast visitor centre is set back into the side of a hill, *Teletubbies* style. As part of the development, however, the

Cliffs of Moher Visitor Centre

Need to Know

Cliffs of Moher Visitor Centre (☎065-708 6141; www.cliffsofmoher.ie; adult/child incl parking €6/free, O'Brien's Tower €2/1; ☺9am-9pm Jul & Aug, 9am-7.30pm Mon-Fri, to 8pm Sat & Sun Jun & Sep, shorter hours rest of year)

✕ Take A Break

Escape the overcrowded cafes in the visitor centre by taking a picnic and dining on the cliff tops.

★ Top Tip

Bring binoculars – more than 30 species of birds, including darling little puffins, can be spotted here.

main walkways and viewing areas along the cliffs have been surrounded by a 1.5m-high wall that's too high and set too far back from the edge.

Walking Trails

There are good rewards if you're willing to walk for 10 minutes. Past the end of the 'Moher Wall' south, a trail runs along the cliffs to Hag's Head (about 5.5km) – few venture this far, yet the views are uninhibited. From here you can continue on to Liscannor for a total walk of 12km (about 3½ hours). To the north, you can follow the Doolin Trail via O'Brien's Tower right to the village of Doolin (about 7km and 2½ hours). The entire Liscannor to Doolin walking path via the cliffs is now signposted; note that there are a lot of ups and downs and narrow, cliff-edge stretches.

Visitor Centre

The modern visitor centre contains numerous shops and a few cafes, plus a rewarding exhibition regarding the fauna, flora, geology and climate of the cliffs. There is also an audiovisual virtual reality experience called The Ledge, filmed on a loop in an auditorium through the day. Free information booklets on the cliffs are available. The soulless ground floor Puffin's Nest Cafe seems designed to urge you up to the pricier Cliffs View Cafe above.

Musicians playing in McGann's, Doolin

DOOLIN 1

CHRIS HOWES/WILD PLACES PHOTOGRAPHY/ALAMY STOCK PHOTO ©

Trad Music Sessions

From cosy, atmospheric pubs in tiny villages where non-instrument-playing patrons are a minority to rollicking urban boozers in Ennis, Clare is one of Ireland's best counties for traditional music.

Great For...

☑ **Don't Miss**

A session at Vaughan's in Kilfenora, one of Ireland's top trad music venues.

Ennis

You can bounce from one music-filled pub to another on most nights, especially in the summer. Musicians from around the county come here to show off and there are good venues for serious trad pursuits.

Brogan's   Pub

(www.brogansbarandrestaurant.com; 24 O'Connell St; ☺noon-midnight) On the corner of Cooke's Lane, Brogan's is a big pub that rambles from one room to the next with a fine bunch of musicians rattling even the stone floors from about 9pm Monday to Thursday (more nights in summer).

Doolin

A collection of pubs with nightly trad music sessions. However, tourist crowds

Eugene's, Ennistymon

MARIA_JANUS/SHUTTERSTOCK ©

can be intense, so sensations of intimacy or enjoyment can evaporate.

McGann's

Pub

(☎065-707 4133; www.mcgannspubdoolin.com; Roadford; ⏰10am-11.30pm Mon-Wed, to 12.30am Thu-Sat, to 11pm Sun; 📶) McGann's has all the classic touches of a full-on Irish music pub, with action often spilling onto the street. The food here (mains €11 to €18) is the best of Doolin's three famous pubs. Inside you'll find locals playing darts in its warren of small rooms, some with peat fires.

Kilfenora

A small village with a big musical heritage on show at the great local pub Vaughan's.

ℹ Need to Know

Check pub websites ahead of travelling for details of who's playing when; book accommodation nearby.

✖ Take A Break

Most music pubs offer a menu of decent pub grub; McGann's in Doolin is one of the best for food.

★ Top Tip

Arrive at least an hour before the session starts to stand any chance of getting a seat near the action.

Vaughan's Pub

Pub

(www.vaughanspub.ie; Main St; ⏰10.30am-11.30pm, hours can vary) A pub with a big reputation in Irish music circles; seafood, traditional foods and local produce feature on the menu. Have a pint under the big tree out front. There's music in the bar every night during the summer and on many nights at other times. The adjacent barn is the scene of terrific **set-dancing sessions** on Thursday (10pm) and Sunday (9pm).

Ennistymon

A charming village inland from Doolin with a couple of ancient pubs attracting top local talent.

Eugene's

Pub

(Main St; ⏰10.30am-11.30pm Mon-Thu, 10.30am-12.30am Fri & Sat, 12.30-11pm Sun) With one of the most amazing pub frontages you'll ever see, Eugene's is a classic choice. Intimate and cosy, with a trademark collection of visiting cards covering its walls, it has a great whiskey collection and some fab stained glass.

Traditional Music Festivals

Ennis Trad Festival (www.ennistradfest. com; ⊘mid-Nov) Traditional music in venues across town keeps spirits high during November's five-day festival.

Fleadh Nua (www.fleadhnua.com; ⊘May) Singing, dancing and workshops are part of this lively eight-day traditional music festival.

Russell Memorial Weekend (www. michorussellweekend.ie; ⊘Feb) Held on the last weekend in February, this festival celebrates the work of legendary Doolin musician Micho Russell and his brothers, and features workshops, dancing classes and trad music sessions throughout town.

Fiddler playing Irish trad music
MICHAEL KEVIN DALY/FUSE/GETTY IMAGES ©

Ennis

Clare's charming commercial hub, Ennis (Inis) lies on the banks of the fast-moving River Fergus. Sights are few, but the town centre, with its narrow, pedestrian-friendly streets, is enjoyable to wander. Handily situated 23km north of **Shannon Airport** (SNN; ☑061-712 000; www.shannonairport.ie; ⚘), it makes an ideal base for exploring the county: you can reach any part of Clare in under two hours from here.

◎ SIGHTS

Ennis Friary   Church
(www.heritageireland.ie; Abbey St; adult/ child €5/3; ⊘10am-6pm Easter-Sep, to 5pm

Oct) North of the Square, Ennis Friary was founded by Donnchadh Cairbreach O'Brien, a king of Thomond, between 1240 and 1249. A mix of structures dating between the 13th and 19th centuries, the friary has a graceful five-section window dating from the late 13th century, a McMahon tomb (1460) with alabaster panels depicting scenes from the Passion, and a particularly fine *Ecce Homo* panel portraying a stripped and bound Christ.

⊗ EATING & DRINKING

Food Heaven   Cafe €
(www.food-heaven.ie; 21 Lower Market St; dishes €5-11; ⊘8.30am-6pm Mon-Sat; ⚘) This small cafe-deli does a good job of living up to its ambitious name with creative and fresh fare. Omelettes such as goat's cheese and cherry tomato or mushroom and thyme are a highlight at breakfast. Be ready to queue at lunch for renowned brown-bread sandwiches, hand-rolled sausage rolls with homemade tomato relish, and potato cakes with sweet chilli mayo.

Nora Culligans   Pub
(Abbey St; ⊘noon-midnight Mon-Thu, to 2am Fri & Sat, to 1am Sun; ⚘) Magnificently restored, cavernous pub Nora Culligans retains original features including the front bar's ornate two-storey-high whiskey cabinets and timber panelling in the back bar. It's an atmospheric venue for live music across a diverse array of genres, from jazz and blues to acoustic singer-songwriters and reggae as well as trad.

Poet's Corner Bar   Pub
(www.flynnhotels.com; Old Ground Hotel, O'Connell St; ⊘11am-11.30pm Mon-Thu, 11am-12.30am Fri & Sat, noon-11pm Sun; ⚘) Trad sessions Thursday to Sunday year-round and every night from June to August make this timber-panelled, coffered-ceilinged bar in the Old Ground Hotel, a favourite with locals and visitors.

ⓘ INFORMATION

Ennis' **tourist office** (☏065-682 8366; www.visitennis.com; Arthur's Row; ☺9am-5.30pm Mon-Fri, to 5pm Sat) is housed in the same building as the **Clare Museum** (www.clarelibrary.ie; Arthur's Row; ☺9.30am-1pm & 2-5.30pm Mon-Sat Jun-Sep, 9.30am-1pm & 2-5.30pm Tue-Sat Oct-May) **FREE**.

ⓘ GETTING THERE & AWAY

The M18 bypass east of the city lets traffic between Limerick and Galway zip right past.

BUS

Bus Éireann (www.buseireann.ie) services operate from the **bus station** (Station Rd) beside the train station. Connect in Galway or Limerick for Dublin.

Destinations include the following:

Cork €19, three hours, hourly

Doolin €14.30, 50 minutes, four daily, via Corofin, Ennistimon, Lahinch, Liscannor and Cliffs of Moher

Galway €12.50, 1½ hours, hourly, via Gort

Limerick €10, one hour, hourly, via Bunratty

Shannon Airport €8.60, 30 minutes, hourly

TRAIN

Irish Rail (www.irishrail.ie) trains from the **train station** (Station Rd) serve Limerick (€15, 40 minutes, seven daily), where you can connect to trains to places further afield, including Dublin.

The line to Galway (€7.50, 1¾ hours, seven daily) takes in some superb Burren scenery.

Bunratty

Bunratty (Bun Raite) is home to a splendid castle that abuts a theme park recreating an Irish village of yore. It's a double act that draws in countless visitors, particularly given its proximity to Shannon Airport (p144), 13km to Bunratty's west.

Ennis Friary

From left: Loop Head Lighthouse; Bunratty Castle; Bunratty Folk Park

⊙ SIGHTS

Bunratty Castle & Folk Park Castle
(📞061-360 788; www.shannonheritage.com/
BunrattyCastleAndFolkPark; castle & folk park
adult/child €16.50/14; ⊙castle 9am-4pm,
folk park 9am-5.50pm) Dating from the
15th century, square, hulking Bunratty
Castle is only the latest of several edifices
to occupy its location beside the River
Ratty. Vikings founded a settlement here
in the 10th century, and later occupants
included the Norman Thomas de Clare in
the 1270s. It's accessed via the folk park,
a reconstructed traditional Irish village
with smoke coiling from thatched-cottage
chimneys, a forge and working blacksmith,
weavers, post office, grocery-pub, small
cafe and more. Tickets are cheaper online.

✪ ENTERTAINMENT

Irish Evening at
Bunratty   Live Performance
(📞061-360 788; www.shannonheritage.com/
IrishEvening; adult/child €50/27.50; ⊙7-9.30pm
Apr-Oct) High-spirited Irish nights lift the
roof of a corn barn in the folk park adjacent
to Bunratty Castle. Waitstaff serve Irish
classics (stews, poached salmon, apple
pie) amid traditional storytelling, music and
dancing, while wine gets you in the mood
for the singalong.

Bunratty Castle
Medieval Banquet   Live Performance
(📞061-360 788; www.shannonheritage.com/
BunrattyCastleMedievalBanquet; adult/child
€58/38; ⊙5.30pm & 8.45pm) Candlelit
medieval banquets at Bunratty Castle
are replete with harp-playing maidens,
court jesters and meaty medieval fare
(vegetarian options available), washed
down with goblets of mead (honey wine).
The banquets are extremely popular with
groups, so book well ahead. You can often
find savings online.

Loop Head

A sliver of land between the Shannon Estuary and the pounding Atlantic, windblown
Loop Head Peninsula has an ends-of-the-
earth feel. As you approach along the R487,

sea begins to appear on both flanks as land tapers to a narrow shelf. On a clear day, the lighthouse-capped headland at Loop Head (Ceann Léime), Clare's southernmost point, has staggering views to counties Kerry and Galway. The often-deserted wilds of the head are perfect for exploration, but be extra careful near the cliff edge.

On the northern side of the cliff near the point, a dramatic crevice has been cleaved from the coastal cliffs where you'll first hear and then see a teeming bird-breeding area. Guillemots, choughs and razorbills are among the squawkers nesting in rocky niches.

A long hiking trail runs along the cliffs to the peninsula's main town, Kilkee. A handful of other tiny settlements dot the peninsula.

◎ SIGHTS & ACTIVITIES

Bog Road Bike Tours Cycling
(☎086 278 0161; www.bogroadbiketours.com; Erin St; 2-/4-hour tour €25/45; ◷tours 10am & 4pm Sat & Sun) Explore the narrow laneways denied to cars around Loop Head on these entertaining tours run by Cillian Murphy, who fills you

in on Kilkee and Loop Head history, from the Famine to storms and shipwrecks. Two-hour tours cover 16km; four-hour tours cover 40km. Bike rental is included in the price.

Loop Head Lighthouse Lighthouse
(adult/child €5/2; ◷10am-6pm mid-Mar–early Nov) On a 90m-high cliff, this 23m-tall working lighthouse, complete with a Fresnel lens, rises up above Loop Head. Guided tours (included in admission) take you up the tower and onto the balcony – in fine weather you can see as far as the Blasket Islands and Connemara. There's been a lighthouse here since 1670; the present structure dates from 1854. It was converted to electricity in 1871 and automated in 1991.

Miltown Malbay

Miltown Malbay has a thriving music scene and hosts the annual Willie Clancy Summer School (p148), one of Ireland's great traditional music events. The town was a favoured resort for well-to-do Victorians, though it isn't actually on the sea: the beach is 2km south at **Spanish Point**.

Clare's Best Music Festival

Miltown Malbay's tribute to native son Willie Clancy, one of Ireland's greatest pipers, is one of the best traditional music festivals in the country. During the nine-day festival, which usually begins in the first or second week in July, impromptu sessions occur day and night and the town pubs are packed. Workshops and classes at the **Willie Clancy Summer School** (☏065-708 4148; http://scoilsamhraidhwillieclancy.com; ◷Jul) underpin the event.

ANATOLII BROHOVSKYI/SHUTTERSTOCK ©

🍺 DRINKING & NIGHTLIFE

Miltown Malbay's traditional Irish pubs have wonderful trad sessions throughout the year.

Hillery's   Pub

(Main St; ◷noon-11pm Mon-Thu, to midnight Fri & Sat, to 6pm Sun) Opened in 1891, Miltown Malbay's oldest pub has stained-glass windows and framed photos on the walls. Live trad sessions take place every weekend year-round and most nights in summer.

Friel's Bar   Pub

(Lynch's; Mullagh Rd; ◷6pm-midnight Mon-Thu, 6pm-1am Fri & Sat, 1pm-midnight Sun) This old-style charmer has regular trad sessions most nights in summer and up to four nights a week the rest of the year.

The Burren

Stretching across northern Clare, the rocky, windswept Burren region is a unique striated lunar-like landscape of barren grey limestone that was shaped beneath ancient seas, then forced high and dry by a great geological cataclysm. It covers 250 sq km of exposed limestone, and 560 sq km in total.

Wildflowers in spring give the Burren brilliant, if ephemeral, colour amid its stark beauty. Villages throughout the region include the music hub of Doolin on the west coast, Kilfenora inland and charming Ballyvaughan in the north, on the shores of Galway Bay.

Flora & Fauna

Soil may be scarce on the Burren, but the small amount that gathers in the cracks and faults is well drained and nutrient-rich. This, together with the mild Atlantic climate, supports an extraordinary mix of Mediterranean, Arctic and alpine plants. Of Ireland's native wildflowers, 75% are found here, including 24 species of beautiful orchids, the creamy-white burnet rose, the little starry flowers of mossy saxifrage and the magenta-coloured bloody cranesbill. Lime-detesting plants such as heathers can be found living alongside those that thrive on lime. One of the biggest threats to this diversity is the proliferation of hazel scrub and blackthorn, which needs to be controlled.

The Burren is a stronghold of Ireland's most elusive mammal, the rather shy weasel-like pine marten. Badgers, foxes and even stoats are common throughout the region. Otters and seals inhabit the shores around Bell Harbour, New Quay and Finavarra Point. The Burren Code is an initiative to educate people as to how they can protect the environment of the Burren when they visit.

⚡ ACTIVITIES

The Burren is a walker's paradise. The stark, beautiful landscape, plentiful trails and ancient sites are best explored on foot. 'Green roads' are the old highways of the Burren, crossing hills and valleys to some of the most remote corners of the region. Many of these unpaved ways were built during the Famine as part of relief work, while some date back possibly thousands of years. Now used mostly by hikers and the occasional farmer, some are signposted.

Beginning in Lahinch and ending in Corofin, the **Burren Way** is a 123km network of marked hiking routes throughout the region.

Guided nature, history, archaeology and wilderness walks are great ways to appreciate this unique region. Typically the cost of the walks averages €10 to €35 and there are many options, including private trips. Operators include Burren Guided Walks & Hikes (p150), Heart of Burren Walks (p150) and Burren Wild Tours (p150).

🔭 Clare's Other Cliffs

On the way to and from the southern tip of Loop Head, take in the jaw-dropping sea vistas and drama of the sensational cliffs along the coast roads.

From Carrigaholt, drive south down Church St for around 2km till you reach the junction, then turn right along the L2002. Part of the Wild Atlantic Way, with directional signs, this scenic route is the Coast Rd, hugging the coastline and offering splendid panoramas of the sea, running through the village of Rhinevilla and eventually rejoining the R487 at Kilbaha.

Heading west from Loop Head, drive along the R487 to Cavan and then take a left along the Coast Rd (L2000) and follow the signs, making your way to Kilkee. You'll rejoin the R487 but can head north again along small roads north from just after either Oughterard or Cross for stunning views of soaring coastal cliffs.

Loop Head cliffs
NORADOA/SHUTTERSTOCK ©

ℹ️ GETTING THERE & AWAY

On its Limerick–Galway route, which runs via Ennis, **Bus Éireann** (www.buseireann.ie) stops at key Burren destinations including Ballyvaughan, Corofin, Doolin, Fanore and Lisdoonvarna.

Kilfenora has limited services to Ennis and some coastal Clare destinations, while New Quay has limited services to Galway city. For Carron, you'll need your own transport.

Doolin

Doolin is hugely popular due to its reputation as a centre of Irish traditional music, owing to year-round trad sessions at its famous trio of music pubs. Located 6km northeast of the Cliffs of Moher in a landscape riddled with caves and laced with walking paths, it's also a jumping-off point for cliff cruises and ferries out to the Aran Islands.

Without a centre, this scattered settlement consists of three infinitesimally small neighbouring villages. Charming **Fisherstreet** has some picturesque traditional cottages, there are dramatic surf vistas at the harbour 1.5km west along the coast. **Doolin** itself is about 1km east on the little River Aille. **Roadford** is another 1km east. None of the villages has more than a handful of buildings.

While the music pubs give Doolin a lively vibe, the heavy concentration of visitors means standards don't always hold up to those in some of Clare's less-frequented villages.

Guided Walks

Burren Guided Walks & Hikes (☑087 244 6807, 065-707 6100; www.burrenguidedwalks.com; from €20; ☺by reservation) Long-time guide Mary Howard leads groups on a variety of rambles, off-the-beaten-track hikes and rugged routes.

Heart of Burren Walks (☑087 292 5487; www.heartofburrenwalks.com; €20; ☺by reservation Tue-Sat) Local Burren author Tony Kirby leads walks and archaeology hikes lasting two hours. Cash only.

Burren Wild Tours (☑087 877 9565; www.burrenwalks.com; L1014, Oughtmama, Bellharbour; €20-30; ☺by appointment) John Connolly offers a broad range of walks, from gentle to more strenuous. Walks start from the cafe at Hazel Mountain Chocolate (☑065-707 8847; www.hazelmountainchocolate.com; L1014, Oughtmama; tour adult/child €12/5; ☺shop & cafe 10am-5.30pm, tours 1pm Sat & Sun).

Limestone rocks, The Burren
MARTIN FOWLER/SHUTTERSTOCK ©

🍷 DRINKING & NIGHTLIFE

Doolin's famed music pubs – Gus O'Connor's in Fisherstreet, and McGann's (p143) and McDermott's in Roadford – have sessions throughout the year, as does Fitz's.. To experience trad music in the intimate surrounds of an Irish home, reserve ahead to visit the **Doolin Music House** (☑065-707 4584; www.doolinmusichouse.com; R478, Caherkinalla; €20; ☺by reservation 7-8.30pm Mon, Wed & Fri).

Gus O'Connor's   Pub

(https://gusoconnorspubdoolin.net; Fisherstreet; ☺10am-midnight Mon-Thu, to 2am Fri-Sun) Right on the river where it runs into the sea, this sprawling place dating from 1832 has a rollicking atmosphere when the music is in full swing. On some summer nights you won't squeeze inside. Music plays from 9.30pm nightly from late February to November and every Sunday from 6pm year-round.

McDermott's   Pub

(MacDiarmada's; Roadford; ☺bar 11am-midnight, kitchen 9am-9.30pm) This simple red-and-white traditional pub is a rowdy favourite. Picnic tables face the street; the inside is pretty basic, as is the menu of sandwiches and roasts. Music kicks off at 9.30pm nightly from Easter to October, and several nights a week the rest of the year.

Fitz's   Pub

(www.hoteldoolin.ie; Doolin; ☺noon-11.30pm Mon-Thu, to 12.30am Fri & Sat, to 11pm Sun) At Hotel Doolin, relative newcomer Fitz's has trad sessions twice nightly from April to October and at least three times a week from November to March. In addition to a superb whiskey selection it has great craft beers and ciders (tasting flights available), and brews its own Dooliner beers. Bar food (mains €13 to €24) is first rate.

ℹ️ INFORMATION

The website www.doolin.ie has comprehensive tourist information.

ℹ️ GETTING THERE & AWAY

BOAT

From mid-March to October, **Doolin Pier** (off R439) is one of two ferry departure points to the Aran Islands (along with **Rossaveal Ferry Terminal** (Rossaveal), 37km west of Galway city). Sailings are often cancelled due to high seas or tides that make the small dock inaccessible.

Doolin 2 Aran Ferries (☑065-707 5949; www.doolin2aranferries.com; Doolin Pier; ☺mid-Mar–

Gus O'Connor's

Oct) and **O'Brien Line** (☎065 707 5618; www.
obrienline.com; Doolin Pier; ☻mid-Mar–Oct)
each have sailings to Inisheer (one way/return
€10/20, 30 minutes, four daily), Inishmore
(€15/25, 1¼ hours, two daily) and Inishmaan
(€20/25, 45 minutes, two daily). Interisland
ferry tickets cost €10 per crossing.

The boats also offer one-hour **Cliffs of Moher
cruises** (€15), which are best done late in the
afternoon when the light is from the west.

There are various combination tickets and
online discounts.

BUS

Four **Bus Éireann** (www.buseireann.ie) buses
daily serve Ennis (€14.30, 50 minutes), via the
Cliffs of Moher (€3.30, 10 minutes); and Galway
(€19.50, two hours) via Ballyvaughan (€8.60,
one hour).

In summer, various backpacker shuttles often
serve Doolin from Galway and other points in
Clare.

THE ANTRIM COAST

The Antrim Coast at a Glance...

Northern Ireland's north coast is a giant geology classroom. The ocean has laid bare the black basalt and white chalk that underlie much of County Antrim, and dissected the rocks into a scenic extravaganza of sea stacks, pinnacles, cliffs and caves. Extraordinary rock formations and ruined castles have made the region an atmospheric backdrop for the hit TV series Game of Thrones, with numerous filming locations here.

To the west lies the spirited city of Derry. Ireland's only walled city sits alongside a broad sweep of the River Foyle and echoes with centuries of often-turbulent history.

Antrim Coast in One Day

With one day to spare between Belfast and Derry, drive the Antrim coast road (including the Torr Head Scenic Road) to Ballycastle. After a lunch of fish and chips at **Morton's** (p166) continue to the Giant's Causeway and spend the afternoon exploring the fantastic coastal scenery before continuing the scenic drive to Derry.

Antrim Coast in Two Days

With two days you can afford to relax with an overnight at the Giant's Causeway or Bushmills. On day one do the coastal drive to Ballycastle; in the afternoon visit **Carrick-a-Rede Rope Bridge** (p165) and the pretty harbour at Ballintoy. Explore the Causeway in the relative peace of evening and/or the following morning, then take in **Dunluce Castle** (p162) and Portrush next day.

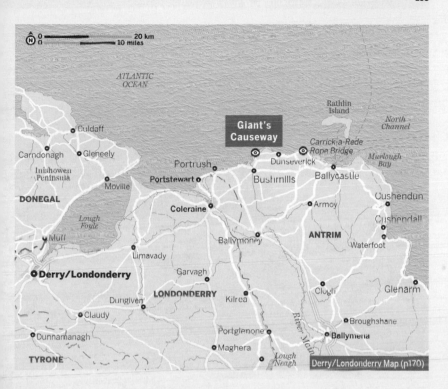

Derry/Londonderry Map (p170)

Arriving in the Antrim Coast

Bus Ulsterbus services connect the region's towns and villages. Contact **Translink** (p236) for timetable and fare information. Additional connections are provided by the seasonal bus services **Antrim Coaster** (p159) and **Causeway Rambler.** (p159)

Train The Londonderry line links Derry to Belfast, stopping in Coleraine (with connections to Portrush), Ballymena and Antrim Town. For information on train fares and timetables, contact Translink.

Sleeping

The greatest breadth of accommodation options can be found in Derry/Londonderry; as well as hotels, there are B&Bs aplenty, often located in beautiful Georgian or Victorian buildings. If you want to be closer to sights such as the Giant's Causeway and the Carrick-a-Rede Rope Bridge (particularly if you're relying on public transport), the coastal towns of Portrush and Ballycastle offer plenty of good lodgings.

Giant's Causeway

This spectacular rock formation – a national nature reserve and Northern Ireland's only Unesco World Heritage Site – is one of Ireland's most impressive and atmospheric landscape features.

Great For...

☑ **Don't Miss**

The cliff-top views from the Chimney Tops headland.

When you first see it you'll understand why the ancients believed the Causeway was not a natural feature. The vast expanse of regular, closely packed, hexagonal stone columns beneath the waves looks for all the world like the handiwork of giants.

Visiting the Giant's Causeway itself is free of charge but you pay to use the car park on a combined ticket with the **Giant's Causeway Visitor Experience** (☎028-2073 1855; www.nationaltrust.org.uk; 60 Causeway Rd; adult/child £10.50/5.25; ☉9am-7pm Jul & Aug, to 6pm Mar-Jun, Sep & Oct, to 5pm Nov-Feb) ✐; parking-only tickets aren't available.

The Making of the Causeway

The story goes that the Irish giant Finn McCool built the Causeway so he could

Giant's
Causeway

Portballintrae

❶ Need to Know

www.nationaltrust.org.uk, ☉dawn-dusk)
FREE

✕ Take A Break

There's a cafe in the visitor centre, but
the nearby **Nook** (📞028-2073 2993;
48 Causeway Rd; mains £9-18; ☉kitchen
11am-9pm Mar-Oct, to 6pm Nov-Feb) offers
a more convivial atmosphere.

★ Top Tip

Try to visit midweek or out of season to
experience the Causeway at its most
evocative.

cross the sea to fight the Scottish giant
Benandonner. Benandonner pursued
Finn back across the Causeway, but in
turn took fright and fled back to Scotland,
ripping up the Causeway as he went. All
that remains are its ends – the Giant's
Causeway in Ireland, and the island of
Staffa in Scotland (which has similar rock
formations).

The more prosaic scientific explanation
is that the Causeway rocks were formed
60 million years ago, when a thick layer of
molten basaltic lava flowed along a valley
in the existing chalk beds. As the lava flow
cooled and hardened – from the top and
bottom surfaces inward – it contracted,
creating a pattern of hexagonal cracks at
right angles to the cooling surfaces (think
of mud contracting and cracking in a hexagonal pattern as a lake bed dries out).

As solidification progressed towards the
centre of the flow, the cracks spread down
from the top and up from the bottom, until the lava was completely solid. Erosion
has cut into the lava flow, and the basalt
has split along the contraction cracks,
creating the hexagonal columns.

Exploring the Causeway

From the car park, it's an easy 10- to
15-minute walk downhill on a tarmac road
(wheelchair accessible) to the Giant's
Causeway itself (a shuttle bus also
plies the route). However, a much more
interesting approach on foot is to follow
the cliff-top path northeast for 2km to the
Chimney Tops headland, which has an
excellent view of the Causeway and the
coastline to the west, including Inishowen
and Malin Head.

This pinnacled promontory was bom-
barded by ships of the Spanish Armada in

1588, who thought it was Dunluce Castle, and the wreck of the Spanish galleon *Girona* lies just off the tip of the headland. Return towards the car park and about halfway back descend the **Shepherd's Steps** (signposted) to a lower-level footpath that leads down to the Causeway. Allow 1½ hours for the round trip.

Alternatively, you can visit the Causeway first, then follow the lower coastal path as far as the **Amphitheatre** viewpoint at Port Reostan, passing impressive rock formations such as the **Organ** (a stack of vertical basalt columns resembling organ pipes), and return by climbing the Shepherd's Steps.

You can also follow the cliff-top path east as far as Dunseverick or beyond.

The superb, ecofriendly Giant's Causeway Visitor Experience (p156), built into the hillside and walled in by tall black basalt slabs that mimic the basalt columns of the Causeway, houses an exhibition explaining the geology of the region, as well as a tourist information desk, restaurant and shop. It's cheaper if you arrive on foot, bicycle or by public transport; admission includes an audio guide.

Wreck of the Girona

The little bay 1km to the northeast of the Giant's Causeway is called Port na Spaniagh – Bay of the Spaniards. It was here, in October 1588, that the *Girona* – a ship of the Spanish Armada – was driven onto the rocks by a storm.

The *Girona* had escaped the famous confrontation with Sir Walter Raleigh's fleet in the English Channel but, along with many other fleeing Spanish ships,

had been driven north around Scotland and Ireland by bad weather. Though designed for a crew of 500, when she struck the rocks she was loaded with 1300 people – mostly survivors gathered from other shipwrecks – including the cream of the Spanish aristocracy. Barely a dozen survived.

Somhairle Buidhe (Sorley Boy) MacDonnell (1505–90), the constable of nearby Dunluce Castle salvaged gold and cannons from the wreck, and used the money to extend and modernise his for-

> ★ **Did You Know**
>
> More than 850,000 people visited the Giant's Causeway in 2016, seeing it regain the title of Northern Ireland's most popular tourist attraction from Titanic Belfast.

tress – cannons from the ship can still be seen on the castle's landward wall. But it wasn't until 1968 that the wreck site was excavated by a team of archaeological divers. They recovered magnificent treasure of gold, silver and precious stones, as well as everyday sailors' possessions, which are now on display in Belfast's Ulster Museum (p226).

Getting There & Away

Antrim Coaster (Bus 252; 020-9066 6630; www.translink.co.uk; Bus Rambler unlimited day travel adult/child £9/4.50, Easter, May bank-holiday weekends, Jul & Aug;), **Causeway Rambler** (Bus 402; 028-9066 6630; www.translink.co.uk; Bus Rambler unlimited day travel adult/child £9/4.50; Easter-Sep), and the Giant's Causeway & Bushmills Railway (p163) run to the Causeway seasonally. Bus 172 runs from Ballycastle (£4.40, 30 minutes, eight daily Monday to Friday, three Saturday and Sunday) to Coleraine (£4.40, 25 minutes) and Bushmills (£2, five minutes) stops here year-round. From Coleraine, trains run to Belfast or Derry.

> **Local Knowledge**
>
> A pleasant way to reach the Giant's Causeway is the 45-minute walk from Bushmills on the footpath running alongside the Giant's Causeway & Bushmills Railway.

Causeway Coast Walking Tour

This spectacular stretch of the Causeway Coast Way is one of the finest coastal walks in Ireland. Be prepared; check tide times in advance.

Start Carrick-a-Rede Rope Bridge
Distance 16.5km
Duration Four to six hours

Take a Break...
Bring a picnic lunch with you and stop at one of the viewpoints along the way; if the weather isn't too wild, Dunseverick Castle is the perfect spot for a scenic meal.

4 The path at Dunseverick crosses a footbridge above a waterfall before reaching ruined **Dunseverick Castle**.

Benbane Head

Port na Spaniagh

5

Chimney Tops

Port Noffer

Giant's Eyes

The Harp

Giant's Causeway

The Organ

Croyer Hill

Dunseverick Harbour

4

6

FINISH

B146

DUNSEVERICK

P

Giant's Causeway & Bushmills Railway (seasonal)

A2

5 Named after an 18th-century clergyman and amateur geologist, **Hamilton's Seat** viewpoint enjoys a spectacular panorama of 100m-high sea cliffs, stacks and pinnacles.

6 The winding **Shepherd's Steps** (p158) cut a staircase into steep cliffs, descending to the shore where a path leads to the Giant's Causeway.

Classic photo Carrick-a-Rede Rope Bridge

1 Test your nerve on the swaying **Carrick-a-Rede Rope Bridge** (p165) slung between seacliffs and an island.

2 Next up is **White Park Bay** (p165), a dramatic 2km-long sweep of white sand. The going here is easiest at low tide, when you can walk on the firm sand.

Boheeshane Bay

Sheep Island

Ballintoy Harbour

Larrybane Head

Carrick-a-Rede Island

Larrybane Bay

1

START

White Park Bay **2**

B15

BALLINTOY

3

PORTBRADDEN

A2

3 Continue on to **Portbradden** (p164), a picturesque cluster of tiny cottages squeezed between the cliffs and the sea.

Ⓝ 0 ————— 2 km
0 ————— 1 mile

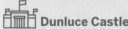

Dunluce Castle

The ruins of **Dunluce Castle** (87 Dunluce Rd; adult/child £5/3; ⊙10am-5pm Mar-Nov, to 4pm Dec & Jan, last entry 30min before closing) perch atop a dramatic basalt crag 5km east of Portrush, a one-hour walk away along the coastal path. A narrow bridge leads from the mainland courtyard across a dizzying gap to the main part of the fortress. Below, a path leads down from the gatehouse to the Mermaid's Cave beneath the castle crag. All coastal buses stop here.

In the 16th and 17th centuries the castle was the seat of the MacDonnell family (the earls of Antrim from 1620), who built a Renaissance-style manor house within the walls. Part of the castle, including the kitchen, collapsed into the sea in 1639, taking seven servants and that night's dinner with it.

RAINBOW79/GETTY IMAGES ©

Portrush

The seaside resort of Portrush (Port Rois) bursts at the seams with holidaymakers in high season and, unsurprisingly, many of its attractions are focused unashamedly on good old-fashioned family fun. It's also one of Ireland's top surfing centres and home to the North's most prestigious golf club.

◉ SIGHTS & ACTIVITIES

East Strand   Beach
(Curran Strand) Portrush's main attraction is the beautiful sandy East Strand beach that stretches for 3km to the east of the town, ending at the scenic chalk cliffs of Whiterocks.

Royal Portrush Golf Club   Golf
(☎028-7082 2311; www.royalportrushgolfclub. com; Dunluce Rd; green fees May-Sep £190, Apr & Oct £100, Nov-Mar £60) Spectacularly situated alongside the Atlantic at the town's eastern edge, 1888-founded Royal Portrush hosted the Open Championship in 1951 and will host again in 2019. It's home to two courses: the par-72 Dunluce, with its water's-edge White Rock (5th) and ravine-set Calamity (14th) holes, and the par-70 Valley. See the website for visitor times.

EATING

Arcadia   Cafe £
(www.arcadiaportrush.co.uk; East Strand; dishes £3-6; ⊙9am-5pm Apr-Sep) A Portrush landmark, this 1920s art deco pavilion houses a breezy beach cafe on the ground floor, serving big breakfasts, bagels, salads and ice cream for a post-surf refuel, and a free art gallery on the upper floor, which also hosts workshops and classes (yoga, painting, etc).

55 Degrees North   International ££
(☎028-7082 2811; www.55-north.com; 1 Causeway St; mains £10-19; ⊙12.30-2.30pm & 5-8.30pm Mon-Fri, to 9pm Sat, noon-8.30pm Sun; 🖼) Floor-to-ceiling windows allow you to soak up a spectacular panorama of sand and sea from this stylish restaurant. The food concentrates on clean, simple flavours. Downstairs, licensed **Café North** (mains lunch £6-8, dinner £10-14; ⊙9am-9pm Mon, Tue & Sat, to 6pm Wed-Fri Easter-Sep, reduced hours Oct-Easter) has a beach-facing terrace.

❶ GETTING THERE & AWAY

The bus terminal is near the Dunluce Centre. Buses 140A and 140B link Portrush with Portstewart (£2.30, 10 minutes, every 20 minutes Monday to Saturday, five Sunday) and

Coleraine (£2.70, 20 minutes). It's also served by seasonal buses **Antrim Coaster** (p159) and **Causeway Rambler** (p159).

The train station is just south of the harbour. Portrush is served by trains from Coleraine (£2.40, 12 minutes, hourly), where there are connections to Belfast and Derry.

Bushmills

The nearest town to the Giant's Causeway (5km), Bushmills has long been a place of pilgrimage for connoisseurs of Irish whiskey, and is an attractive stop for hikers exploring the Causeway Coast.

SIGHTS & ACTIVITIES

Old Bushmills Distillery   Distillery

(028-2073 3218; www.bushmills.com; 2 Distillery Rd; tour adult/child £8/4; 9.15am-4.45pm Mon-Sat, noon-4.45pm Sun Mar-Oct, 10am-4.45pm Mon-Sat, noon-4.45pm Sun Nov-Feb) Bushmills is the world's oldest legal distillery, having been granted a licence by King James I in 1608. The whiskey is made with Irish barley and water from St Columb's Rill, a tributary of the River Bush, and matured in oak barrels. During ageing, the alcohol content drops from around 60% to 40%; the spirit lost through evaporation is known as 'the angels' share'. After the tour, you can try a free sample of your choice from Bushmills' range.

Giant's Causeway & Bushmills Railway   Train

(028-2073 2844; infogcbr@btconnect.com; return adult/child £5/3) Trains run hourly between 10am and 5.30pm, departing on the hour from the Causeway, on the half-hour from Bushmills, daily in July and August, and on weekends only from Easter to June and September to October.

Brought from a private line on the shores of Lough Neagh, the narrow-gauge line and locomotives (two steam and one diesel) follow the route of a 19th-century tourist tramway for 3km from Bushmills to below the Giant's Causeway Visitor Experience.

A path alongside the full length of the Giant's Causeway & Bushmills Railway track makes for a pleasant 5km walk or cycle.

Portstewart Strand

The broad, 2.5km beach of **Portstewart Strand** (www.nationaltrust.org.uk/portstewart-strand) is a 20-minute walk south of the centre along a coastal path, or a short bus ride along Strand Rd. Parking is allowed on the firm sand, which can accommodate over 1000 cars (open year-round, £5 per car from Easter to October).

Bang on Portstewart Strand beach, this National Trust–owned, wooden **Harry's Shack** (028-7083 1783; www.facebook.com/HarrysShack; Portstewart Strand; mains £12-17; 11am-3pm & 5-8.30pm Tue-Thu, 10am-9pm Fri & Sat, to 7pm Sun) has one of the north coast's best restaurants (book ahead for lunch and dinner). Harry's uses fruit, vegetables and herbs from its own organic farm plus local meat and seafood in simple but sensational dishes like megrim sole with cockles and seaweed butter, and Mulroy Bay mussels in Irish cider.

WWW.DEIRDREGREGG.COM/GETTY IMAGES ©

✖ EATING

Bushmills Inn
Irish ££

(📞028-2073 3000; www.bushmillsinn.com; 9 Dunluce Rd; mains lunch £12-15, dinner £13-25; ⏱noon-5pm & 6-9.30pm Mon-Sat, noon-2.30pm & 6-9.30pm Sun; 🛜) Set in the old 17th-century stables of the Bushmills Inn, this haven has intimate wooden booths and blazing fires, and uses fresh local produce in dishes like Atlantic seafood chowder, wild Irish venison and traditional Dalriada Cullen Skink (wood-smoked haddock poached in cream, with poached eggs and new potatoes). Book ahead.

Tartine
Irish ££

(📞028-2073 1044; www.distillersarms.com; 140 Main St; mains £12-22; ⏱5-8.30pm Wed & Thu, to 9pm Fri, to 9.30pm Sat, 12.30-2pm & 5-8.30pm Sun) Inside a former pub, with bare boards, exposed stone and glowing fire, Tartine's three interconnecting dining rooms are adorned with Irish art. Local produce is given a French twist: Ballycastle crab crème brûlée and roast pork with braised beef bourguignon.

Giant's Causeway to Ballycastle

The pretty village of Ballintoy (Baile an Tuaighe) tumbles down the hillside to a picture-postcard harbour, better known to *Game of Thrones* fans as the Iron Islands' Lordsports Harbour (among other scenes filmed here). The restored lime kiln on the quayside once made quicklime using stone from the chalk cliffs and coal from Ballymoney.

Ballintoy lies roughly halfway between Ballycastle and the Giant's Causeway on the most scenic stretch of the Causeway Coast, with sea cliffs of contrasting black basalt and white chalk, rocky islands and broad sweeps of sandy beach.

The main attractions can be reached by car or bus, but the 16.5km stretch between the Carrick-a-Rede car park and the Giant's Causeway is best enjoyed on a walk (p160) following the waymarked **Causeway Coast Way** (www.walkni.com).

About 9.5km east of the Giant's Causeway is the tiny seaside hamlet of **Portbradden**, with half a dozen harbour-

BARTKOWSKI/SHUTTERSTOCK ©

side houses. Visible from Portbradden and accessible via the next junction off the A2 is the spectacular **White Park Bay**, with its wide, sweeping sandy beach. Some 3km further east is **Ballintoy**.

◎ SIGHTS

Carrick-a-Rede
Rope Bridge
Bridge

(☏028-2076 9839; www.nationaltrust.org. uk/carrick-a-rede; 119 Whitepark Rd, Ballintoy; adult/child £7/3.50; ⊙9.30am-6pm Apr-Oct, to 3.30pm Nov-Mar) This 20m-long, 1m-wide bridge of wire rope spans the chasm between the sea cliffs and the little island of Carrick-a-Rede, swaying 30m above the rock-strewn water. Crossing the bridge is perfectly safe, but frightening if you don't have a head for heights, especially if it's breezy (in high winds the bridge is closed). From the island, views take in Rathlin Island and Fair Head to the east.

There's a small National Trust information centre and cafe at the car park.

The impetus for the crossing first came from fishers, who would stretch their nets out from the tip of the island to intercept the passage of salmon migrating along the coast to their home rivers.

Now firmly on the tour-bus route, Carrick-a-Rede has become so popular that the National Trust has introduced ticketed one-hour time slots to visit the bridge. Turn up early to be sure of securing a ticket in high season.

✖ EATING

Red Door Cottage
Cafe £

(☏028-2076 9048; www.facebook.com/ thereddoortearoom; 14a Harbour Rd, Ballintoy; mains £6-10; ⊙11am-4pm Tue-Fri, 10am-4pm Sat & Sun May-Oct, 10am-4pm Sat & Sun Mar & Apr) Fronted by a fire-engine-red door, this little cottage sits 200m off the main coast road along the side road to Ballintoy Harbour. Everything is homemade: soups, chowders, Irish stew, burgers and cakes. The garden's picnic tables are idyllic in the sunshine; when it's chilly there's a turf fire indoors. It's worth booking ahead in peak holiday seasons.

Top Five Antrim Coast Photo Ops

Giant's Causeway (p156)
Dunluce Castle (p162)
White Park Bay (p165)
Carrick-a-Rede Rope Bridge (p165)
Torr Head Scenic Road (p168)

From left: Carrick-a-Rede rope bridge; Puffins can be seen on Rathlin Island (p167); Ballintoy harbour

Roark's Kitchen
Cafe £

(Harbour Rd, Ballintoy Harbour; mains £6.25-7.50; 11am-7pm daily Jun-Aug, Sat & Sun only May & Sep;) On the quayside at Ballintoy Harbour, this cute little chalk-built tearoom serves teas, coffees, ice cream, home-baked apple, cherry and rhubarb tart, and lunch dishes such as Irish stew or chicken and ham pie. Cash only.

ⓘ GETTING THERE & AWAY

Bus 172 (eight daily Monday to Friday, three daily Saturday and Sunday) connects Ballintoy with Coleraine (£4.40, 40 minutes), Ballycastle (£3, 20 minutes), Giant's Causeway (£3.20, 20 minutes) and Bushmills (£3.50, 25 minutes). The **Antrim Coaster** (p159) and **Causeway Rambler** (p159) buses cover the route in season.

Ballycastle

The harbour town and holiday resort of Ballycastle (Baile an Chaisil) marks the eastern end of the Causeway Coast. It's a pretty town with a family-friendly promenade and a good bucket-and-spade beach. Ferries to Rathlin Island depart from here.

◉ SIGHTS
Marconi Memorial
Monument

In the harbour car park, a plaque at the foot of a rock pinnacle commemorates the day in 1898 when Guglielmo Marconi's assistants contacted Rathlin Island by radio from Ballycastle to prove to Lloyds of London that wireless communication was a viable proposition. The idea was to send notice to London or Liverpool of ships arriving safely after a transatlantic crossing – most vessels on this route would have to pass through the channel north of Rathlin.

✕ EATING
Morton's Fish & Chips
Fish & Chips £

(028-2076 1100; The Harbour, Bayview Rd; mains £6-10; noon-8pm Sun-Thu, to 9pm Fri & Sat) Fish and chips don't come fresher: local boats unload their daily catch right along-

Cushendun

side this little harbourside hut. The cod, haddock, scallops, scampi and crab cakes along with chips made from locally farmed potatoes draw long queues in summer (expect to wait).

Ursa Minor Bakery, Cafe £

(www.ursaminorbakehouse.com; 45 Ann St; ⏰10am-4pm Tue-Sat) Specialising in sourdough and friands (sweet almond cakes), Ursa Minor is the kind of bakery-cafe you might hope to find in a hip Sydney suburb rather than the seaside town of Ballycastle. When Dara and Ciara Ó Hartghaile returned from New Zealand they decided to give artisan baking a shot; the resulting bakery is a hit with locals and visitors alike.

ⓘ GETTING THERE & AWAY

The bus station is on Station Rd, just east of the Diamond (the diamond-shaped area at the heart of the city, within the four main gates of the city walls). Bus 217 links Ballycastle with Ballymena (£6.70, 50 minutes, hourly Monday to Friday, five Saturday), where you can connect to Belfast.

Bus 172 goes along the coast to Coleraine (£6.50, one hour, eight daily Monday to Friday, three Saturday and Sunday) via Ballintoy, the Giant's Causeway and Bushmills.

The seasonal **Antrim Coaster bus** (p159) also stops here.

Glens of Antrim

The northeastern corner of Antrim is a high plateau of black basalt lava overlying beds of white chalk. Along the coast, between Cushendun and Glenarm, the plateau has been dissected by a series of scenic, glacier-gouged valleys known as the Glens of Antrim.

Cushendun & Cushendall

The pretty seaside village of Cushendun is famous for its distinctive Cornish-style cottages, now owned by the National Trust. Built between 1912 and 1925 at the behest of the local landowner, Lord Cushendun, they were designed by

 Rathlin Island

Rathlin is famous for its spectacular coastal scenery and the seabirds, especially puffins, which nest on the sea cliffs at the island's western tip. From the harbour in Church Bay there are three main walking routes: to the **Rathlin West Light Seabird Centre** (☎028-2076 3948; www.rspb.org.uk; adult/child £5/2.50; ⏰10am-5pm Mar-Sep) (7km), to the **East Lighthouse** (3km) and to the **South Lighthouse** (4.5km). The roads are all suitable for cycling. There are also some fabulous off-road walking trails including the **Ballyconagan Trail** to the Old Coastguard Station on the north coast.

Getting There & Around

Rathlin Island Ferry (☎028-2076 9299; www.rathlinballycastleferry.com; return trip adult/child/bicycle £12/6/3.30) runs daily from Ballycastle; advance bookings are essential. From April to mid-September there are up to 10 crossings a day, half of which are fast catamaran services (20 minutes), the rest via a slower car ferry (45 minutes). Reduced service in winter.

McGinn's **Puffin Bus** (☎07759 935192, 07752 861788; tickets per adult/child £5/3) shuttles visitors between the ferry and Rathlin West Light Seabird Centre from April to September; contact the company for other transport requests.

Bicycle hire (☎028-2076 3954; john_jennifer@btinternet.com; Soerneog View Hostel; per day £10; ⏰10am-5pm) is available at Soerneog View Hostel, south of the harbour.

East Lighthouse
ROGERBRADLEY/GETTY IMAGES ©

 Torr Head Scenic Road

A few kilometres east of Ballycastle, a minor road signposted 'Scenic Route' branches north off the A2. This alternative route to Cushendun is not for the faint-hearted driver (nor for caravans), as it clings, precarious and narrow, to steep slopes high above the sea. Side roads lead off to the main points of interest. On a clear day, there are superb views across the sea to Scotland, from the Mull of Kintyre to the peaks of Arran.

The first turn-off ends at the National Trust car park at Coolanlough, the starting point for a waymarked 5km return hike to **Fair Head**. The second turn-off leads steeply down to **Murlough Bay**. From the parking area at the end of this road, you can walk north along the shoreline to some ruined miners' cottages (10 minutes); coal and chalk were once mined in the cliffs above, and burned in a lime kiln (south of the car park) to make quicklime.

The third turn-off leads you past some ruined coastguard houses to the rocky headland of **Torr Head**, crowned with a 19th-century coastguard station (abandoned in the 1920s). This is Ireland's closest point to Scotland – the Mull of Kintyre is a mere 19km away across the North Channel. In late spring and summer, a fixed-net salmon fishery operates here. The ancient ice house beside the approach road was once used to store the catch.

Murlough Bay
JOE DANIEL PRICE/GETTY IMAGES ©

Clough Williams-Ellis, the architect of Portmeirion in north Wales.

Cushendall is a holiday centre with a small and shingly beach. The village, which can be a traffic bottleneck, sits at the foot of Glenballyeamon, overlooked by the prominent flat-topped hill of Lurigethan.

SIGHTS & ACTIVITIES

Cushendun has a wide sandy **beach**, various short **coastal walks** and some impressive **caves** – a *Game of Thrones* filming location – cut into the overhanging conglomerate sea cliffs south of the village (follow the trail around the far end of the holiday apartments south of the river mouth).

Some 6km north of the village on the A2 road to Ballycastle is **Loughareema**, also known as the Vanishing Lake. Three streams flow in but none flow out. The lough fills up to a respectable size (400m long and 6m deep) after heavy rain, but the water gradually drains away through fissures in the underlying limestone, leaving a dry lake bed.

Curfew Tower   Historic Building
The unusual red sandstone Curfew Tower at the central crossroads was built in 1817 and based on a building the landowner had seen in China. It was originally a prison. The tower is closed to the public.

EATING

Harry's Restaurant   Bistro ££
(📱028-2177 2022; http://harryscushendall. com; 10 Mill St; mains lunch £8-13, dinner £10-20; ⏰noon-9pm; 📶) With its cosy lounge-bar atmosphere and friendly welcome, Harry's is a local institution, serving pub grub staples from noon to 6pm plus an à la carte evening menu that ranges from steak to lobster.

ℹ️ GETTING THERE & AWAY

Bus 150 links Cushendun with Cushendall (£2.70, 15 minutes, six daily Monday to Friday, three Saturday), Glenariff Forest Park (£3.80, 30 minutes) and Ballymena (£6.70, one hour).

Glenarm

The seasonal **Antrim Coaster** (p159) stops here.

Glenarm

Delightful little Glenarm (Gleann Arma) is the oldest village in the Glens of Antrim. It's well worth a visit for the fabulous gardens at Glenarm Castle, rows of pretty Georgian houses and forest park.

⊙ SIGHTS & ACTIVITIES

Take a stroll into the old village of neat Georgian houses (off the main road, immediately south of the river). Where the street opens into the broad expanse of Altmore St, look right to see the **Barbican Gate** (1682), the entrance to the grounds of Glenarm Castle (p169).

Up steep Vennel St, turn left after the last house along the Layde Path to the viewpoint, which has a grand view of the village and the coast.

Glenarm Castle & Walled Garden   Castle

(www.glenarmcastle.com; 2 Castle Lane; walled garden adult/child £6/3; ⊙garden 10am-5pm Mon-Sat, 11am-5pm Sun Apr–mid-Oct) Since 1750 Glenarm has been the family seat of the McDonnell family, earls of Antrim; it's currently the home of Lord and Lady Dunluce. The castle itself is closed to the public – except during the Tulip Festival on the May bank-holiday weekend, and during the **Dalriada Festival** (www.dalriadafestival.co.uk; 1-day pass adult/child £15/6; ⊙Jul) in July – but you can visit the lovely walled garden and take a walk around the estate along the castle trail.

The estate's organic farm is renowned for its award-winning Glenarm shorthorn beef; the smokehouse produces organic smoked salmon. Both are sold at the **Glenarm Castle Tea Room & Shop** (☑028-2884 1984; mains £4.85-9.25; ⊙10am-5pm Mon-Sat, 11am-5pm Sun Apr–mid-Oct).

ⓘ GETTING THERE & AWAY

The seasonal bus **Antrim Coaster** (p159) stops in the village.

Derry (Londonderry)

Northern Ireland's second-largest city continues to flourish as an artistic and cultural hub. Derry's city centre was given a striking makeover for its year as the UK City of Culture 2013, with the new Peace Bridge, Ebrington Sq, and the redevelopment of the waterfront and Guildhall area making the most of the city's splendid riverside setting.

There's lots of history to absorb here, along with taking in the burgeoning live-music scene in the city's lively pubs.

◎ SIGHTS

Derry's walled city is Ireland's earliest example of town planning. It's thought to have been modelled on the French Renaissance town of Vitry-le-François, designed in 1545 by Italian engineer Hieronimo

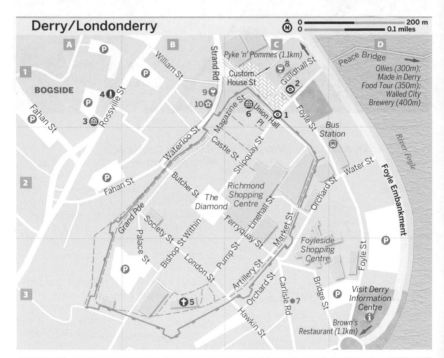

Derry/Londonderry

Derry's City Walls

Marino – both are based on the grid plan of a Roman military camp, with two main streets at right angles to each other, and four city gates, one at either end of each street.

Derry's City Walls   Walls
(⊙dawn-dusk) **FREE** The best way to get a feel for Derry's layout and history is to walk the 1.5km circumference of the city's walls. Completed in 1619, Derry's city walls are 8m high and 9m thick, and are the only city walls in Ireland to survive almost intact. The four original gates (Shipquay, Ferryquay, Bishop's and Butcher's) were rebuilt in the 18th and 19th centuries, when three new gates (New, Magazine and Castle) were added.

Tower Museum   Museum
(www.derrystrabane.com/towermuseum; Union Hall Pl; adult/child £4/2; ⊙10am-5.30pm, last entry 4pm) Head straight to the 5th floor of this award-winning museum inside a replica 16th-century tower house for a view from the top. Then work your way down

through the excellent **Armada Shipwreck** exhibition, and the **Story of Derry**, where well-thought-out exhibits and audiovisuals lead you through the city's history, from the founding of the monastery of St Colmcille (Columba) in the 6th century to the Battle of the Bogside in the late 1960s. Allow at least two hours.

Guildhall   Notable Building
(☎028-7137 6510; www.derrystrabane.com/Guildhall; Guildhall St; ⊙10am-5.30pm) **FREE** Standing just outside the city walls, the neo-Gothic Guildhall was originally built in 1890, then rebuilt after a fire in 1908. Its fine stained-glass windows were presented by the London livery companies, and its clock tower was modelled on London's Big Ben. Inside, there's a historical exhibition on the Plantation of Ulster, and a tourist information point.

St Columb's Cathedral   Cathedral
(www.stcolumbscathedral.org; 17 London St; suggested donation £2; ⊙9am-5pm Mon-Sat) Built between 1628 and 1633 from the

From left: Peace Bridge (p170); Fish tacos at Pyke 'n' Pommes; Derry

same grey-green schist as the city walls, this was the first post-Reformation church to be erected in Britain and Ireland, and is Derry's oldest surviving building.

In the **porch** (under the spire, by the St Columb's Court entrance) you can see the original foundation stone of 1633 that records the cathedral's completion. The smaller stone inset comes from the original church built here in 1164.

Museum of Free Derry   Museum

(www.museumoffreederry.org; 55 Glenfada Park; adult/child £4/3; ☉9.30am-4.30pm Mon-Fri year-round, plus 1-4pm Sat Apr-Sep, 1-4pm Sun Jul-Sep) Just off Rossville St, this excellent museum chronicles the history of the Bogside, the Civil Rights Movement and the events of Bloody Sunday through photographs, newspaper reports, film clips, interactive displays and first-hand accounts from witnesses, including some of the original photographs that inspired the murals of the nearby People's Gallery.

People's Gallery Murals   Public Art

(www.bogsideartists.com; Rossville St) The 12 murals that decorate the gable ends of houses along Rossville St, near Free Derry Corner, are popularly referred to as the People's Gallery. They are the work of 'the Bogside Artists' (Kevin Hasson, and brothers Tom and Will Kelly, the second of whom died in 2017). The three men lived through the worst of the Troubles in Bogside. The murals can be clearly seen from the northern part of the City Walls.

⊙ TOURS

City Walking Tours   Walking

(☎028-7127 1996; www.derrycitytours.com; Carlisle Stores, 11 Carlisle Rd; adult/child £4/ free; ☉Historic Derry tours 10am, noon, 2pm and 4pm year-round) One-hour Historic Derry walking tours start from Carlisle Stores. There are also tours of the Bogside and of Derry's murals. Recommended.

Free Derry Tours   Cultural

(☏07793 285972; adult/student £6/5; ⊙10am, noon & 2pm Mon-Fri Mar-Sep plus 11am & 2pm Sat, Apr-Sep, 2pm Sun Jul-Sep) The Museum of Free Derry (p172) runs these hour-long walking tours of the Bogside taking in the People's Gallery murals, Free Derry Corner, the Hunger Strikers' Memorial and the Bloody Sunday Memorial.

Made in Derry
Food Tour   Food & Drink

(https://madeinderryfoodtours.com; per person £47; ⊙noon Sat) Four-hour tours of Derry's emerging artisan food and drink scene, meeting chefs and producers and sampling 20 local specialities – such as cheeses and craft beer – along the way. The tour starts outside the Eighty81 building on Ebrington Sq. Book ahead.

✪ EATING

Pyke 'n' Pommes   Street Food £

(behind Foyle Marina, off Baronet St; mains £4-16; ⊙noon-5pm Fri & Sat, to 4pm Sun-Thu; ⌖⌖) ✔
Derry's single-best eatery is this quayside shipping container. Chef Kevin Pyke's delectable, mostly organic burgers span his signature Notorious PIG (pulled pork, crispy slaw, beetroot and crème fraîche) and Veganderry (chickpeas, lemon and co-riander) to his Legenderry Burger (wagyu beef, pickled onions and honey-mustard mayo). His Pykeos fish tacos are another hit. Seasonal specials might include mackerel or oysters.

Brown's Restaurant   Irish ££

(☏028-7134 5180; https://brownsrestaurant. com; 1 Bond's Hill, Waterside; 3-course lunch £15, dinner mains £17-24; ⊙noon-3pm Tue-Sat, 5.30-9pm Tue-Thu, 5-10pm Fri & Sat, noon-3pm Sun; ⌖) ✔ From the outside Brown's may not have the most promising appearance, but stop inside and you're in an elegant little enclave of brandy-coloured banquettes and ornate metal light fittings, with vintage monochrome prints adorning the walls. The ever-changing menu is a gastronome's delight, making creative use of fresh local produce.

Walled City Brewery

Housed in the former army barracks on Ebrington Sq, **Walled City Brewery** (028-7134 3336; www.walledcitybrewery.com; 70 Ebrington Sq; 5-11pm Tue-Thu, 2.30-11.30pm Fri & Sat, 2-10pm Sun) is an exciting new craft brewery and restaurant run by master brewer and Derry local James Huey. As well as having 10 craft beers on tap, Walled City serves top-notch grub, such as house-smoked beer-braised pulled pork (mains £14 to £24). Also runs home-brewing courses.

ANDREW MONTGOMERY/LONELY PLANET ©

Ollies   Irish ££

(028-7132 9751; www.facebook.com/love-ollies; 59 Ebrington Sq; mains lunch £4.50-8, dinner £10-15; 9am-9pm;) All the food at this bright cafe/bistro is homemade using local ingredients, from the fluffy pancakes and waffles at breakfast to the creamy Greencastle seafood chowder and the breads, cakes and pastries. There's a good range of vegetarian and gluten-free options, too. It's BYO (there's a small fee for corkage).

DRINKING & NIGHTLIFE

Peadar O'Donnell's   Pub

(www.peadars.com; 59-63 Waterloo St; 11.30am-1.30am Mon-Sat, 12.30pm-12.30am Sun) Done up as a typical Irish pub/grocery (with shelves of household items, shopkeeper's scales on the counter and a mu-

seum's-worth of old bric-a-brac), Peadar's has rowdy traditional music sessions every night and often on weekend afternoons as well. Its adjacent **Gweedore Bar** (www.peadars.com; 59-63 Waterloo St; 11.30am-1.30am Mon-Sat, noon-12.30am Sun) hosts live rock bands every night, and a Saturday night disco upstairs.

Guildhall Taphouse   Bar

(www.facebook.com/Guildhalltaphouse; 4 Custom House St; noon-1am Mon-Sat, to midnight Sun) Housed in a wooden-beamed, 19th-century building brightened with fairy lights, the Taphouse is a cosy place to sample an excellent selection of local and international craft beers or a sophisticated cocktail. There's regular live music including trad sessions every Wednesday.

INFORMATION

Visit Derry Information Centre (028-7126 7284; www.visitderry.com; 44 Foyle St; 9am-5.30pm Mon-Fri, 10am-5pm Sat & Sun;) A large tourist information centre with helpful staff and stacks of brochures for attractions in Derry and beyond. Also sells books and maps and can book accommodation. **Claudy Cycles** (028-7133 8128; www.claudycycles.com; Visit Derry Information Centre; bike hire per half-/full day £8/12) can be rented here.

GETTING THERE & AWAY

AIR

City of Derry Airport (028-7181 0784; www.cityofderryairport.com; Airport Rd, Eglinton) is about 13km east of Derry along the A2 towards Limavady. There are direct flights to London Stansted (daily), Liverpool (twice weekly) and Glasgow International (four days a week), plus summer routes to Spain.

BUS

The **bus station** (028-7126 2261; Foyle St) is just northeast of the walled city.

Guildhall (p171)

Services to Northern Ireland destinations are operated by **Translink** (www.translink.co.uk); destinations in the Republic are served by **Bus Éireann** (www.buseireann.ie).

Belfast Europa Bus Centre £12, 1¾ hours, half-hourly Monday to Friday, hourly Saturday and Sunday

Galway £16.50, 5½ hours, five daily

Airporter (☑028-7126 9996; http://airporter. co.uk; 1 Bay Rd, off Culmore Rd; ☎) buses run directly from Derry to Belfast International Airport (£20, 1½ hours) and George Best Belfast City Airport (£20, two hours) at least once an hour Monday to Friday and slightly less frequently Saturday and Sunday. Buses depart from the Airporter office, 1.5km north of the city centre, next to Da Vinci's Hotel.

TRAIN

Derry's train station is on the eastern side of the River Foyle; a free Rail Link bus connects it with the bus station.

Belfast £12, 2¼ hours, nine daily Monday to Saturday, six on Sunday

Coleraine £9.60, 45 minutes, 11 daily Monday to Saturday, six on Sunday

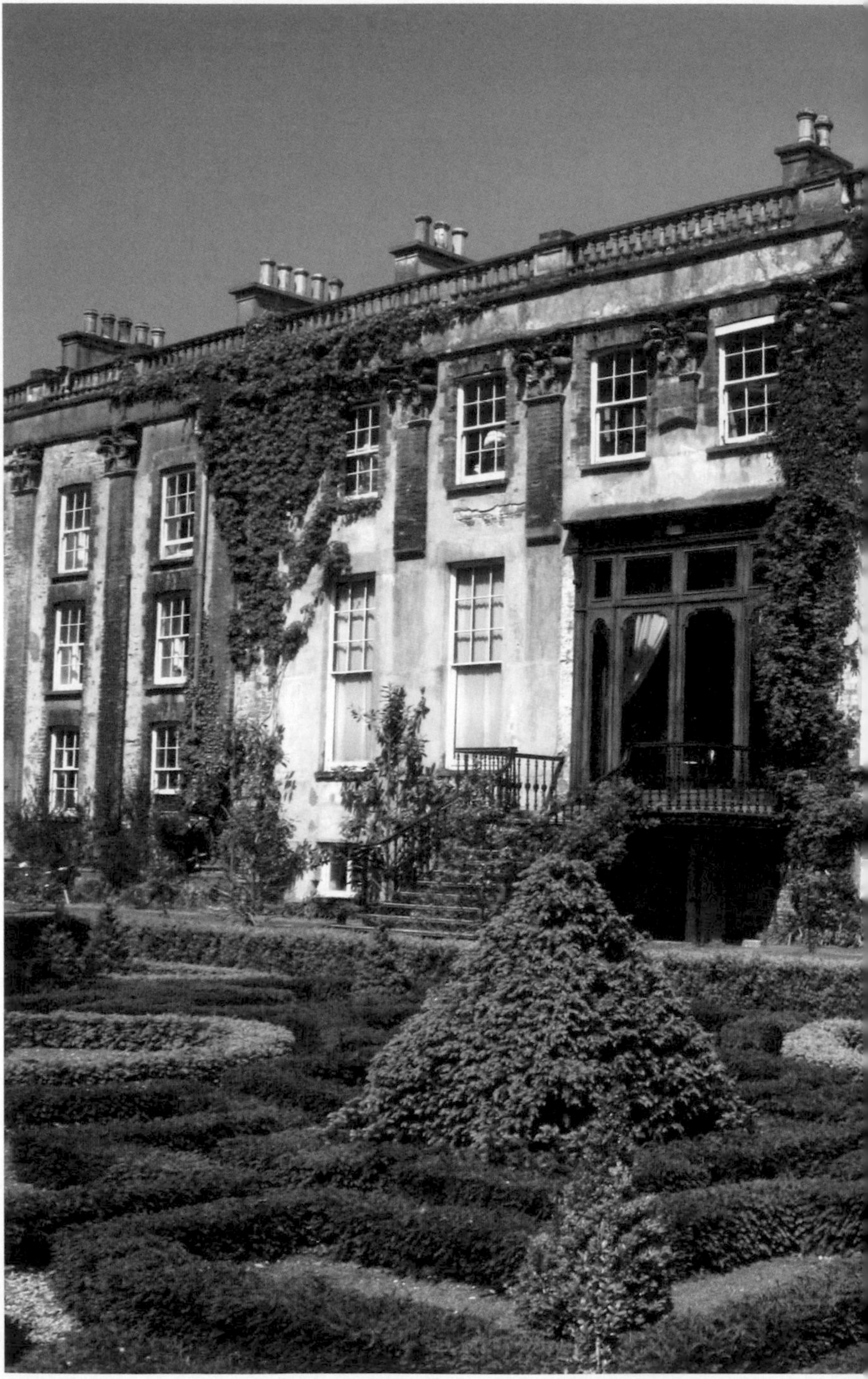

Bantry House (p194)

COUNTY CORK

County Cork at a Glance...

Everything good about Ireland can be found in County Cork. Surrounding the country's second city – a thriving metropolis made glorious by location and its almost Rabelaisian devotion to the finer things of life – is a lush landscape dotted with villages that offer days of languor and idyll. The city's understated confidence is grounded in its plethora of food markets and ever-evolving cast of creative eateries, and in its selection of pubs, entertainment and cultural pursuits. Further afield, you'll pass inlets along eroded coastlines and a multitude of perfectly charming old fishing towns and villages.

County Cork in Two Days

Visit **Blarney Castle** (p182) first thing, then explore Cork city, taking in **Cork City Gaol** (p185) and making sure not to miss the **English Market** (p180). Lunch at the **Farmgate Cafe** (p180) is a must, as is dinner at one of Cork's many restaurants. Day two is for a boat trip from nearby Cobh to fascinating **Spike Island** (p189).

County Cork in Four Days

Head to the coast at **Kinsale** (p191), and spend a day exploring its sea-scented streets, including a walk out to **Charles Fort** (p192), followed by dinner at one of its fine seafood restaurants. On day four, take a drive along the scenic Cork coast to visit **Bantry House** (p194). Enjoy fine food at **Manning's Emporium** (p195) before continuing on the road to Killarney.

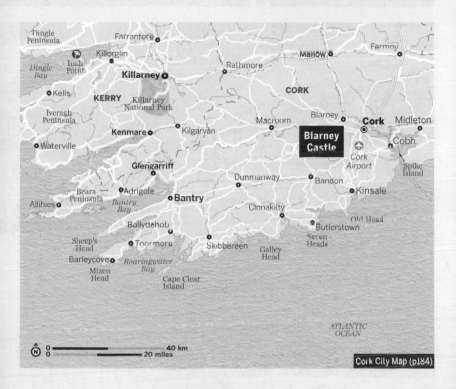

Cork City Map (p184)

Arriving in County Cork

Cork Airport is 8km south of the city centre. Buses shuttle between the airport, the train station and bus station every half hour between 6am and 10pm (€5.00, 30 minutes).

Kent Train Station is north of the River Lee, a 10- to 15-minute walk from the city centre.

Cork Bus Station is on Parnell Pl in the city centre.

Sleeping

Cork city offers the full range of accommodation, from backpacker hostels and budget chain hotels to suburban B&Bs, boutique guesthouses and luxury hotels. The Cork coast has long been a holiday playground and is well endowed with farmhouse B&Bs, camping grounds and seaside hotels but, especially in the more remote areas, many places close down for the winter.

GABRIELL17/SHUTTERSTOCK ©

Gourmet Cork

Ireland's largest county can fairly lay claim to being the foodie capital of Ireland. Farmers markets and fine dining are the highlights of a visit.

Great For...

☑ Don't Miss

The farmhouse cheeses and Irish charcuterie at **On the Pig's Back** (☎021-427 0232; www.onthepigsback.ie; English Market; ☺9am-5.30pm Mon-Sat) ✎ in the English Market.

English Market   Market

(www.englishmarket.ie; main entrance Princes St; ☺8am-6pm Mon-Sat) It could just as easily be called the Victorian Market for its ornate vaulted ceilings and columns, but the English Market is a true gem, no matter what you name it. Scores of vendors sell some of the region's very best local produce, meats, cheeses and takeaway food. On a sunny day, take your lunch to nearby Bishop Lucey Park, a popular al fresco eating spot.

Farmgate Cafe   Cafe, Bistro €

(☎021-427 8134; www.farmgate.ie; Princes St, English Market; mains €8-14; ☺8.30am-5pm Mon-Sat) ✎ An unmissable experience at the heart of the English Market, the Farmgate is perched on a balcony overlooking the food stalls below, the source of all that fresh local produce on your

Farmgate Cafe

JAMES SMART/LONELY PLANET ©

plate – everything from crab and oysters to the lamb for an Irish stew. Head up the stairs and turn left for table service, right for counter service.

Midleton Farmers Market   Market

(Main St; ☺9am-1pm Sat) 🌱 Midleton's farmers market is one of Cork's best, with bushels of local produce on offer and producers who are happy to chat. It's behind the big roundabout at the north end of Main St.

Farmgate Restaurant   Irish €€

(☑021-463 2771; www.farmgate.ie; Broderick St; mains lunch €11-18, dinner €15-26; ☺9am-5pm Tue & Wed-Sat, 6.30-9.30pm Thu-Sat) 🌱 The original, sister establishment to Cork city's Farmgate Cafe (p180), the Midleton restaurant offers the same superb blend of traditional and modern Irish cuisine.

Squeeze through the deli selling amazing baked goods and local produce, to the subtly lit, art-clad, 'farmhouse shed' cafe-restaurant, where you'll eat as well as you would anywhere in Ireland.

Ballymaloe Cookery School   Cooking

(☑021-464 6785; www.ballymaloecookeryschool.com; Shanagarry) TV personality Darina Allen (daughter-in-law of Myrtle Allen of Ballymaloe House (p190) runs this famous cookery school. Darina's own daughter-in-law, Rachel Allen, is also a high-profile TV chef and author, and regularly teaches at the school. Demonstrations cost €75; lessons, from half-day sessions (€95 to €135) to 12-week certificate courses (€10,995), are often booked out well in advance. For overnight students, there are pretty cottages amid the 100 acres of grounds. It's 3km east of Ballymaloe House (p190).

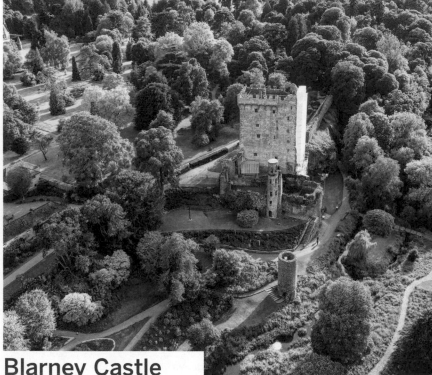

Blarney Castle

If you need proof of the power of a good yarn, then join the queue to get into this 15th-century castle, one of Ireland's most popular tourist attractions.

Great For...

☑ **Don't Miss**

While kissing the stone is the main focus for most visitors, the Poison Garden and Rock Close offer some stunning scenery and are must-sees.

The crowds are here, of course, to plant their lips on the Blarney Stone, which supposedly gives one the gift of the gab – a cliché that has entered every lexicon and tour route.

The Blarney Stone is perched at the top of a steep climb up claustrophobic spiral staircases within the castle. On the battlements, you bend backwards over a long, long drop (with safety grill and attendant to prevent tragedy) to kiss the stone; as your shirt rides up, coach loads of onlookers stare up your nose. Once you're upright again, don't forget to admire the stunning views before descending. Try not to think of the local lore about all the fluids that drench the stone other than saliva. Better yet, just don't kiss it.

The custom of kissing the stone is a relatively modern one, but Blarney's association

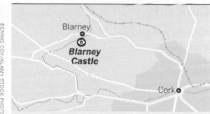

KISSING THE BLARNEY STONE

ℹ️ Need to Know

📞021-438 5252; www.blarneycastle.ie; adult/child €15/6; 🕐9am-7pm Mon-Sat, to 6pm Sun Jun-Aug, shorter hours Sep-May; 🅿️)

✕ Take a Break

There's a cafe next to the castle's stable yard; also, the **Lemon Tree Restaurant** (📞021-438 5116; www.blarneycastlehotel. com; Blarney Castle Hotel, The Square, Blarney; mains €10-17; 🕐7.30-11am, noon to 4.30pm, 6-9.30pm; 🅿️🛜♿) at Blarney Castle Hotel is a 700m walk from the castle and offers breakfasts, lunches and pub meals.

★ Top Tip

Book your tickets via the castle's website and receive a discount. If you want to explore Blarney House, the nearby mansion, it's open from the beginning of June to the end of August (closed Sundays).

with smooth talking goes back a long time. Queen Elizabeth I is said to have invented the term 'to talk blarney' out of exasperation with Lord Blarney's ability to talk endlessly without ever actually agreeing to her demands.

The famous stone aside, Blarney Castle itself is an impressive 16th-century tower set in gorgeous grounds. Escape the crowds on a walk around the Arboretum, which showcases specimen trees from around the world (including yews and Spanish chestnuts up to 600 years old), and the Fern Garden, an atmospheric jungle of 2m-tall tree ferns.

The Harry-Potterish Poison Garden is tucked beneath the castle battlements, and is home to some of the world's most toxic plants, including deadly nightshade hemlock, and mandrake which, as any Harry

Potter fan will know, is said to scream when its human-shaped root is ripped from the soil (the specimen here is kept behind bars to protect visitors from its narcotic and hallucinogenic effects).

You can also explore the landscaped nooks and crannies of the Rock Close, where trails laid out in the 18th century wend their way among ancient trees and manmade features that include standing stones, the Wishing Steps, the Fairy Glade and a bog garden.

Blarney is 8km northwest of Cork and buses run every half hour from Cork bus station (€7.80 return, 20 minutes).

Cork City

Ireland's second city is first in every important respect – at least according to the locals, who cheerfully refer to it as the 'real capital of Ireland'. It's a liberal, youthful and cosmopolitan place that was badly hit by economic recession but is now busily reinventing itself with spruced-up streets, revitalised stretches of waterfront, and – seemingly – an artisan coffee bar on every corner. There's a bit of a hipster scene, but the best of the city is still happily traditional – snug pubs with live-music sessions, restaurants dishing up top-quality local produce, and a genuinely proud welcome from the locals.

◎ SIGHTS

The best sight in Cork is the city itself – soak it up as you wander the streets. A new conference and events centre, complete with 6000-seat concert venue,

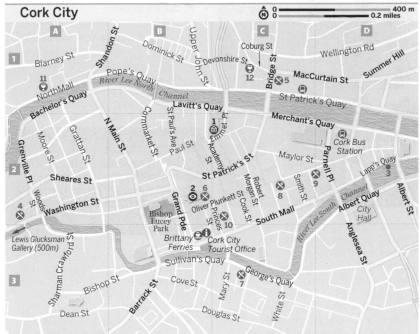

Cork City

STEPHEN LONG/SHUTTERSTOCK ©

View of Cork City

tourist centre, restaurants, shops, galleries and apartments, is scheduled to open in 2019 as the focus of the new **Brewery Quarter** (the former Beamish & Crawford brewery site, fronted by the landmark mock-Tudor 'counting house'), a block west of the English Market.

Shandon, perched on a hillside over-looking the city centre to the north, is a great spot for the views alone, but you'll also find galleries, antique shops and ca-fes along its old lanes and squares. Those tiny old row houses, where generations of workers raised huge families in very basic conditions, are now sought-after urban pieds-à-terre. Pick up a copy of the *Cork Walks – Shandon* leaflet from the tourist office (p188) for a self-guided tour of the district.

Cork City Gaol   Museum
(021-430 5022; www.corkcitygaol.com; Convent Ave; adult/child €8/5; 9.30am-5pm Apr-Sep, 10am-4pm Oct-Mar) This imposing former prison is well worth a visit, if only to get a sense of how awful life was for prisoners a century ago. An audio tour

(€2 extra) guides you around the restored cells, which feature models of suffering prisoners and sadistic-looking guards. Take a bus to University College Cork (UCC) – from there walk north along Mardyke Walk, cross the river and follow the signs uphill (10 minutes).

The tour is very moving, bringing home the harshness of the 19th-century penal system. The most common crime was that of poverty; many of the inmates were sen-tenced to hard labour for stealing loaves of bread. Atmospheric evening tours take place every weekday at 5.45pm (€10).

The prison closed in 1923, reopening in 1927 as a radio station that operated until the 1950s. The Governor's House has been converted into a **Radio Museum** (021-430 5022; www.corkcitygaol.com/radio-museum; Cork City Gaol, Convent Ave; incl Cork City Gaol adult/child €8/5; 9.30am-5pm Apr-Sep, 10am-4pm Oct-Mar;) where, alongside collec-tions of beautiful old radios, you can hear the story of Guglielmo Marconi's conquest of the airwaves.

Crawford Municipal
Art Gallery   Gallery
(☏021-480 5042; www.crawfordartgallery.ie;
Emmet Pl; ⊙10am-5pm Mon-Wed, Fri & Sat, to
8pm Thu) **FREE** Cork's public gallery houses
a small but excellent permanent collection covering the 17th century through to
the modern day. Highlights include works
by Sir John Lavery, Jack B Yeats and
Nathaniel Hone, and a room devoted to
Irish women artists from 1886 to 1978 –
don't miss the pieces by Mainie Jellet and
Evie Hone.

Lewis Glucksman Gallery   Gallery
(☏021-490 1844; www.glucksman.org; University College Cork, Western Rd; suggested
donation €5; ⊙10am-5pm Tue-Sat, 2-5pm Sun;
👪) **FREE** This award-winning building is a
startling construction of limestone, steel
and timber. Two floors of galleries with
suitably paint-spattered floors display the
best in both national and international
contemporary art and installation. Don't
miss the free fortnightly curatorial tours.

The on-site **cafe** (☏021-490 1848; www.
glucksman.org; Lewis Glucksman Gallery,
Western Rd; mains €6-12; ⊙10am-5pm Tue-Sat,
noon-5pm Sun; 👪) is excellent.

⊕ TOURS
Atlantic Sea Kayaking   Kayaking
(☏028-21058; www.atlanticseakayaking.com;
Lapp's Quay; €50) Offers guided 'urban
kayaking' trips around Cork's waterways
from 6.30pm to 9pm (book in advance,
minimum two people). They also offer
a four-hour trip (minimum four people,
€65) to Cobh and Spike Island (p189).

Cork City Tour   Bus
(☏021-430 9090; www.corkcitytour.com;
adult/student/child €15/13/5; ⊙Mar-Nov) A
hop-on-hop-off open-top bus linking the
city's main points of interest. Longer tours
(€23 per adult) head to the Jameson
Experience (p190) in Midleton.

🍴 EATING

Cork Coffee Roasters   Cafe €

(📞021-731 9158; www.facebook.com/CorkCoffee; 2 Bridge St; mains €3-6; ⏰7.30am-6.30pm Mon-Fri, 8am-6.30pm Sat, 9am-5pm Sun; 📶) In this foodiest of foodie towns it's not surprising to find a cafe run by artisan coffee roasters. The brew on offer in this cute and often crowded corner is some of the best in Ireland, guaranteed to jump start your morning along with a buttery pastry, scone or tart.

Filter   Cafe €

(📞021-455 0050; filtercork@gmail.com; 19 George's Quay; mains €4-7; ⏰8am-6pm Mon-Fri, 9am-6pm Sat, 10am-5pm Sun; 📶) 🍴 The quintessential Cork espresso bar, Filter is a carefully curated shrine to coffee nerdery, from the rough-and-ready retro decor to the highly knowledgeable baristas serving up expertly brewed shots made with single-origin, locally roasted beans. The sandwich menu is a class act, too, offering a choice of fillings that includes pastrami, chorizo and ham hock on artisan breads.

Nash 19   International €€

(📞021-427 0880; www.nash19.com; Princes St; mains €10-17; ⏰7.30am-4.30pm Mon-Fri, 8.30am-4.30pm Sat) 🍴 A superb bistro and deli where locally sourced food is honoured at breakfast and lunch, either sit-in or take away. Fresh scones draw in the crowds early; daily lunch specials (soups, salads, desserts, etc), free-range chicken pie and platters of smoked fish from Frank Hederman (p188) keep them coming for lunch – the Producers Plate, a sampler of local produce, is sensational.

Market Lane   Irish, International €€

(📞021-427 4710; www.marketlane.ie; 5 Oliver Plunkett St; mains €12-27; ⏰noon-9.30pm Mon-Thu, noon-10.30pm Fri & Sat, 1-9.30pm Sun; 📶👪) 🍴 It's always hopping at this bright corner bistro. The menu is broad and hearty, changing to reflect what's fresh at the English Market: perhaps roast cod with seaweed butter sauce, or pea and barley risotto with goat's cheese? No reservations for fewer than six diners; sip a drink at the bar till a table is free. Lots of wines by the glass.

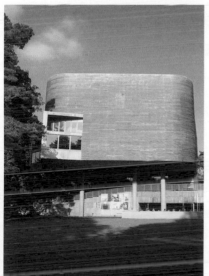

Top Five Cork Restaurants
Nash 19 (p187)
Bastion (p193)
Manning's Emporium (p195)
Farmgate Cafe (p180)
Finn's Table (p193)

From left: Cork City Gaol (p185); Lewis Glucksman Gallery; Jameson Experience, Midleton (p190)

⦿¡ Smokin'

No trip to Cork is complete without a visit to an artisan food producer, and the effervescent Frank Hederman is more than happy to show you around **Belvelly Smokehouse** (☑021-481 1089; www.frankhederman.com; Belvelly; free for individuals, charge for groups; ☺by reservation 10am-5pm Mon-Fri), the oldest traditional smokehouse in Ireland – indeed, the only surviving one. The smokehouse is 19km east of Cork on the R624 towards Cobh; call ahead to arrange a visit.

Alternatively, stop by Frank's stall at the Cobh (☑086 199 7643; www.facebook.com/cobhfarmers; The Promenade; ☺10am-2pm Fri) or **Midleton** (p181) farmers markets; you can also buy his produce at Cork's **English Market** (p180).

Seafood and cheese are smoked here – even butter – but the speciality is fish, particularly salmon. In a traditional process that takes 24 hours from start to finish, the fish is filleted and cured before being hung to smoke over beech woodchips. The result is subtle and delectable.

Smoked salmon
MATEUSZ GZIK/SHUTTERSTOCK ©

Cafe Paradiso — Vegetarian €€

(☑021-427 7939; www.cafeparadiso.ie; 16 Lancaster Quay; 2-/3-course menus €33/40; ☺5.30-10pm Mon-Sat; ☑) ✔ A contender for best restaurant in town of any genre, Paradiso serves contemporary vegetarian dishes, including vegan fare: how about confit artichokes, broad beans and scallions with lemon risotto and hazelnut crumb? Reservations are essential.

Rates for dinner, bed and breakfast, staying in the funky upstairs rooms, start from €180/220 per single/double.

Jacques Restaurant — Modern Irish €€

(☑021-427 7387; www.jacquesrestaurant.ie; 23 Oliver Plunkett St; mains lunch €7-14, dinner €22-26; ☺10am-4pm Mon, to 10pm Tue-Sat) ✔ Sisters Jacqueline and Eithne Barry draw on a terrific network of local suppliers that they've built up over three decades to help them realise their culinary ambitions – the freshest Cork food cooked simply, without frills. The menu changes daily: smoked quail with celeriac remoulade, perhaps, or Castletownbere crab with spaghetti and herbs. Two-course dinners (€24) are served Tuesday to Thursday, and pre-6.30pm Friday and Saturday.

🍷 DRINKING & NIGHTLIFE

Sin É — Pub

(☑021-450 2266; www.facebook.com/sinecork; 8 Coburg St; ☺12.30-11.30pm Mon-Thu, to 12.30am Fri & Sat, to 11pm Sun) You could easily spend an entire day at this place, which is everything a craic-filled pub should be – long on atmosphere and short on pretension (Sin É means 'that's it!'). There's music every night from 6.30pm May to September, and regular sessions Tuesday, Friday and Sunday the rest of the year, much of them traditional but with the odd surprise.

Franciscan Well Brewery — Pub

(☑021-439 3434; www.franciscanwellbrewery.com; 14 North Mall; ☺1-11.30pm Mon-Thu, to 12.30am Fri & Sat, to 11pm Sun; ☏) The copper vats gleaming behind the bar give the game away: the Franciscan Well brews its own beer. The best place to enjoy it is in the enormous beer garden at the back. The pub holds regular beer festivals together with other small independent Irish breweries.

ℹ INFORMATION

Cork City Tourist Office (☑021-425 5100; www.discoverireland.ie/corkcity; Grand Pde; ☺9am-5pm Mon-Sat year-round, plus 10am-5pm Sun Jul

& Aug) Souvenir shop and information desk. Sells Ordnance Survey maps.

ℹ️ GETTING THERE & AWAY

AIR

Cork Airport (☎021-431 3131; www.corkairport. com) Airlines servicing the airport include Aer Lingus and Ryanair.

BOAT

Brittany Ferries (☎021-427 7801; www.brittany ferries.ie; 42 Grand Pde) sails to Roscoff (France) weekly from the end of March to October. The crossing takes 14 hours; fares vary widely. The ferry terminal is at Ringaskiddy, 15 minutes by car southeast of the city centre along the N28.

BUS

Bus Éireann (☎021-455 7178; www.buseire ann.ie) operates from the **bus station** (cnr Merchant's Quay & Parnell Pl), while **Aircoach** (☎01-844 7118; www.aircoach.ie) and **Citylink** (☎001 504 104, www.citylink.ie; ☎) services depart from **St Patrick's Quay**, across the river. **GoBus** (☎091-564 600; www.gobus.ie; ☎) uses a stop around the corner on Parnell Pl.

Dublin (€15, 3¾ hours, six daily)

Dublin (Aircoach; €16, three hours, hourly)

Dublin (GoBus; €17, three hours, six to nine daily)

Dublin airport (Aircoach; €20, 3½ hours, hourly)

Galway (Citylink; €21, three hours, five daily)

Kilkenny (€21, three hours, two daily)

Killarney (€27, two hours, hourly)

Limerick (Citylink; €17, 1½ hours, five daily)

Waterford (€23.50, 2¼ hours, hourly)

TRAIN

Kent Train Station (☎021-450 6766) is north of the River Lee on Lower Glanmire Rd, a 10- to 15-minute walk from the city centre. Bus 205 runs into the city centre (€2, five minutes, every 15 minutes).

🏛️ Spike Island

This low-lying green **island** (☎085 851 8818; www.spikeislandcork.com; Cork Harbour; adult/child incl ferry €18/10; ☺11am-5.30pm Jun-Aug, noon-4.30pm May, noon-4.30pm Sat & Sun Apr & Sep only, noon-4.30pm Sun Oct only) in Cork Harbour was once an important part of the port's defences, topped by an 18th-century artillery fort. In the second half of the 19th century, during the Irish War of Independence, and from 1984 to 2004 it served as a prison, gaining the nickname 'Ireland's Alcatraz'. Today you can enjoy a guided walking tour of the former prison buildings, then go off and explore on your own; the ferry departs from Kennedy Pier, Cobh.

The guided tour takes in the modern prison, the old punishment block, the shell store (once used as a children's prison) and No 2 bastion with its massive 6in gun. Other highlights include the **Gun Park**, with a good display of mostly 20th-century artillery, the **Mitchel Hall**, with an exhibit on the *Aud,* a WWI German gun-running ship that was sunk in the entrance to Cork Harbour; and the **Glacis Walk**, a 1.5km trail that leads around the walls of the fortress, with great views of Cobh town and the harbour entrance. You'll need around four hours to make the most of a visit.

Above: Mitchel Hall

 **Ireland's Teardrop**

So named because it was the last sight of the 'ould country' for emigrants sailing to America, the **Fastnet Rock** is the most southerly point of Ireland.

This isolated fang of rock, topped by a spectacular lighthouse, stands 6.5km southwest of Cape Clear Island, and in clear weather is visible from many places on the coastline from Baltimore to Mizen Head. Its image – usually with huge waves crashing around it – graces a thousand postcards, coffee-table books and framed art photographs.

The Fastnet lighthouse, widely considered the most perfectly engineered lighthouse in the world, was built in 1904 from ingeniously interlocked blocks of Cornish granite – there are exhibits about its construction at **Mizen Head Visitor Centre** (⌂028-35115; www.mizenhead.ie; Mizen Head; adult/child €7.50/4.50; ☺10am-6pm Jun-Aug, 10.30am-5pm mid-Mar–May, Sep & Oct, 11am-4pm Sat & Sun Nov–mid-Mar; 🖢) and **Cape Clear Museum** (⌂028-39119; www.capeclearmuseum.ie; €3; ☺2.30-5pm Jun-Aug).

From May to August, **Fastnet Experience** (⌂087 389 9711; www.fastnettour. com; adult/family €35/80) operates boat trips to the rock, departing from Schull, Baltimore and Cape Clear Island. Tours are weather-dependent and last 2½ to three hours (1½ hours if departing from Cape Clear).

Fastnet Lighthouse
MATTHIAS OESTERLE/GETTY IMAGES ©

GETTING AROUND

TO/FROM THE AIRPORT

Bus Éireann (p189) service 226A shuttles between the train station, bus station and Cork Airport every half-hour between 6am and 10pm (€5.60, 30 minutes). A taxi to/from town costs €22 to €26.

BUS

Most places are within easy walking distance of the centre. Single bus tickets cost €2.05 each; a day pass is €5. Buy all tickets on the bus.

CAR

You can avoid city centre parking problems by using **Black Ash Park & Ride** on the South City Link Rd, on the way to the airport. Parking costs €5 a day, with buses into the city centre at least every 15 minutes (10-minute journey time).

TAXI

Cork Taxi Co-op (⌂021-427 22 22; www. corktaxi.ie)

Shandon Cabs (⌂021-450 22 55)

Midleton

Aficionados of a particularly fine Irish whiskey will recognise the name Midleton, and the main reason to linger in this bustling market town is to visit the old Jameson whiskey distillery, along with sampling a meal at one of the town's famously good restaurants. The surrounding region is full of pretty villages, craggy coastlines and heavenly rural hotels such as **Ballymaloe House** (⌂021-465 2531; www.ballymaloe.ie; Shanagarry; r from €250; 🅿🛜🏊🐾).

◉ SIGHTS

Jameson Experience Museum
(⌂021-461 3594; www.jamesonwhiskey.com; Old Distillery Walk; tours adult/child €18/9; ☺shop 10am-6pm; 🅿) Coachloads pour in to tour this restored 200-year-old distillery building. Exhibits and tours (run between 10am and 4pm) explain the process of taking barley and creating whiskey (Jameson is

today made in a modern factory in Cork). There's a well-stocked gift shop, and the **Malt House Restaurant** (open noon to 3pm) has live music on Sundays.

GETTING THERE & AWAY

Midleton is 20km east of Cork. The train station is 1.5km (20 minutes' walk) north of the **Jameson Experience** (p190). There are frequent trains from Cork (€6.25, 25 minutes, at least hourly).

There are also frequent buses from Cork bus station (€8, 30 minutes, every 15 to 45 minutes). You'll need a car to explore the surrounding area.

Cobh

Cobh (pronounced 'cove') is a charming waterfront town on a glittering estuary, dotted with brightly coloured houses and overlooked by a splendid cathedral. It's a far cry from the harrowing Famine years when more than 70,000 people left Ireland through the port in order to escape the ravages of starvation. Cobh was also the final port of call for the *Titanic;* a poignant museum commemorates the fatal voyage's point of departure.

SIGHTS

Cobh, The Queenstown Story
Museum

(☎021-481 3591; www.cobhheritage.com; Lower Rd; adult/child €9.50/5; ◉9.30am-6pm May-Oct, to 5pm Nov-Apr) The howl of the storm almost knocks you off-balance, there's a bit of fake vomit on the deck, and the people in the pictures all look pretty miserable – that's just one room at Cobh Heritage Centre. Housed in the old train station (next to the current station), this interactive museum is way above average, chronicling Irish emigrations across the Atlantic in the wake of the Great Famine.

Titanic Experience Cobh
Museum

(☎021-481 4412; www.titanicexperiencecobh. ie; 20 Casement Sq; adult/child €9.50/6.50; ◉9am-6pm Apr-Sep, 10am-5.30pm Oct-Mar; ♿) The original White Star Line offices, where

 County Cork Food Festivals

Kinsale Gourmet Festival (www.kinsalerestaurants.com; ◉Oct) comprises three days of tastings, cookery demonstrations and competitions, kicking off with the Cork heat of the All-Ireland seafood chowder cook-off (the final of which takes place in Kinsale in April).

Downtown Kinsale
TYLER W. STIPP/SHUTTERSTOCK ©

123 passengers embarked on (and one lucky soul absconded from) the RMS *Titanic*, now house this powerful insight into the ill-fated liner's final voyage. Admission is by tour, which is partly guided and partly interactive, with holograms, audiovisual presentations and exhibits, allow at least an hour. The technical wizardry is impressive but what's most memorable is standing on the spot from where passengers were ferried to the waiting ship offshore, never to return.

GETTING THERE & AWAY

Car By road, Cobh is 23km southeast of Cork, off the main N25 Cork–Rosslare road; Great Island is linked to the mainland via a causeway.

Train Hourly trains connect Cobh with Cork (€6.15, 25 minutes) via Fota.

Kinsale

The picturesque yachting harbour of Kinsale (Cionn tSáile) is one of many colourful gems strung along the coastline of County Cork. Narrow, winding streets lined with galleriesand gift shops, lively bars and superb restaurants, and a handsome natural harbour filled with yachts and guarded by a huge 17th-century fortress make it an engrossing place to spend a day or two.

◎ SIGHTS

Charles Fort   Fort

(☏021-477 2263; www.heritageireland.ie; Summercove; adult/child €5/3; ⊙10am-6pm mid-Mar–Oct, to 5pm Nov–mid-Mar; [P]) One of Europe's best-preserved star-shaped artillery forts, this vast 17th-century fortification would be worth a visit for its spectacular views alone. But there's much more here: the 18th- and 19th-century ruins inside the walls make for some fascinating wandering. It's 3km southeast of Kinsale along the minor road through Scilly; if you have time, hike there along the lovely coastal **Scilly Walk**.

Signal Tower & Lusitania Museum   Museum

(☏021-419 1285; www.oldheadofkinsale.com; Signal Tower, Old Head of Kinsale; adult/concession €4/3; ⊙10am-6pm daily Apr-Oct) This 200-year-old signal tower has been restored and converted into a museum dedicated to the RMS *Lusitania,* which was torpedoed by a German U-boat in 1915 with the loss of 1200 lives. You can walk to the nearby cliff tops for impressive views south towards the Old Head, the nearest point of land to the disaster; a privately owned **golf club** (☏021-477 8444; www.oldhead.com; Old Head of Kinsale; green fees €160-230) prevents you from reaching the lighthouse at the tip of the headland. The tower is 13km south of town via the R604.

✗ EATING

Black Pig Wine Bar   Irish €€

(☏021-477 4101; www.facebook.com/theblack-pigwinebar; 66 Lower O'Connell St; mains €10-18; ⊙5.30-11pm Wed, Thu & Sun, to 11.30pm Fri & Sat) ✔ This sophisticated hideaway is set in an 18th-century coach house with a charming cobbled courtyard out the back, and offers a mouth-watering menu of gourmet nibbles, charcuterie platters and cheese boards sourced from artisan local suppliers. The award-winning wine list offers no fewer than

From left: Charles Fort; Lobster thermidor at Fishy Fishy Cafe; Kinsale harbour

200 wines by the bottle and 100 by the glass, including many organic varieties. Reservations recommended.

Bastion Modern Irish **€€€**
(021-470 9696; www.bastionkinsale.com; cnr Main & Market Sts; mains €18-31; 5-10pm Wed-Sun;) Awarded a Bib Gourmand in 2016, the newest addition to Kinsale's lengthy list of top restaurants offers diners a relaxed and informal entry into the world of haute cuisine. Waitstaff will guide you through the concise à la carte menu of local oysters, beef, fish and venison, but it's best to go for the seven-course tasting menu (€65) or the five-course early-bird menu (pre-6pm; €45).

Finn's Table Modern Irish **€€€**
(021-470 9636; www.finnstable.com; 6 Main St; mains €23-34; 6-10pm Mon, Tue & Thu-Sat) John and Julie Finn's gourmet restaurant is elegant but unstuffy, and Finn's Table's warm welcome and menu of seasonal, locally sourced produce rarely fails to please. Seafood (including lobster when in season) is from West Cork, while meat is from the Finn family's butchers.

Fishy Fishy Cafe Seafood **€€€**
(021-470 0415; www.fishyfishy.ie; Crowley's Quay; mains €16-27; noon-9pm Mar-Oct, shorter hours rest of year) One of the most famous seafood restaurants in the country, Fishy Fishy has a wonderful setting with stark white walls splashed with bright artwork and striking steel fish sculptures, and a terrific decked terrace at the front. All the fish is caught locally, and dishes include lobster thermidor and a chilled seafood platter served with homemade mayonnaise.

INFORMATION

Tourist Office (021-477 2234; www.kinsale.ie; cnr Pier Rd & Emmet Pl; 9.15am-5pm Tue-Sat year-round, 9.15am-5pm Mon Apr-Oct, 10am-5pm Sun Jul & Aug) Has a good map detailing walks in and around Kinsale.

GETTING THERE & AWAY

Bus Éireann (021-450 8188; www.buseireann.ie) service 226 connects Kinsale with Cork bus station (€9.60, one hour, hourly) via Cork

PHIL DARBY/SHUTTERSTOCK ©

Bantry Bay

Airport, and continues to Cork train station. The **bus stop** is on Pier Rd, near the tourist office.

Bantry

Framed by the Sheep's Head hills and the craggy Caha Mountains, magnificent, sprawling Bantry Bay is one of the country's most attractive seascapes. Sheltered by islands at the head of the bay, Bantry town is neat and respectable, with narrow streets of old-fashioned, one-off shops and a picturesque harbourfront.

Pride of place goes to Bantry House (p194), the former home of one Richard White, who earned his place in history when, in 1798, he warned authorities of the imminent landing of Irish patriot Wolfe Tone and his French fleet, in support of the United Irishmen's rebellion. In the end storms prevented the fleet from landing and the course of Irish history was definitively altered – all Wolfe Tone got for his troubles was a square and a statue bearing his name.

◎ SIGHTS

Bantry House & Garden   Historic Building

(☏027-50047; www.bantryhouse.com; Bantry Bay; house & garden adult/child €11/3, garden only €5/free; ☉10am-5pm daily Jun-Aug, Tue-Sun Apr, May, Sep & Oct; ℗) With its melancholic air of faded gentility, 18th-century Bantry House makes for an intriguing visit. From the Gobelin tapestries in the drawing room to the columned splendour of the library, it conjures up a lost world of aristocratic excess. But the gardens are its greatest glory, with lawns sweeping down towards the sea, and the magnificent Italian garden, with its staircase of 100 steps, at the back, offering spectacular views. The entrance is 1km southwest of the town centre on the N71.

The house has belonged to the White family since 1729 and every room brims with treasures brought back from each generation's travels. The entrance hall is paved with mosaics from Pompeii, French and Flemish tapestries adorn the walls, and Japanese chests sit next to Russian shrines. Upstairs, worn bedrooms look out wanly over an astounding view of the bay. Experienced pianists are invited to tinkle the ivories of the ancient grand piano in the library.

The owners also offer B&B accommodation in one of the wings.

⊗ EATING

Organico   Cafe €

(☑027-55905; www.organico.ie; 2 Glengarriff Rd; mains €7-11; ☺9am-6pm Mon-Sat; 🛜🖉) ✔ This bright and lively wholefood shop and cafe serves tinglingly fresh salads, sandwiches and soups, and lunch specials such as felafel platters with hummus and tahini. Great coffee and cakes, too.

Manning's Emporium   Cafe, Deli €

(☑027-50456; www.manningsemporium.ie; Ballylickey; mains €8-13; ☺7.30am-6pm Tue, Thu & Fri, 9am-9pm Sat, 9am-6pm Sun, brunch 10am-3pm Sat & Sun; 🅿🛜) ✔ This gourmet deli and cafe is an Aladdin's cave of West Cork's finest food. Grab a menu, choose a table, and order at the counter – tasting plates are the best way to sample the local artisan produce

and farmhouse cheeses. Foodie events take place regularly. It's on the N71 in Ballylickey (on the right approaching from Bantry).

Fish Kitchen   Seafood €€

(☑027-56651; http://thefishkitchen.ie; New St; mains lunch €8-12, dinner €15-28; ☺noon-3pm & 5.30-9pm Tue-Sat) This outstanding little restaurant above a fishmonger's shop does seafood to perfection, from the live-tank local oysters (served with lemon and Tabasco sauce) to Bantry Bay mussels in white wine. If you don't fancy seafood, it does a juicy steak, too. Friendly, unfussy and delicious.

ⓘ INFORMATION

Tourist Office (☑027-50229; www.visitbantry. ie; Wolfe Tone Sq; ☺10am-6pm Mon-Sat Apr-Oct) Staffed by volunteers, so hours may vary.

ⓘ GETTING THERE & AWAY

Bus Éireann (www.buseireann.ie) runs four to six buses daily between Bantry and Cork (€22, two hours).

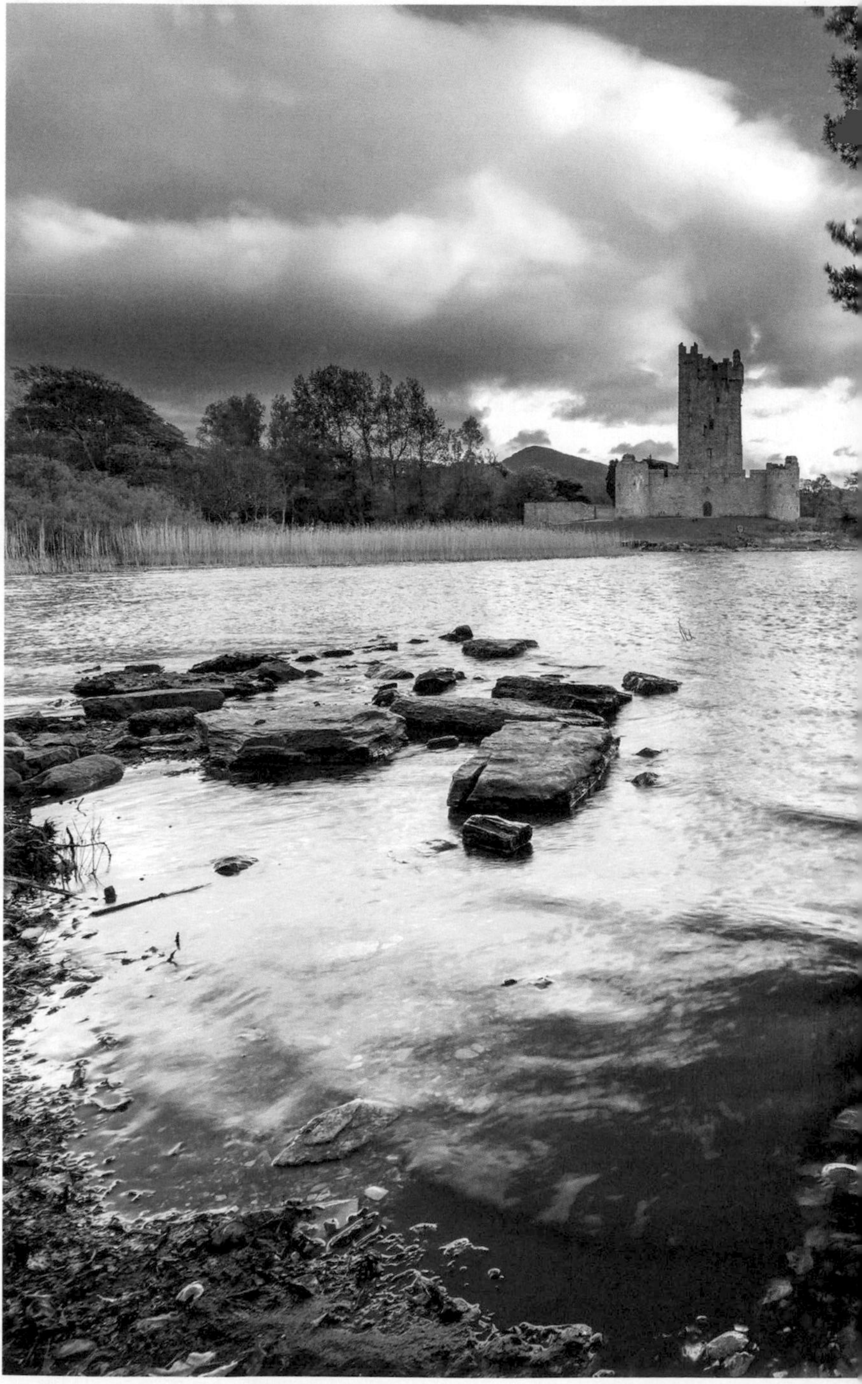

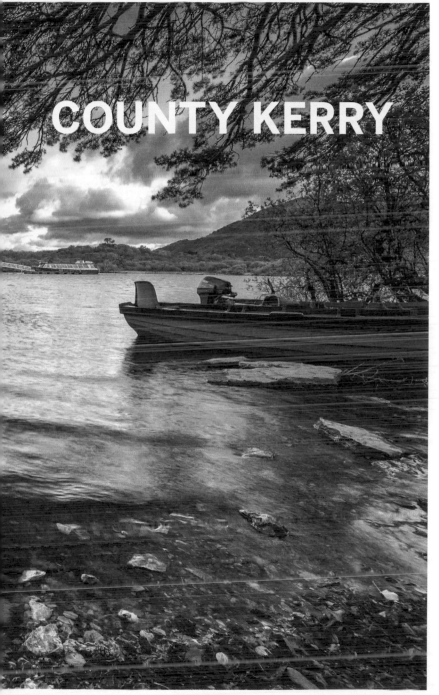

COUNTY KERRY

County Kerry at a Glance...

County Kerry contains some of Ireland's most iconic scenery: surf-pounded sea cliffs and soft golden strands, emerald-green farmland criss-crossed by tumbledown stone walls, mist-shrouded bogs and cloud-torn mountain peaks. With one of the country's finest national parks as its backyard, the lively tourism hub of Killarney spills over with colourful shops and pubs loud with spirited trad music. The town is the jumping-off point for Kerry's two famed loop drives: the larger Ring of Kerry skirts the mountainous, island-fringed Iveragh Peninsula; the more compact Dingle Peninsula is like a condensed version of its southern neighbour.

County Kerry in Two Days

Begin with a wander around Killarney town then take a **jaunting car ride** (p208) out to **Muckross House** (p205), followed by a boat trip on Lough Leane. On day two embark on a driving tour of the **Ring of Kerry** (p200), stopping for something to eat either at **QCs** (p212) in Cahersiveen or the **Boathouse** (p213) in Kenmare.

County Kerry in Four Days

On day three you have a choice. If the weather is kind (May to September), make the once-in-a-lifetime boat trip to magnificent **Skellig Michael** (p202). Otherwise, enjoy a more leisurely boat-and-bike (or bus and jaunting car) trip to the scenic **Gap of Dunloe** (p212). On day four head to **Dingle town** (p213) for lunch, and an afternoon drive around Slea Head.

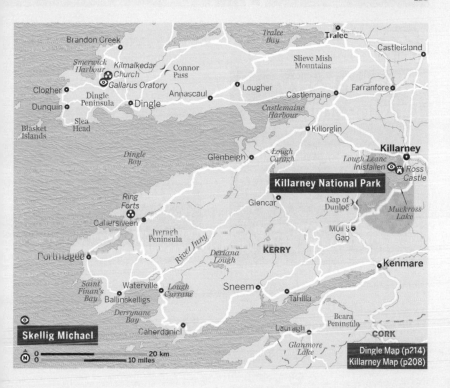

Killarney National Park

Skellig Michael

Dingle Map (p214)
Killarney Map (p208)

20 km
10 miles

Arriving in County Kerry

Kerry Airport (p211) is at Farranfore, about 17km north of Killarney on the N22.

Killarney's train station is behind the Malton Hotel, just east of the centre.

Bus Éireann runs one or two services a day to Killarney and Dingle town from Dublin and Cork. Citylink also runs a service to Killarney from Galway.

Sleeping

Killarney makes an excellent base for exploring the county and has a wealth of accommodation options, from camping grounds to hostels, B&Bs and large hotels. Dingle town also has plenty of choices. Be sure to book ahead in summer and during festivals. Elsewhere, you'll find some charming rural B&Bs, inns and pub accommodation, although some close during the winter months.

Ring of Kerry Driving Tour

Windswept beaches, waves crashing against rugged cliffs, medieval ruins, soaring mountains and glinting loughs are some of the stunning distractions along the Ring of Kerry circle drive.

Start Killorglin
Distance 179km
Duration One to two days

Classic Photo: Valentia Island

3 Take the ferry to **Valentia Island**, a beautiful and under-visited place with a rich and fascinating history

4 Take the scenic detour via the little travelled **Skellig Ring** which links Portmagee and Waterville via a Gaeltacht (Irish-speaking) area.

Take a Break...
The Bridge Bar (☎066-947 7108; www.moorings.ie; ⏰11am-11.30pm Mon-Sat, noon-11pm Sun) in **Portmagee** is a great place to stop for lunch.

0 — 20 km
0 — 10 miles
Ⓝ

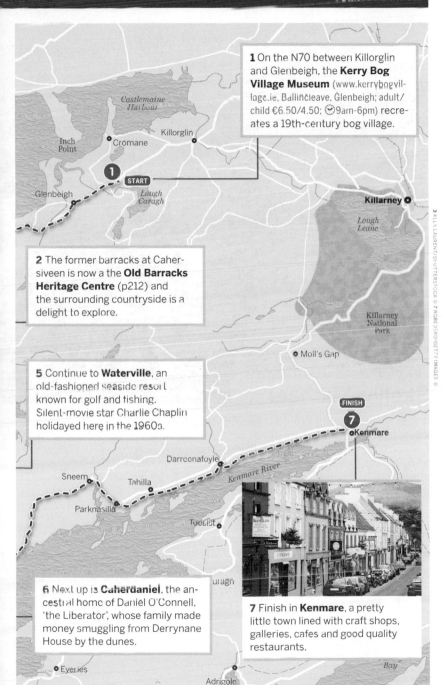

1 On the N70 between Killorglin and Glenbeigh, the **Kerry Bog Village Museum** (www.kerrybogvillage.ie, Ballincleave, Glenbeigh; adult/child €6.50/4.50; ☺9am-6pm) recreates a 19th-century bog village.

2 The former barracks at Cahersiveen is now a the **Old Barracks Heritage Centre** (p212) and the surrounding countryside is a delight to explore.

5 Continue to **Waterville**, an old-fashioned seaside resort known for golf and fishing. Silent-movie star Charlie Chaplin holidayed here in the 1960s.

6 Next up is **Caherdaniel**, the ancestral home of Daniel O'Connell, 'the Liberator', whose family made money smuggling from Derrynane House by the dunes.

7 Finish in **Kenmare**, a pretty little town lined with craft shops, galleries, cafes and good quality restaurants.

START

FINISH

Castlemaine Harbour

Inch Point

Cromane

Killorglin

Glenbeigh

Lough Caragh

Killarney

Lough Leane

Killarney National Park

Moll's Gap

Kenmare

Darreenafoyle

Kenmare River

Sneem

Tahilla

Parknasilla

Tousist

Eyeries

Adrigole

Bay

3 ALLA LAURENT/SHUTTERSTOCK © 7 RGB3/ROY/GETTY IMAGES ©

STEFAN MISSING/SHUTTERSTOCK ©

Skellig Michael

A trip to the Skellig Islands, two wave-battered pinnacles of rock 12km off the coast, and the site of Ireland's most remote and spectacular ancient monastery, is an unforgettable experience.

The jagged, 217m-high rock of Skellig Michael (Archangel Michael's Rock; like St Michael's Mount in Cornwall and Mont St Michel in Normandy) is the larger of the two Skellig Islands and a Unesco World Heritage Site. Early Christian monks established a community and survived here from the 6th until the 12th or 13th century. The monastic buildings perch on a saddle in the rock, some 150m above sea level, reached by 600 steep steps cut into the rock face.

The astounding 6th-century oratories and **beehive cells** vary in size; the largest cell has a floor space of 4.5m by 3.6m. You can see the monks' south-facing vegetable garden and their cistern for collecting rainwater. The most impressive structural achievements are the settlement's foundations – platforms built on the steep

Great For...

☑ **Don't Miss**

The 6th-century, stone-built beehive cells at the very summit of Skellig Michael.

View from Skellig Michael to Little Skellig

Portmagee

Ballinskelligs

Skellig Michael Small Skellig

❶ Need to Know

www.heritageireland.ie; ☺May–Sep; `FREE`

✕ Take A Break

There are no facilities on Skellig Michael – take a packed lunch with you.

★ Top Tip

To see the islands up close without landing, consider a cruise with Skellig Experience (☎066-947 6306; www.skellig experience.com; adult/child €5/3, incl cruise €35/20; ☺10am-7pm Jul & Aug, to 6pm May, Jun & Sep, to 4.30pm Fri-Wed Mar, Apr, Oct & Nov) from Valentia Island.

slope using nothing more than earth and drystone walls.

Influenced by the Coptic Church (founded by St Anthony in the deserts of Egypt and Libya), the monks' determined quest for ultimate solitude led them to this remote, windblown edge of Europe. Not much is known about the life of the monastery, but there are records of Viking raids in AD 812 and 823. Monks were kidnapped or killed, but the community recovered and carried on. In the 11th century a rectangular oratory was added to the site, but although it was expanded in the 12th century, the monks abandoned the rock around this time.

After the introduction of the Gregorian calendar in 1582, Skellig Michael became a popular spot for weddings. Marriages were forbidden during Lent, but since

Skellig used the old Julian calendar, a trip to the islands allowed those unable to wait for Easter to tie the knot.

Skellig Michael famously featured as Luke Skywalker's Jedi temple in *Star Wars: The Force Awakens* (2015) and *Star Wars: The Last Jedi* (2017), attracting a whole new audience to the island's dramatic beauty.

While Skellig Michael looks like two triangles linked by a spur, Small Skellig is longer, lower and much craggier. From a distance it looks as if someone battered it with a feather pillow that burst. Close up you realise you're looking at a colony of over 20,000 pairs of breeding gannets, the second largest breeding colony in the world. Most boats circle the island so you can see the gannets and you may see basking seals as well. **Small Skellig** is a bird sanctuary; no landing is permitted.

NICOLAS KIPOURAX PAQUET/GETTY IMAGES ©

Killarney National Park

Any cynicism engendered by Killarney's shamrock-filled souvenir stores evaporates when you begin to explore the lakes and woods of sublime Killarney National Park.

Great For...

☑ **Don't Miss**

A boat tour of the Killarney lakes.

The core of the national park is the Muckross Estate, donated to the state by Arthur Bourn Vincent in 1932; the park was designated a Unesco Biosphere Reserve in 1982. The Killarney Lakes – Lough Leane (the Lower Lake, or 'Lake of Learning'), Muckross (or Middle) Lake and the Upper Lake – make up about a quarter of the park, surrounded by natural oak and yew woodland, and overlooked by the high crags and moors of Purple Mountain (832m) to the west and Knockrower (552m) to the south.

The park is rich in wildlife as well as scenic beauty: deer swim out to graze on the lake islands, red squirrels and pine martens scamper in the woods, and salmon and brown trout thrive in the clean waters. Fifteen white-tailed eagles were reintroduced here in 2007; by 2015 at least four nesting pairs were established

Red deer stag

GABE9OOIC/GETTY IMAGES ©

ℹ️ Need to Know

www.killarneynationalpark.ie; FREE

✕ Take A Break

There's a good cafe in the visitor centre near Muckross House.

★ Top Tip

Take binoculars, and look out for rare white-tailed eagles circling above the Middle Lake.

Muckross Traditional Farms €15/10.50; ⊙9am-7pm Jul & Aug, to 5.30pm Sep-Jun; P) This impressive Victorian mansion is crammed with fascinating objects (70% of the contents are original). Portraits by John Singer Sargent adorn the walls alongside trophy stags' heads and giant stuffed trout, while antique Killarney furniture, with its distinctive inlaid scenes of local beauty spots, graces the grand apartments along with tapestries, Persian rugs, silverware and china specially commissioned for Queen Victoria's visit in 1861. It's 5km south of Killarney, signposted from the N71.

in County Kerry, with one pair breeding successfully in the national park.

Ross Castle — Castle

(☎064-663 5851; www.heritageireland.ie; Ross Rd; adult/child €5/3; ⊙9.30am-5.45pm early Mar-Oct; P) Lakeside Ross Castle dates back to the 15th century, when it was a residence of the O'Donoghue family. It was the last place in Munster to succumb to Cromwell's forces, thanks partly to its cunning spiral staircase, every step of which is a different height in order to break an attacker's stride. The castle is a lovely 3km walk or bike ride from the pedestrian park entrance; you may well spot deer along the way.

Muckross House — Historic Building

(☎064-667 0144; www.muckross-house. ie; Muckross Estate; adult/child €9/6, incl

Muckross Traditional Farms — Museum

(☎064-663 0804; www.muckross-house. ie; Muckross Estate; adult/child €9/6, incl Muckross House €15/10.50; ⊙10am-6pm Jun-Aug, 1-6pm May & Sep, 1-6pm Sat & Sun Mar, Apr & Oct) These recreations of 1930s farms evoke the sights, sounds and smells of real farming – cow dung, hay, wet earth and peat smoke, plus a cacophony of chickens, ducks, pigs and donkeys.

Costumed guides bring the traditional farm buildings to life, and the petting area allows kids to get up close and personal with piglets, lambs, ducklings and chicks. The farms are immediately east of Muckross House; you'll need at least two hours to do justice to the self-guided tour.

Muckross Abbey   Ruins
(www.muckross-house.ie; Muckross Estate; ⊙24hr) FREE This well-preserved ruin (actually a friary, though everyone calls it an abbey) was founded in 1448 and burned by Cromwell's troops in 1652. There's a square-towered church and a small, atmospheric cloister with a giant yew tree in the centre (legend has it that the tree is as old as the abbey). In the chancel is the tomb of the McCarthy Mòr chieftains, and an elaborate 19th-century memorial

to local philanthropist Lucy Gallwey. The abbey is 1.5km north of Muckross House (signposted).

Inisfallen   Island
The first monastery on Inisfallen (the largest of the lake's islands) was founded by St Finian the Leper in the 7th century. The extensive ruins of a 12th-century **Augustinian priory** and an oratory with a carved Romanesque doorway stand on the site of St Finian's original. You can hire a motor boat with boatman (around €10) from Ross Castle for the 10-minute trip to the island. In calm weather you can hire a rowing boat (€5 per hour; allow 30 minutes each way).

Muckross House (p205)

Knockreer House & Gardens

Gardens

(⊙8am-7pm Jun-Aug, to 6pm Apr-May & Oct, to 5pm Nov-Mar) **FREE** Killarney House, built for the Earl of Kenmare in the 1870s, burned down in 1913; the present Knockreer House was built on the same site in 1958 and is now home to a national park education centre. It isn't open to the public, but its gardens, featuring a terraced lawn and a summerhouse, have magnificent views across the lakes to the mountains.

From the park entrance opposite St Mary's Cathedral, follow the path to your right for about 500m.

MANUEL CAPELLARI/SHUTTERSTOCK ©

Killarney Lake Tours

Cruise

(☎064-663 2638; www.killarneylaketours.ie; Ross Castle Pier; adult/child €10/5; ⊙Apr-Oct) One-hour tours of Lough Leane in a comfortable, enclosed cruise boat depart four times daily from the pier beside Ross Castle, taking in the island of Inisfallen (no landing) and O'Sullivan's Cascade (a waterfall on the west shore).

Getting Around

Walking, cycling and boat trips are the best ways to explore the park. There are two pedestrian/bike entrances in Killarney town: opposite St Mary's Cathedral (24-hour access); and the so-called **Golden Gates** at the roundabout on Muckross Rd (open 8am to 7pm June to August, to 6pm April, May and October, to 5pm November to March).

Jaunting cars depart from Kenmare Pl in Killarney town centre, and from the Jaunting Car Entrance to Muckross Estate, at a car park 3km south of town on the N71. Expect to pay around €15 to €20 per person for a tour from Killarney to Ross Castle and back. There are no set prices; haggle for longer tours.

★ Muckross Lake Loop Trail

This hiking trail takes in some of the best scenery in the park, including the Meeting of the Waters where channels from all three of Killarney's lakes merge.

Killarney

In the tourism game for more than 250 years, Killarney is a well-oiled machine set in the midst of sublime scenery spanning lakes, waterfalls and woodland spreading beneath a skyline of 1000m-plus peaks. Competition keeps standards high and visitors on all budgets can expect to find good restaurants, great pubs and comfortable accommodation.

Mobbed in summer, Killarney is perhaps at its best in the late spring and early autumn when the crowds are manageable, but the weather is still good enough to enjoy its outdoor activities.

TOURS

Jaunting Car Tours   Tours

(☑064-663 3358; http://killarneyjauntingcars. ie; Kenmare Pl; per jaunting car €30-80) Killarney's traditional horse-drawn jaunting cars provide tours from the town to Ross Castle and Muckross Estate, complete with amusing commentary from the driver (known as a 'jarvey'). The cost varies depending on distance; cars can fit up to four

---

Killarney

Map

Killarney — scale: 0–400 m / 0–0.2 miles (N)

Rock Rd · High St · Chapel Pl · New Market La · New St · Lower New St · Beech Rd · Main St · Muckross Rd · College St · Scotts St · Fair Hill · St Anthony's Pl · East Avenue Rd · Lewis Rd · Kenmare Pl · Countess Rd · Countess Gve · Plunkett St

Killarney Coach Park · Bus Station · Train Station · Knockreer House & Gardens (650m) · Killarney Shuttle Bus · O'Sullivan's Bike Hire · Killarney National Park

---

Killarney

Jaunting car tour through Killarney National Park

people. The pick-up point, nicknamed 'the Ha Ha' or 'the Block', is on Kenmare Pl.

Killarney Guided Walks   Walking

(☏087 639 4362; www.killarneyguidedwalks. com; adult/child €9/5) Guided two-hour walks through the national park woodlands leave at 11am daily from opposite St Mary's Cathedral at the western end of New St; advance bookings are required from November to April. Tours meander through Knockreer gardens, then to spots where Charles de Gaulle holidayed, David Lean filmed *Ryan's Daughter* and Brother Cudda slept for 200 years.

Tours are available at other times on request.

Killarney Golf & Fishing Club   Golf

(☏064-663 1034; www.killarneygolfclub.com; green fees €65-110) This historic club, which has hosted the Irish Open on several occasions, has three championship golf courses with lakeside settings and mountain views. It's 3.4km west of Killarney on the N72.

🍴 EATING

Khao   Asian €

(☏064-667 1040; 66 High St; mains €11-17; ⊙noon-10.30pm; 🖉) Fiery spices waft from this cosy spot, which sizzles up authentic stir-fries and wok-fried noodles along with rich curries, rice dishes and noodle soups. All of its produce is organic, and vegetarian choices abound. The two-course lunch menu, served between noon and 5pm, is a fantastic deal. Takeaway is available.

Mareena's Simply Food   Irish €€

(☏066-663 7787; www.mareenassimplyfood. com; East Avenue Rd; mains €19-29; ⊙6-9pm Tue-Sun mid-Feb–Dec) Mareena's serves locally sourced produce, from scallops and sea bass to neck of lamb and pork fillet, cooked plainly and simply to let the quality of the food speak for itself. The contemporary oyster-toned decor matches the cuisine – unfussy and understated.

Fishing Killarney's Lakes

Trout Fishing for brown trout in the lakes of Killarney National Park is free (no permit needed). The season runs from 15 February to 12 October. Fishing from the bank is allowed, but the best sport is to be had from a boat, which you can hire at **Ross Castle** (☑085 174 2997; Ross Castle Pier; ⊙9.30am-5pm Apr-Oct, by reservation Nov-Mar) or at **Sweeney's** (☑064-664 4207; www.theinvicta.com; Invicta B&B, Tomies, Beaufort), at the west end of Lough Leane, for €40 a day (including outboard motor; up to three people).

Salmon The River Laune, which flows from Lough Leane to the sea, is one of Ireland's best salmon rivers. The season runs from 17 January to 30 September, with the best fishing from late July onwards. Both a permit (one day €20) and a state rod licence (one day/three weeks €20/40) are required. You can also fish for salmon in the Killarney lakes (no permit needed, but state rod licence is still required).

O'Neill's (☑064-663 1970; 6 Plunkett St; ⊙10am-9.30pm Mon-Fri, 10am-9pm Sat & Sun) angling centre in Killarney provides information, rents rods and tackle, and sells permits and licences.

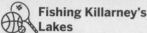

Ross Castle
STEFANO_VALERI/SHUTTERSTOCK ©

Smoke House Steak, Seafood €€
(☑064-663 9336; www.thesmokehouse.ie; 8 High St; mains €13-31; ⊙5-10pm Mon-Fri, noon-10pm Sat & Sun) One of Killarney's busiest restaurants, this switched-on bistro was the

first establishment in Ireland to cook with a Josper (superhot Spanish charcoal oven). The Kerry surf 'n' turf platter – a half-lobster and fillet steak – is outstanding; other options include rack of Kerry mountain lamb and wild local venison. Weekend brunch, served from noon till 3pm, includes eggs Florentine and Benedict.

Gaby's Seafood Restaurant Seafood €€€

(☑064-663 2519; www.gabys.ie; 27 High St; mains €30-50; ⊙6-10pm Mon-Sat) Gaby's is a refined dining experience serving superb seafood in a traditional manner. Peruse the menu by the fire before drifting past the wine racks to the low-lit dining room to savour exquisite dishes such as lobster in cognac and cream. The wine list is long and the advice unerring.

🍷 DRINKING & NIGHTLIFE

O'Connor's Pub

(http://oconnorstraditionalpub.com; 7 High St; ⊙10.30am-11pm Mon-Thu, to 12.30am Fri & Sat, 12.30-11pm Sun) Live music plays every night at this tiny traditional pub with leaded-glass doors, which is one of Killarney's most popular haunts. In warmer weather, the crowds spill out onto the adjacent lane.

Celtic Whiskey Bar & Larder Bar

(☑064-663 5700; www.celticwhiskeybar.com; 93 New St; ⊙10.30am-11.30pm Mon-Thu, to 12.30am Fri & Sat, to 11pm Sun) Of the thousand-plus whiskeys stocked at this stunning contemporary bar, over 500 are Irish, including the 1945 Willie Napier from County Offaly and 12-year-old Writers' Tears from County Carlow. One-hour courses (from €15) include the introductory Distiller's Apprentice and a blend-your-own Blender's Challenge. A dozen Irish craft beers are on tap; sensational food (mains €10.50 to €24.50) is served until 10pm.

ℹ️ INFORMATION

Killarney's **tourist office** (☑064-663 1633; http://killarney.ie; Beech Rd; ⊙9am-5pm

Mon-Sat;) can handle most queries and is especially good with transport intricacies.

ⓘ GETTING THERE & AWAY

AIR

Bus Éireann (www.buseireann.ie) has hourly services (€5.60, 20 minutes) between Killarney and **Kerry Airport** (KIR; ☏066-976 4644; http://kerryairport.ie; Farranfore).

Tralee–Killarney **trains** (☏064-663 1067; www.irishrail.ie) stop at Farranfore station (€7.50, 20 minutes, every two hours), 1.3km southwest of the airport (a 10-minute walk at minimum).

A taxi to Killarney costs about €20.

BUS

Bus Éireann operates from the **bus station** (Park Rd). For Dublin you need to change at Cork – the train is much faster.

Cork €25, two hours, hourly

Limerick €14.25, 1½ hours, every two hours

Tralee €10.45, 40 minutes, six daily

Waterford €29, 4¾ hours, hourly Monday to Saturday, every two hours Sunday

From April to October, **Go Coach** (http://gocoach.ie) serves Dingle town (€10, 1½ hours, three daily) from **Killarney Coach Park** (Lewis Rd)

TRAIN

Killarney's **train station** (Fair Hill) is behind the Malton Hotel, just east of the centre.

There are one or two direct services per day to Cork and Dublin; otherwise you'll have to change at Mallow.

Cork €10, 1½ hours

Dublin €21, 3¼ hours

Tralee €9.20, 40 minutes, every two hours

ⓘ GETTING AROUND

BICYCLE

Bicycles are ideal for exploring the scattered sights of the Killarney region, many of which are accessible only by bike or on foot.

 Aghadoe

On a hilltop 5km west of town, Aghadoe's sweeping views of Killarney, the lakes and Inisfallen Island have made jaws drop for centuries. At the eastern end of the hilltop meadow are the ruins of a Romanesque church and the 13th-century Parkavonear Castle. Parkavonear's keep, still standing, is one of the few cylindrical keeps built by the Normans in Ireland.

There's no public transport, but several tour buses stop here.

Church ruins
JOHN FREEMAN/GETTY IMAGES ©

Many of Killarney's hostels and hotels offer bike rental. Alternatively, try **O'Sullivan's Bike Hire** (☏064-663 1282; www.osullivanscycles.com; Beech Rd; per day/week €15/80).

BUS

The **Killarney Shuttle Bus** (☏087 138 4384; www.killarneyshuttlebus.com; return €6, day pass €10; ☉Mar-Oct) service runs daily from the tourist office to all the main tourist spots, including Gap of Dunloe, Cronin's Yard, Ross Castle, Muckross House, Torc Waterfall and Ladies' View. Buy tickets from the driver. A day pass giving unlimited travel on the shuttle bus offers the best value.

Cahersiveen

The main town of the Iveragh Peninsula, Cahersiveen (pronounced caar-suh-*veen*; from *cathair saidhbhín*, Little Sarah's Ring Fort) is indelibly linked with the fight for Irish independence – it was the birthplace

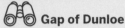 **Gap of Dunloe**

The Gap of Dunloe is a wild and scenic mountain pass – studded with crags and bejewelled with lakes and waterfalls – that lies to the west of Killarney National Park, squeezed between Purple Mountain and the high summits of Macgillycuddy's Reeks (Ireland's highest mountain range).

A boat trip through the Killarney lakes followed by a bike ride through the Gap of Dunloe is the classic Killarney region experience. Your hostel, hotel or campsite can arrange it for you (€15 per person, plus bike hire €12 to €15 per day).

Gap of Dunloe Tours (☎064-663 0200; www.gapofdunloetours.com; 7 High St; ☺Mar-Oct) can arrange a walking tour (€13.50), highly recommended bike-and-boat circuit (€15), or bus-and-boat tour (€30) taking in the Gap. Trips depart from **O'Connor's pub**.

JOE DUNCKLEY/SHUTTERSTOCK ©

of Daniel O'Connell, 'the Great Liberator', and was where the first shots of the 1867 Fenian Rising were fired.

◎ SIGHTS

Ring Forts   Ruins
(Ballycarbery) FREE Some 3km northwest of Cahersiveen, two extraordinary stone ring forts situated 600m apart are reached from a shared parking area. **Cahergal**, the larger and more impressive, dates from the 10th century and has stairways on the inside walls, a *clochán* (beehive hut), and the remains of a roundhouse.

The smaller, 9th-century **Leacanabuile** contains the outlines of four houses. Both have a commanding position overlooking Ballycarbery Castle and Valentia Harbour, with superb views of the Kerry mountains.

**Old Barracks
Heritage Centre**   Museum
(☎066-401 0430; www.oldbarrackscahersiveen.com; Bridge St; adult/child €4/2; ☺10am-5.30pm Mon-Sat, 11am-5.30pm Sun) Established in response to the Fenian Rising of 1867, the Royal Irish Constabulary barracks at Cahersiveen were built in an eccentric Bavarian-schloss style, complete with pointy turret and stepped gables. Burnt down in 1922 by anti-Treaty forces, the imposing building has been restored and now houses fascinating exhibitions on the Fenian Rising and the life and works of local hero Daniel O'Connell.

⊗ EATING

**QCs Seafood
Restaurant & Bar**   Seafood €€
(☎066-947 2244; http://qcbar.com; 3 Main St; mains €16-26.50, bar food €9-15; ☺kitchen 12.30-2.30pm & 6-9.30pm Mon-Sat, 5-9pm Sun, bar 12.30pm-midnight Mon-Sat, 5pm-midnight Sun; ☏) QCs is a modern take on a classic pub and as such is open pub hours for pints and craic. But some of the finest food on the Ring pours forth, particularly locally sourced seafood from its own fishing fleet, such as Valentia crab and Dingle Bay prawn bisque. Upstairs are six boutique B&B bedrooms (doubles from €159).

Kenmare

Kenmare (pronounced 'ken-*mair*') is the thinking person's Killarney. Ideally positioned for exploring the Ring of Kerry (and the Beara Peninsula), but without the coach-tour crowds of its more famous neighbour, Kenmare (Neidín, meaning 'little nest' in Irish) is a pretty spot with a neat triangle of streets lined with craft shops, galleries, cafes and good-quality restaurants.

EATING

Boathouse Bistro Bistro €€

(☑064-664 2889; www.dromquinnamanor.com; Dromquinna Manor, Sneem Rd; mains €15-32; ☉12.30-9pm) At the water's edge, this 1870s boathouse 4.5km west of Kenmare has been stunningly converted to a beach-house-style blue-and-white bistro specialising in local seafood delivered daily to its own wharf. Expertly cooked dishes (sautéed Kenmare Bay crab claws in garlic butter, grilled Beara scallops with Sneem black pudding) are accompanied by 33 by the-glass wines and 28 different gins.

Tom Crean Fish & Wine Irish €€

(☑064-664 1589, http://tomcrean.ie; Main St; mains €14.50-28; ☉5-9.30pm Wed-Mon Sep-Jun, daily Jul & Aug; 🐕) 🍴 Named for Kerry's pioneering Antarctic explorer, and run by his granddaughter, this venerable restaurant uses only the best of local organic produce, cheeses and fresh seafood. Sneem lobster is available in season, the oysters *au naturel* capture the scent of the sea, and the seafood gratin served in a scallop shell is divine.

ⓘ GETTING THERE & AWAY

Bus Éireann (www.buseireann.ie) serves Killarney (€12.40, 45 minutes, three daily) and Sneem (€9.70, 35 minutes, one daily) year-round, and runs a daily Ring of Kerry loop service from late June to late August.

Dingle Peninsula

One of the highlights of the Wild Atlantic Way, the Dingle Peninsula (Corca Dhuibhne) culminates in the Irish mainland's westernmost point. In the shadow of sacred Mt Brandon, a maze of fuchsia-fringed *boreens* (country lanes) weaves together an ancient landscape of prehistoric ring forts and beehive huts, early Christian chapels, crosses and holy wells, picturesque hamlets and abandoned villages.

But it's where the land meets the ocean – whether in a welter of wave-pounded

👓 Moll's Gap

Built in the 1820s to replace an older track to the east (the Old Kenmare Road, now followed by the Kerry Way hiking trail), the vista-crazy N71 Killarney to Kenmare road (32km) winds between rock and lake, with plenty of lay-bys to stop and admire the views (and recover from the switchback bends). Watch out for the buses squeezing along the road.

About 17km south of Killarney is the panoramic viewpoint **Ladies' View** (N71).

A further 5km south is the summit of the pass at Moll's Gap, which is worth a stop for great views and refreshments at **Avoca Cafe** (☑064-663 4720; www.avocahandweavers.com; N71, Moll's Gap; dishes €5.50-13; ☉9.30am-5pm Mon-Fri, 10am-5pm Sat & Sun; 🐕).

POM POM/SHUTTERSTOCK ©

rocks, or where the surf laps secluded, sandy coves – that Dingle's beauty truly reveals itself.

Centred on charming Dingle town, the peninsula has long been a beacon for those of an alternative bent, attracting artists, craftspeople, musicians and idiosyncratic characters who can be found in workshops, museums, festivals and unforgettable trad sessions throughout Dingle's tiny settlements.

Dingle Town

Framed by its fishing port, the peninsula's charming little 'capital' manages to be quaint without even trying. Some pubs

Dingle

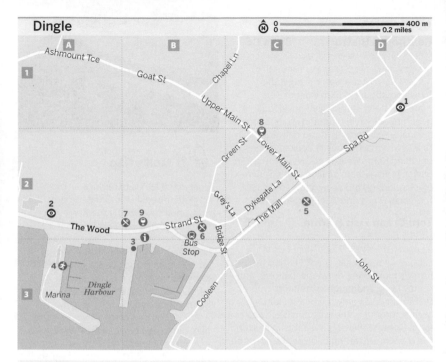

Dingle

◉ Sights
1 Dingle Brewing Company..........................D1
2 Dingle Oceanworld A2

◉ Activities, Courses & Tours
3 Dolphin Trips...B3
4 Naomhòg Experience................................A3

◉ Eating
5 Idás..C2
6 Murphy's...B2
7 Out of the Blue...B2

◉ Drinking & Nightlife
8 Curran's..C2
9 John Benny's B2

double as shops, so you can enjoy Guinness and a singalong among screws and nails, wellies and horseshoes. It has long drawn runaways from across the world, making it a cosmopolitan, creative place. In summer its hilly streets can be clogged with visitors; in other seasons its authentic charms are yours for the savouring.

Although Dingle is one of Ireland's largest Gaeltacht (Irish-speaking) towns, the locals have voted to retain the name Dingle rather than go by the officially sanctioned – and signposted – Gaelige name of An Daingean.

◉ SIGHTS & ACTIVITIES

Dingle Oceanworld   Aquarium
(☑066-915 2111; www.dingle-oceanworld.ie; The Wood; adult/child €13.50/8.75; ☺10am-7pm Jul & Aug, to 6pm Sep-Jun) Dingle's aquarium is a lot of fun, and includes a walk-through tunnel and a touch pool. Psychedelic fish glide through tanks that recreate such environments as Lake Malawi, the River Congo and the piranha-filled Amazon. Reef sharks and stingrays cruise the shark tank; water is pumped from the harbour for the spectacularly ugly wreck fish.

Dingle Brewing Company Brewery
(066-915 0743; http://dinglebrewing
company.com; Spa Rd; self-guided tour €6;
⏰by reservation) Housed in a 19th-century
creamery building, this terrific craft brewery was launched in 2011 on 20 July – not
coincidentally Tom Crean's birthday (its
single brew, a crisp, hoppy lager, is named
after the local Antarctic explorer). Admission includes a self-guided brewery tour
followed by a pint. It's on the road towards
the Connor Pass.

Naomhòg Experience Boating
(087/ 699 2925; http://dinglerowing.com;
Dingle Marina; lessons €25) *Naomhòg* is the
Kerry name for a *currach*, a traditional
Irish boat made from a wooden frame
covered with tarred canvas (originally
animal hides). They were used by the
Blasket islanders for fishing, and are now
maintained and raced by local enthusiasts. You can book a one-hour session in
Dingle Harbour (minimum two people) to
learn how to row one.

Dolphin Trips Cruise
(066-915 2626; www.dingledolphin.com; The
Pier; adult/child €16/8) Boats run by the
Dingle Boatmen's Association cooperative
leave the pier daily for one-hour trips to
see Dingle's most famous resident, Fungie
the dolphin. It's free if Fungie doesn't
show, but he usually does. The ticket
office is next to the tourist office.

❌ EATING

Murphy's Ice Cream €
(www.murphysicecream.ie; Strand St; 1/2/3
scoops €4/5.50/7; ⏰11am-9pm May-Oct, to
8pm Nov-Apr; 📶) Made here in Dingle, Murphy's sublime ice cream comes in a daily
changing range of flavours that include
brown bread, sea salt, Dingle gin, and
whiskey-laced Irish coffee, along with sor-
bets made with rainwater. In addition to a
second Dingle branch at the pier opposite
the tourist office, its runaway success has
seen it expand Ireland wide.

 Fungie the Dolphin

In 1983 a bottlenose dolphin swam into
Dingle Bay and local tourism hasn't been
the same since. Showing an unusual
affinity for human company, he swam
with the local fishing fleet. Eventually
somebody got the idea of charging tourists to go out on boats to see the friendly
dolphin (nicknamed Fungie). Today up to
12 boats at a time and more than 1000
tourists a day ply the waters with Dingle's
mascot, now a cornerstone of the local
economy (there's even a bronze statue of
him outside the tourist office).

In the wild, bottlenose dolphins live
for an average of 25 years, though they
have been known to live to over 40 in
captivity. As Fungie has been around for
well over 30 years (yes, it's still the same
dolphin, recognisable by his distinctive
markings), speculation is rife about how
long it will be before he finally glides into
the deep for the last time. And what will
Dingle do without its dolphin?

Idás Irish €€€
(066-915 0885; www.idasdingle.com; John St;
5-course veg/nonveg menu €40/50, with wine
€90/100; ⏰6-10pm Wed-Sun) ✦ Chef Kevin
Murphy is dedicated to promoting produce
solely from the Dingle Peninsula, taking
lamb, seafood and foraged herbs to create
delicately flavoured concoctions such as
braised John Dory fillet with fennel dashi
cream, pickled cucumber and wild garlic,
which are served as part of a set vegetarian
or nonvegetarian menu (no à la carte).

Out of the Blue   Seafood €€€
(066-915 0811; www.outoftheblue.ie; The
Wood; mains lunch €12.50-20, dinner €21-37; 5-
9.30pm Mon-Sat, 12.30-3pm & 5-9.30pm Sun)
Occupying a bright blue-and-yellow waterfront fishing shack, this rustic spot is in
fact one of Dingle's top restaurants, with an
intense devotion to fresh local seafood (and
only seafood). If staff don't like the catch,
they don't open, and they resolutely don't
serve chips. Highlights might include Dingle
Bay prawn bisque with lobster or chargrilled
whole sea bass flambéed in cognac.

Charthouse   Modern Irish €€€
(066-915 2255; www.thecharthousedingle.
com; The Mall; mains €19.50-30; 6-10pm
Jun-Sep, hours vary Oct-Dec & mid-Feb–May)
Window boxes frame this free-standing
stone cottage, while inside dark-red walls,
polished floorboards and flickering candles
create an intimate atmosphere. Creative
cooking uses Irish produce: Beara Peninsula
scallops with Castlegregory chorizo, Dingle
vodka–marinated hake, and butter bean
cassoulet with hazelnut-crusted Toons

Bridge halloumi. Book up to several weeks
ahead at busy times.

The Irish cheeseboard comes with a
glass of vintage port.

🍷 DRINKING & NIGHTLIFE

John Benny's   Pub
(066-915 1215; www.johnbennyspub.com;
Strand St; noon-11pm) A toasty cast iron
woodstove, stone slab floor, memorabilia
on the walls, great staff and no intrusive TV
make this one of Dingle's most enjoyable
traditional pubs. Glenbeigh oysters and
Cromane mussels are highlights of its
excellent pub menu (mains €13 to €19.50;
kitchen open to 9.30pm). Local musos pour
in most nights for rockin' trad sessions.

Curran's   Pub
(Main St; 10am-11pm) One of Dingle's most
traditional shop-pubs, stocking everything
from wellies to bags of potatoes, Curran's
has nooks and crannies including original
stained-glass snugs. Its Guinness is some of
the best for miles around. Spontaneous trad
sessions regularly take place.

Gallarus Oratory

ℹ INFORMATION

Busy but helpful, Dingle's **tourist office** (☎066-915 1188; www.dingle-peninsula.ie; The Pier; ⏱9am-5pm Mon-Sat) has maps, guides and plenty of information on the entire peninsula.

ℹ GETTING THERE & AWAY

The **bus stop** (The Tracks) is outside the car park behind the supermarket. Up to four **Bus Éireann** (www.buseireann.ie) buses a day serve Tralee (€14.80, 1¼ hours) year-round.

From April to October only, **Go Coach** (http://gocoach.ie) serves Killarney (€10, 1½ hours, three daily).

Dingle Shuttle Bus (☎087 250 4767; http://dingleshuttlebus.com) runs a minibus service between Kerry and Shannon airports (book in advance) and offers private Dingle Peninsula and Ring of Kerry tours.

Slea Head Drive

A cache of superbly preserved structures from Dingle's ancient past including beehive huts, ring forts, inscribed stones and early Christian sites are a highlight of Slea Head, set against staggeringly beautiful coastal scenery. The landscape is especially dramatic in shifting mist, although it's obliterated when thick sea fog rolls in.

The signposted Slea Head Drive is a 50km loop that passes through the villages and sights of Ventry, Dunquin, Ballyferriter and Ballydavid to the west of Dingle town.

◎ SIGHTS

Gallarus Oratory Historic Site

(www.heritageireland.ie; Gallarus) ᴴᴿᴱᴱ One of Ireland's most beautiful ancient buildings, Gallus Oratory has withstood the elements in this lonely spot beneath the brown hills for some 1200 years. There's a narrow doorway on the western side and a single, round-headed window on the east. Gallarus is clearly signposted off the R559, 8km northwest of Dingle town, and is 400m east of the **Gallarus Visitor Centre** (www.gallarusoratory.ie; €3; ⏱9am-6pm Easter-Oct) car park.

 Connor Pass

Topping out at 456m, the R560 across the Connor (or Conor) Pass from Dingle town to Cloghane and Stradbally is Ireland's highest public road. On a foggy day you'll see nothing but the tarmac just in front of you, but in fine weather it offers phenomenal views of Dingle Harbour to the south and Mt Brandon to the north The road is in good shape, but narrow in places and steep and twisting on the north side (signs portend doom for buses and trucks; caravans are forbidden).

The summit car park yields views down to glacial lakes in the rock-strewn valley below, where you can see the remains of walls and huts where people once lived impossibly hard lives. From the smaller, lower car park on the north side, beside a waterfall, you can make a 10-minute climb to Pedlar's Lake and the kind of vistas that inspire climbers.

ROLF G WACKENBERG/SHUTTERSTOCK ©

Kilmalkedar Church Ruins

(Kilmalkedar) ᴴᴿᴱᴱ The Dingle Peninsula's most important Christian site, Kilmalkedar has a beautiful setting with sweeping views over Smerwick Harbour. Built in the 12th century on the site of a 7th-century monastery founded by St Maolcethair, the roofless church is a superb example of Irish Romanesque architecture, its round-arched west door decorated with chevron patterns and a carved human head. In the graveyard you'll find an Ogham stone and a carved stone sundial. It's 7.5km northeast of Ballyferriter.

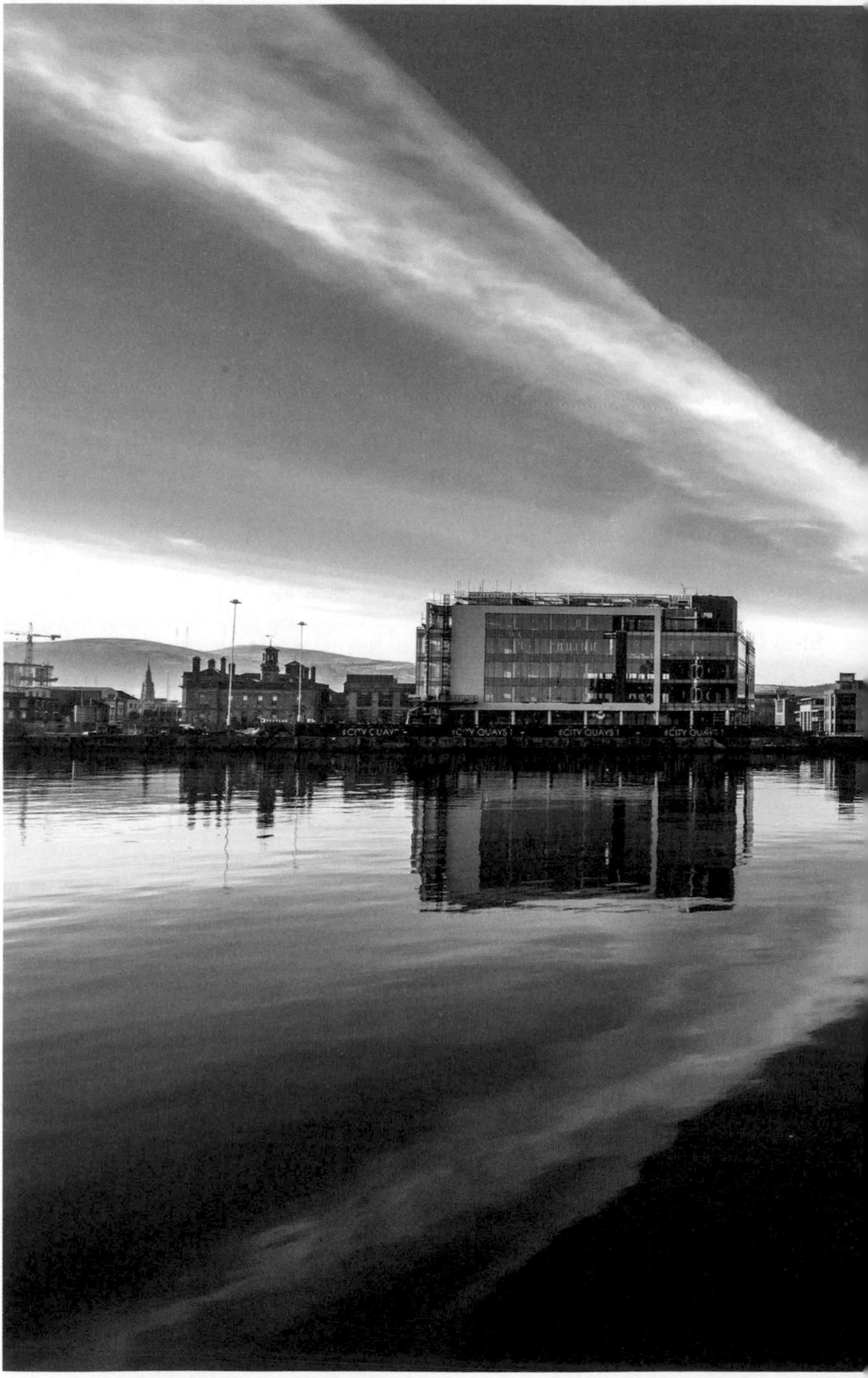

BELFAST

Belfast at a Glance...

Belfast is in many ways a brand-new city. Once shunned by travellers unnerved by tales of the Troubles and sectarian violence, in recent years it has pulled off a remarkable transformation from bombs-and-bullets pariah to a hip-hotels-and-hedonism party town.

The Titanic Quarter's centrepiece, the stunning, star-shaped Titanic Belfast centre, has become the city's number-one tourist draw, adding to a list of attractions that includes beautifully restored Victorian architecture, a glittering waterfront lined with modern art, a fantastic and fast-expanding foodie scene and music-filled pubs.

Belfast in One Day

Start with a free guided tour of **City Hall** (p226). Take a **black taxi tour** (p225) of the West Belfast murals, and ask the taxi driver to drop you off for lunch at **Holohan's** (p231). Afterwards, cruise the river on a **Lagan Boat Company** (p229) tour, then spend the rest of the afternoon exploring **Titanic Belfast** (p222), before dinner at the **Barking Dog** (p233).

Belfast in Two Days

On your second day, explore the fascinating exhibits in the **Ulster Museum** (p226) and take a stroll through the **Botanic Gardens** (p227). In the afternoon either take a guided tour around historic **Crumlin Road Gaol** (p227). Spend the evening crawling traditional pubs such as **Kelly's Cellars** (p234), the **Duke of York** (p234), and **Crown Liquor Saloon** (p226).

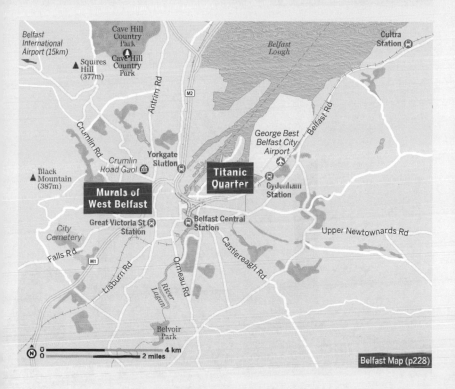

Belfast Map (p228)

Arriving in Belfast

Belfast International Airport Frequent buses to the city (return £10.50, 30 minutes) from 4.30am to 11pm.

George Best Belfast City Airport Frequent buses to the city (return £3.80, 15 minutes) from 6am to 9.30pm.

Europa Bus Station Buses from Dublin arrive here; located right in the city centre.

Belfast Central Station Trains from Dublin arrive here; rail ticket includes free bus ride into the city centre.

Sleeping

From backpacker hostels to boutique havens, the range of places to stay widens every year. Most of Belfast's budget and midrange accommodation is south of the centre, in the leafy university district around Botanic Ave, University Rd and Malone Rd, around a 20-minute walk from City Hall. Business hotels and luxury boutiques proliferate in the city centre.

Book ahead on weekends, in summer and during busy festival periods.

Titanic Belfast

VANDERWOLF IMAGES/SHUTTERSTOCK ©

Titanic Quarter

Belfast's former shipbuilding yards – the birthplace of RMS Titanic – stretch along the east side of the River Lagan, dominated by the towering yellow cranes known as Samson and Goliath.

Great For..

☑ **Don't Miss...**

Taking a peek at the first-class toilets aboard the SS *Nomadic*.

Titanic Belfast

The head of the slipway where the *Titanic* was built is now occupied by the gleaming, angular edifice of **Titanic Belfast** (www. titanicbelfast.com; Queen's Rd; adult/child £18/8; ⊗9am-7pm Jun-Aug, to 6pm Apr, May & Sep, 10am-5pm Oct-Mar; ⬚Abercorn Basin), an unmissable multimedia extravaganza that charts the history of Belfast and the creation of the world's most famous ocean liner. Cleverly designed exhibits enlivened by historic images, animated projections and soundtracks chart Belfast's rise to turn-of-the-20th-century industrial superpower, followed by a high-tech ride through a noisy, smells-and-all recreation of the city's shipyards.

You can explore every detail of the *Titanic*'s construction, from a computer 'fly-through' from keel to bridge, to replicas

SS Nomadic

AVTCN_IVANOV/SHUTTERSTOCK ©

Titanic Quarter ◎

❶ Need to Know

A series of information boards along Queen's Rd describe items and areas of interest.

✕ Take a Break

There are cafes in both Titanic Belfast and the Thompson Pump House.

★ Top Tip

Saver tickets (adult/child £9/6) are available for speedy visits without the shipyard ride one hour before the museum closes.

of the passenger accommodation. Perhaps most poignant are the few flickering images that constitute the only film footage of the ship in existence.

Behind the building you can see the massive slipways where the *Titanic* and her sister ship *Olympic* were built and launched.

SS Nomadic

Built in Belfast in 1911, the **SS Nomadic** (www.nomadicbelfast.com; Hamilton Dock, Queen's Rd; adult/child £7/5; ☺9am-7pm Jun-Aug, to 6pm Apr, May & Sep, 10am-5pm Oct-Mar; 🚇Abercorn Basin) is the last remaining vessel of the White Star Line. The little steamship ferried 1st- and 2nd-class passengers between Cherbourg Harbour and the ocean liners that were too big to dock at the French port. On 10 April 1912

it delivered 172 passengers to the ill-fated *Titanic*. Don't miss the luxurious 1st-class toilets. Entry to the SS *Nomadic* (valid for 24 hours) is included in the ticket for *Titanic* Belfast.

Titanic's Dock & Pump House

At the far end of Queen's Rd is the most impressive monument to the days of the great liners – the vast **Thompson Dry Dock** (www.titanicsdock.com; Queen's Rd; adult/child £5/3.50; ☺10am-5pm Apr-Oct, 10.30am-4pm Nov & Dec, 10.30am-5pm Jan & Feb; 🚇Science Park) where the *Titanic* was fitted out.

Beside it is the **Pump House**, which has an exhibition on Belfast shipbuilding. Self-guided tours include a viewing of original film footage from the shipyards, a visit to the inner workings of the pump house and a walk along the floor of the dry dock.

The dry dock's huge size gives you some idea of the scale of the ship, which could only just fit into it.

Bobby Sands mural, by Danny Devenny

EVERYONE REPUBLICAN OR OTHERWISE HAS THEIR OWN PARTICULAR ROLE TO PLAY

...OUR REVENGE WILL BE THE LAUGHTER OF OUR CHILDREN

Bobby Sands MP
POET, GAEILGEOIR, REVOLUTIONARY, IRA VOLUNTEER.

Murals of West Belfast

The political murals of West Belfast are one of the city's most compelling sights, a colourful and visceral reminder of the tensions that once tore the city apart.

Great For...

☑ Don't Miss

A visit to the Peace Line, the corrugated steel wall that divides West Belfast's Protestant and Catholic communities.

Belfast's tradition of political murals is a century old, dating from 1908 when images of King Billy (William III, Protestant victor over the Catholic James II at the Battle of the Boyne in 1690) were painted by Unionists protesting against home rule for Ireland. The tradition was revived in the late 1970s as the Troubles wore on, with murals used to mark out sectarian territory, make political points, commemorate historical events and glorify terrorist groups.

Republican Murals

The first Republican murals appeared in 1981, when the hunger strike by Republican prisoners – demanding recognition as political prisoners – at the Maze Prison saw the emergence of dozens of murals of support. In later years, Republican muralists broadened their scope to cover wider

Solidarity P.O.W.s mural, by Danny Devenny and Carlos Latuff

VANDERWOLF IMAGES/SHUTTERSTOCK ©

political issues, Irish legends and historical events.

Loyalist Murals

Loyalist murals have traditionally been more militaristic and defiant in tone than the Republican murals. The Loyalist battle cry of 'No Surrender!' is everywhere, along with red, white and blue painted kerbstones, paramilitary insignia and images of King Billy, usually shown on a prancing white horse.

Murals Today

In recent years there has been a lot of debate about what to do with Belfast's murals. There's no doubt they have become an important tourist attraction, but there is now a move to replace the more aggressive and militaristic images with murals dedi-

cated to local heroes and famous figures such as footballer George Best and *The Chronicles of Narnia* novelist CS Lewis.

Taxi Tours

Black taxi tours of West Belfast's murals are offered by a large number of taxi companies and local cabbies. These can vary in quality and content, but in general they're an intimate and entertaining way to see the sights. Drivers will pick you up from anywhere in the city centre.

Paddy Campbell's Famous
Black Cab Tours   Cultural
(☎07990 955 227; www.belfastblackcabtours. co.uk; tour per 1-3 people £30) Popular 1½-hour black cab tour.

Harper Taxi Tours   Cultural
(☎07711 757 178; www.harpertaxitours.com; from £30) Political and historical tours.

Official Black Taxi Tours   Cultural
(☎028-9064 2264; www.belfasttours.com; 1-2 passengers £35, 3 or more per person £15) Customised tours lasting 1½ hours.

◉ SIGHTS

◉ City Centre

City Hall   Historic Building

(www.belfastcity.gov.uk; Donegall Sq; ⊘guided tours 11am, 2pm & 3pm Mon-Fri, noon, 2pm & 3pm Sat & Sun Oct-May, plus 10am & 4pm Mon-Fri, 4pm Sat & Sun Jun-Sep; 🚇Donegall Sq) **FREE** Belfast's classical Renaissance-style City Hall was built in fine, white Portland stone in 1906. Highlights of the free, 45-minute guided tour include the sumptuous, wedding-cake Italian marble and colourful stained glass of the entrance hall and rotunda; an opportunity to sit on the mayor's throne in the council chamber and try on the robes; and the idiosyncratic portraits of past lord mayors. Each is allowed to choose his or her own artist and the variations in personal style are intriguing.

Crown Liquor
Saloon   Historic Building

(www.nationaltrust.org.uk/the-crown-bar; 46 Great Victoria St; ⊘11.30am-11pm Mon-Sat, 12.30-10pm Sun; 🚇Europa Bus Centre) **FREE** There are not many historical monuments that you can enjoy while savouring a pint of beer, but the National Trust's Crown Liquor Saloon is one of them. Belfast's most famous bar was refurbished by Patrick Flanagan in the late 19th century and displays Victorian decorative flamboyance at its best (he was looking to pull in a posh clientele from the train station and Grand Opera House opposite). Despite being a tourist attraction, the bar fills up with locals come 6pm.

◉ South Belfast (Queen's Quarter)

Ulster Museum   Museum

(www.nmni.com; Botanic Gardens; ⊘10am-5pm Tue-Sun; 👪; 🚇Botanic) **FREE** You could spend hours browsing this state-of-the-art museum, but if you're pressed for time don't miss the **Armada Room**, with artefacts retrieved from the 1588 wreck of the Spanish galleon *Girona;* the **Egyptian Room**, with Takabuti, a 2500-year-old Egyptian mummy unwrapped in Belfast in 1835; and the **Early Peoples Gallery**, with the bronze Bann Disc, a superb example of Celtic design from the Iron Age.

City Hall

Botanic Gardens   Gardens

(Stranmillis Rd; ☺7.30am–sunset; 🖳College Green) **FREE** The showpiece of Belfast's green oasis is Charles Lanyon's beautiful **Palm House** (☺10am–5pm Apr–Sep, to 4pm Oct–Mar) built in 1839 and completed in 1852, with its birdcage dome, a masterpiece in cast-iron and curvilinear glass. Nearby is the 1889 **Tropical Ravine** (☺10am–5pm Apr–Sep, to 4pm Oct–Mar) a huge red-brick greenhouse designed by the garden's curator Charles McKimm. Inside, a raised walkway overlooks a jungle of tropical ferns, orchids, lilies and banana plants growing in a sunken glen. It is due to reopen in February 2018 following a £3.8 million restoration.

Queen's University   Historic Building

(University Rd; guided tour £5; 🖳Queen's University) Northern Ireland's most prestigious university was founded by Queen Victoria in 1845. In 1908, the Queen's College became the Queen's University of Belfast and today its campus spreads across some 250 buildings.

Just inside the main entrance is the **Queen's Welcome Centre** (☎028-9097 5252; www.qub.ac.uk/welcomecentre; ☺8.30am–5.30pm Mon–Fri, 11am–4pm Sat & Sun), with an information desk and souvenir shop. Book ahead for **guided tours**, or pick up a free leaflet that outlines a self-guided tour.

◎ West Belfast (Gaeltacht Quarter)

Northwest of Donegall Sq, Divis St leads across the Westlink Motorway to Falls Rd and West Belfast. Though scarred by decades of civil unrest during the Troubles, this former battleground is one of the most compelling places to visit in Northern Ireland. Recent history hangs heavy in the air, but there is a noticeable spirit of optimism and hope for the future.

The main attractions are the powerful murals that chart the history of the conflict, as well as the political passions of the moment.

 Crumlin Road Gaol

Guided tours of Belfast's notorious **Crumlin Road Gaol** (☎028-9074 1500; www.crumlinroadgaol.com; 53-55 Crumlin Rd; tour adult/child £9/6.50; ☺10am–5.30pm, last tour 4.30pm; 🖳Agnes St) take you from the tunnel beneath Crumlin Rd, built in 1850 to convey prisoners from the courthouse across the street (and allegedly the origin of the judge's phrase 'take him down'), through the echoing halls and cramped cells of C-Wing, to the truly chilling execution chamber. Advance tour bookings are recommended. The jail's pedestrian entrance is on Crumlin Rd; the carpark entrance is reached via Clifton park Ave to the north.

TREVOR BUCHANAN/GETTY IMAGES ©

West Belfast grew up around the linen mills that propelled the city into late-19th-century prosperity. It was an area of low-cost, working-class housing, and even in the Victorian era was divided along religious lines. The advent of the Troubles in 1968 solidified the sectarian divide, and since 1970 the ironically named **Peace Line** (🖳Falls Rd) has separated the Loyalist and Protestant Shankill district (from the Irish *sean chill*, meaning 'old church') from the Republican and Catholic Falls district.

Despite its past reputation, the area is safe to visit. The best way to see West Belfast is on an informative and entertaining black taxi tour, but there's nothing to stop you visiting under your own steam, either

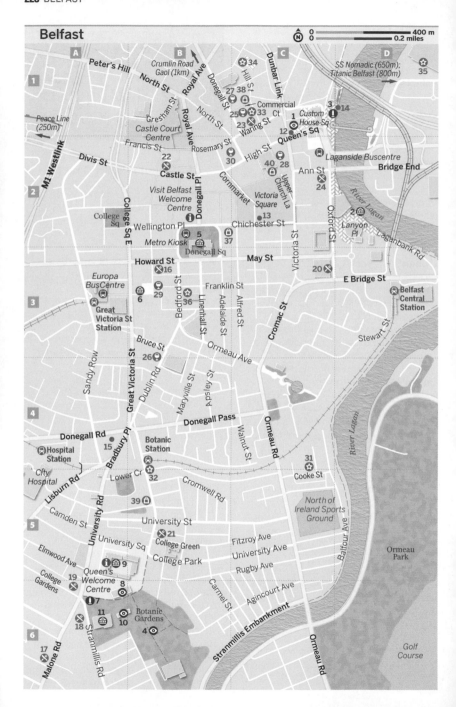

Belfast

0 — 400 m
0 — 0.2 miles

Peter's Hill

Crumlin Road
Gaol (1km)

North St

Royal Ave

Donegall St

Hill St

Dunbar Link

SS Nomadic (650m);
Titanic Belfast (800m)

35

27 38

34

Royal Ave

North St

Gresham St

Castle Court
Centre

Commercial
Ct

25

33

Waring St

Custom
House Sq

3 14

1

Peace Line
(250m)

Francis St

Rosemary St

23

30

High St

12

Queen's Sq

M1 Westlink

Divis St

22

Castle St

Donegall Pl

Cornmarket

40 28

Ann St

24

Laganside Buscentre

Bridge End

River Lagan

Visit Belfast
Welcome
Centre

College
Sq

College Sq E

Upper
Church La

Victoria
Square

13

Wellington Pl

Chichester St

2

Lanyon
Pl

Laganbank Rd

Metro Kiosk

5

37

Donegall Sq

May St

Oxford St

Victoria St

20

Howard St

16

Bedford St

Franklin St

E Bridge St

Belfast
Central
Station

Europa
BusCentre

6

29

36

Linenhall St

Adelaide St

Alfred St

Cromac St

Great
Victoria St
Station

Bruce St

26

Ormeau Ave

Stewart St

Sandy Row

Great Victoria St

Dublin Rd

Maryville St

Apsley St

Donegall Pass

Ormeau Rd

River Lagan

Donegall Rd

15

Bradbury Pl

Botanic
Station

Walnut St

31

Cooke St

Hospital
Station

City
Hospital

Lisburn Rd

Lower Cr

32

Cromwell Rd

North of
Ireland Sports
Ground

Ormeau
Park

39

Camden St

University Rd

University St

University Sq

21

College Green

Fitzroy Ave

University Ave

Balfour Ave

Ormeau
Park

Elmwood Ave

College Park

Rugby Ave

College
Gardens

19

Queen's
Welcome
Centre

9

8

Carmel St

Agincourt Ave

11

18

Malone Rd

Strannillis Rd

7

10

Botanic
Gardens

4

Strannmillis Embankment

Ormeau Rd

Golf
Course

17

Malone Rd

Belfast

walking or using the shared black taxis that travel along the Falls and Shankill Rds. Alternatively, buses 10A to 10F from Queen St will take you along the Falls Rd; buses 11A to 11D from Wellington Pl go along Shankill Rd.

ⓖ TOURS

Belfast Food Tour   Food & Drink
(https://tasteandtour.co.uk; 4hr food tour per person £50; Belfast Central) Starting in St George's Market, these fun tours are a great way to tap into Northern Ireland's flourishing food scene, with plenty of samples of the region's most traditional dishes and innovative new produce along the way.

The company also runs other food and drink tours, including a Belfast Whiskey

Walk (£60) and a Brewery Tour (£45). Book ahead.

Lagan Boat Company   Boating
(☏028-9024 0124; www.laganboatcompany. com; adult/child £10/8; ⊙12.30pm, 2pm & 3.30pm daily Apr-Oct, 12.30pm & 2pm Sat-Mon Nov-Mar; ☐Queen's Sq) The Lagan Boat Company's excellent **Titanic Tour** explores the docklands downstream of Lagan Weir, taking in the slipways where the liners *Titanic* and *Olympic* were launched and the huge dry dock where they could just fit, with nine inches (23cm) to spare. There's also a chance to spot seals. Tours depart from Donegall Quay near the **Bigfish sculpture** (☐Queen's Sq). Book ahead.

Titanic Tours   Tours
(☏028-9065 9971; www.titanictours-belfast.co.uk; 3hr tour per adult/child £30/15) A three-hour

Belfast's Titanic Connection

Perhaps the most famous vessel ever launched, RMS *Titanic* was built in Belfast's Harland & Wolff shipyard for the White Star Line. When the keel was laid in 1909, Belfast was at the height of its fame as a shipbuilding powerhouse, and the *Titanic* was promoted by White Star as the world's biggest and most luxurious ocean liner. Ironically, it was also claimed to be 'unsinkable'.

Titanic was launched from H&W's slipway No 3 on 31 May 1911, and spent almost a year being fitted out in the nearby Thompson Graving Dock before leaving Belfast for the maiden voyage on 2 April 1912. In one of the most notorious nautical disasters of all time, the ship hit an iceberg in the North Atlantic on 14 April 1912, and sank in the early hours of the following day. Of the 2228 passengers and crew on board, only 705 survived; there were only enough lifeboats for 1178 people.

The Titanic Stories website (www.the-titanic.com) contains a wealth of information on the ship and its passengers, and lists all *Titanic*-related museums and memorials throughout Ireland and the rest of the world.

Titanic mural, Newtownards Rd
PAUL J MARTIN/SHUTTERSTOCK ©

luxury tour led by the great-granddaughter of one of the *Titanic's* crew, visiting various *Titanic*-related sites. For groups of two to five people; includes pick-up and drop-off at your accommodation. Also offers custom full-day tours for £40 to £50 per person.

Belfast Pub Crawl　　　Tours

(☎07731 977 774; www.belfastcrawl.com; per person £10; ☺8.30pm Fri & Sat; ☒Queen's Sq) A three-hour tour taking in four of the city's historic pubs (including a drink in each, plus live trad music), departing from the **Albert Memorial Clock Tower** (Queen's Sq; ☒Queen's Sq). Advance booking required.

🛒 SHOPPING

Studio Souk　　　Arts & Crafts

(www.studiosouk.com; 60-62 Ann St; ☺9.30am-5.30pm Mon-Sat, 1-5.30pm Sun; ☒Victoria Sq) With three floors filled with pieces by over 80 local artists and designers, including pottery, printed canvas bags, tea towels and artwork, Souk is the perfect place to pick up Belfast-themed gifts and souvenirs.

Friend at Hand　　　Alcohol

(☎028-9032 9969; 36 Hill St; ☺11.30am-7pm Mon-Sat, noon-6pm Sun; ☒Queen's Sq) This whiskey museum and shop has more than 200 different whiskeys for sale as well as displays of old whiskey paraphernalia and 400 bottles from the private collection of Belfast bar magnate Willie Jack – some more than 100 years old. Whiskeys for sale include an £11,000 bottle of Midleton, but there are more affordable local tipples available, too.

Co Couture　　　Chocolate

(www.cocouture.co.uk; 7 Chichester St; ☺10am-6pm Mon-Sat; ☒Donegall Sq) This small subterranean shop has won prizes for its handcrafted chocolates made using raise trade (a step up from fair trade) chocolate from Madagascar. The range includes dairy-free chocolates, hot chocolate and vegetarian marshmallows. Also runs chocolate-making classes.

No Alibis Bookstore Books

(http://noalibis.com; 83 Botanic Ave; ☺9am-5.30pm Mon-Sat, 1-5pm Sun; 🚊Botanic Ave) Specialising in crime fiction (and even appearing in print in Colin Bateman's *Mystery Man* series), this small, independent bookshop run by friendly and knowledgeable staff hosts regular poetry readings, book signings and monthly jazz nights.

 EATING

 City Centre

Holohan's at the Barge Modern Irish ££

(☎028-9023 5973; www.holohansatthebarge. co.uk; Belfast Barge, Lanyon Quay; mains lunch £5-9, dinner £15-22; ☺5-11pm Tue-Sat, 1-7pm Sun; 🚊Oxford St) Aboard the **Belfast Barge** (www.facebook.com/TheBelfastBarge; ☺10am-4pm Tue-Sat) **FREE**, Holohan's is a sensational find for inspired twists on seafood and superb cooking of traditional Irish recipes such as *crabachain*, a mushroom, chestnut and tarragon fritter. Desserts are excellent too, and wines from around the world are served by the glass.

OX Irish ££

(☎028-9031 4121; http://oxbelfast.com; 1 Oxford St; 3-/7-course lunch £20/25, 5-course dinner £50; ☺noon-2.30pm & 6-9.30pm Tue-Fri, from 1pm Sat; 🚊Oxford St) ✿ A high-ceilinged space with cream-painted brick and warm golden wood creates a theatre-like ambience for the open, Michelin-starred kitchen at the back, which turns out some of Belfast's finest cuisine. The restaurant works with local suppliers and focuses on fine Irish beef, sustainable seafood, and seasonal vegetables and fruit. Book six to eight weeks ahead.

Mourne Seafood Bar Seafood ££

(☎028-9024 8544; http://mourneseafood.com; 34-36 Bank St; mains lunch £9-25; ☺noon-9.30pm Mon-Thu, noon-4pm & 5-10pm Fri & Sat, 1-9pm Sun; 🚊Royal Ave) ✿ Hugely popular, this informal, pub-like place is all red brick and

 Game of Thrones Tours

Game of Thrones Tours (☎028-9568 0023; www.gameofthronestours.com; adult/student £40/36; ☺Wed-Sun Easter-Sep, reduced tours Oct-Easter; 🚊Victoria Sq) Offers two full-day itineraries covering 11 iconic *Game of Thrones* filming locations: the Winterfell Locations Trek taking in Castle Ward and Tollymore Forest Park (where the Starks discover a dead direwolf and her pups), and the Iron Islands and Stormlands Adventure, covering sights in north Antrim including Ballintoy Harbour and the Dark Hedges. Tours depart from Victoria Square mall.

McComb's Game of Thrones Tours (☎028-9031 5333; www.mccombscoaches.com; 22-32 Donegall Rd; £35; ☺9am; 🚊Bradbury Pl) The drivers of these *Game of Thrones* tours have also driven the extras and equipment. Filming locations visited include the Dark Hedges (i.e. King's Road), Cushendun (the sea cave where the shadow assassin was born), Ballintoy Harbour (Lordsport Harbour) and Larrybane (where the shadow assassin kills Renly). Pick-up is from the **Belfast Youth Hostel** (22-32 Donegall Rd; 🚊Shaftesbury Sq) at 9am.

Dark Hedges (King's Road)
ANDY GIBSON/500PX ©

dark wood with old oil lamps dangling from the ceiling. On the menu are oysters meltingly sweet scallops, lobster and langoustines sourced from its own shellfish beds, along with luscious fish such as hake, sea bream and sea bass. Book ahead for dinner.

The attached **Belfast Cookery School** (☎028-9023 4722; www.belfastcookeryschool.com; 53-54 Castle St; classes £40-55; ☒Royal Ave) runs a diverse range of culinary classes. Mourne Seafood Bar's **sister restaurant** (☎028-4375 1377; http://mourneseafood.com; 10 Main St; mains £11-26; ☺12.30-9.30pm Wed & Thu, to 10pm Fri & Sat, to 6pm Sun) ✐ is near County Down's Dundrum Bay.

George's of the Market
Modern Irish ££

(☎028-9024 0014; http://georgesbelfast.com; Oxford St; brunch £3.50-8, express lunch £7, dinner £12.50-25; ☺10am-2.30pm Tue, 10am-2.30pm & 5-9.30pm Wed-Sat, 10am-4pm Sun; ☒Belfast Central) ✐ Many of the ingredients at this 1st-floor restaurant in historic **St George's Market** (www.belfastcity.gov.uk; cnr Oxford & May Sts; ☺6am-3pm Fri, 9am-3pm Sat, 10am-4pm Sun; ☒Belfast Central) are sourced on-site, and on market days, the best seats are on the balcony looking down over the buzz of stall holders and shoppers below. It's revered for its 'Beast of the Market' Ulster fry-up

breakfasts, but steaks and cutlets cooked on the grill are excellent, too.

Muddlers Club
Modern Irish £££

(☎028-9031 3199; www.themuddlersclubbelfast.com; Warehouse Lane, off Waring St; mains £16-24, tasting menu £45; ☺noon-2.45pm & 5.30-10pm Tue-Sat; ☒Queen's Sq) Industrial-style deco, friendly service and rustic dishes that allow fresh local ingredients to shine are a winning combination at one of Belfast's best restaurants. Named after a society of Irish revolutionaries co-founded by Wolfe Tone who held meetings at the same spot in the 1790s, the Muddlers Club is hidden in an alleyway off Commercial Court. Book ahead.

James St South
Modern Irish £££

(☎028-9043 4310; www.jamesstreetsouth.co.uk; 21 James St S; mains lunch £12-20, dinner £15.50-28, 4-/5-course tasting menu £70/80; ☺5.30-9.30pm Mon & Tue, 12.30-2.30pm & 5.30-9.30pm Wed-Sat; ☒Donegall Sq) Graced by a large, impressionistic landscape by Irish artist Clement McAleer, this starkly beautiful dining room with crisp white table linen creates a perfect stage for the presentation of sophisticated local meat

and seafood dishes. The service is relaxed yet highly professional.

Its **Bar & Grill** (028-9560 0700; www.belfastbargrill.co.uk; mains £13.50-28.50; noon-10pm) is less formal but the quality of the food is just as high.

South Belfast

Café Conor
Cafe ££

(028-9066 3266; www.cafeconor.com; 11a Stranmillis Rd; mains £9-19; 9am-10pm Mon-Sat, to 9pm Sun, Ulster Museum) Set in the glass-roofed former studio of William Conor, a Belfast artist, this light-filled, laid-back bistro offers a range of pastas, salads, burgers and stir-fries, along with favourites such as fish and chips with mushy peas and a daily pie special. The breakfast menu, which includes waffles with bacon and maple syrup, is served till 5pm.

Barking Dog
Bistro ££

(028-9066 1885; www.barkingdogbelfast.com; 33-35 Malone Rd; mains £16-30, 5 tapas dishes £15.50; noon-2.30pm & 5-10pm Mon-Thu, to 11pm Fri & Sat, noon-4pm & 5-9pm Sun; ; Eglantine Ave) Chunky hardwood,

bare brick, candlelight and modern design create the atmosphere of a stylishly restored farmhouse. The menu completes the feeling of cosiness and comfort with satisfying dishes such as their signature burger of meltingly tender beef shin with caramelised onion and horseradish cream, and sweet-potato gnocchi.

Molly's Yard
Irish ££

(028-9032 2600; www.mollysyard.co.uk; 1 College Green Mews; mains bistro £10, restaurant £13-25; noon-9.30pm Mon-Sat; ; Queen's University) A restored Victorian stables courtyard is the setting for this charming restaurant, with a cosy bar-bistro on the ground floor, outdoor tables in the yard and a rustic dining room (open from 6pm) in the airy roof space upstairs. The menu is seasonal and sticks to half a dozen each of starters and mains.

It also has its own craft beers, brewed at Lisburn's **Hilden Brewery** (028-9266 0800; www.hildenbrewery.com; Hilden House, Grand St; tour £10; tours by reservation noon Wed-Fri).

Top Five Belfast Restaurants
Holohan's at the Barge (p231)
Muddlers Club
Mourne Seafood Bar (p231
George's of the Market
Barking Dog

From left: Holohan's at the Barge (p231); St George's Market; Crown Liquor Saloon (p226)

 Classic Victorian Pubs

Duke of York (📞028-9024 1062; www.dukeofyorkbelfast.com; 11 Commercial Ct; ⊙11.30am-midnight Mon, to 1am Tue-Sat, 1-9pm Sun; 🚇Queen's Sq) In a cobbled alleyway off buzzing Hill St, the snug, traditional Duke feels like a living museum. There's regular live music; local band Snow Patrol played some of their earliest gigs here. Outside on Commercial Ct, a canopy of umbrellas leads to an outdoor area covered with murals depicting Belfast life; it takes on a street-party atmosphere in warm weather.

Kelly's Cellars (www.kellyscellars.com; 30-32 Bank St; ⊙11.30am-1am Mon-Sat, 1pm-midnight Sun; 🚇Royal Ave) Kelly's is Belfast's oldest pub (1720) – as opposed to tavern – and was a meeting place for Henry Joy McCracken and the United Irishmen when they were planning the 1798 Rising. It pulls in a broad cross-section of Belfast society and is a great place to catch traditional-music sessions, at 4.30pm on Saturdays.

White's Tavern (www.whitesbelfast.com; 1-4 Wine Cellar Entry; ⊙noon-11pm Mon & Tue, to 1am Wed-Sat, to midnight Sun; 🚇Royal Ave) Established in 1630 but rebuilt in 1790, White's claims to be Belfast's oldest tavern (unlike a pub, a tavern provided food and lodging). Downstairs is a traditional Irish bar with an open peat fire and live music nightly; upstairs, **Vandal Geek and Movie Bar** hosts regular retro film nights and Monday-night Dungeons & Dragons games.

Duke of York
MICK HARPER/SHUTTERSTOCK ©

Deanes at Queen's   Bistro ££
(📞028-9038 2111; www.michaeldeane.co.uk; 1 College Gardens; mains lunch £7-12, dinner £14-20; ⊙noon-3pm & 5.30-10pm Mon-Sat, 1-6pm Sun; 🚇Methodist College) A chilled-out bar and grill from Belfast's top chef, Michael Deane, this place was once Queen's University's staff club. The menu focuses on what can be described as good-value, gourmet pub grub, taking full advantage of the newly installed Mibrasa charcoal grill.

🍷 DRINKING & NIGHTLIFE

John Hewitt   Pub
(www.thejohnhewitt.com; 51 Donegall St; ⊙11.30am-1am Mon-Fri, noon-1am Sat, 7pm-1am Sun; 🚇Queen's Sq) Named for the Belfast poet and socialist, the John Hewitt is one of those treasured bars that has no TV or gaming machines, just the murmur of conversation. It's a good place to try Jawbox gin, made by the bar's owner Gerry White, and craft beers from Lisburn's Hilden brewery (p233).There are regular sessions of folk, jazz and bluegrass from 9pm.

Muriel's Cafe-Bar   Bar
(📞028-9033 2445; 12-14 Church Lane; ⊙11.30am-1am Mon-Fri, 10am-1am Sat, 11.30am-midnight Sun; 🚇Queen's Sq) Hats meet harlotry (ask who Muriel was) in this delightfully snug and welcoming bar with retro-chic decor, old sofas and armchairs, heavy fabrics in shades of olive and dark red, gilt-framed mirrors and a cast-iron fireplace. Gin is Muriel's favourite tipple and there's a range of exotic brands to mix with your tonic. The food menu is pretty good, too.

Filthy Quarter   Bar
(www.thefilthyquarter.com; 45 Dublin Rd; ⊙1pm-1am Mon-Sat, to midnight Sun; 🚇Dublin Rd) Four individually and collectively fabulous bars make up the Filthy Quarter: retro-trad-style, bric-a-brac-filled **Filthy McNastys**, hosting local musicians from 10pm nightly; the fairy-lit **Secret Garden**, a two-storey beer garden with watering cans for drinks coolers; **Gypsy Lounge** (Tuesday, Thursday, Friday, Saturday and Sunday nights), with a gypsy

caravan DJ booth; and a chandelier- and candelabra-adorned cocktail bar, **Filthy Chic**.

Perch — Rooftop Bar

(www.theperchbelfast.com; 5th fl, The Gate, 42 Franklin St; ☺1pm-1am Mon-Sat, to midnight Sun; ⚑Bedford St) Piped-in birdsong and flowery murals set the scene as an industrial lift takes you up to the Perch, a lively rooftop bar in the rafters of a Victorian building, with hanging plants and chilled-out tunes. In winter there's boozy hot chocolate and blankets, while the summer cocktail menu includes Pimm's punch and Bellinis. They also have pizzas (£6.50 to £8.50).

⭐ ENTERTAINMENT

MAC — Arts Centre

(Metropolitan Arts Centre; http://themaclive.com; 10 Exchange St West; ⚑Queens Sq) The MAC is a beautifully designed venue overlooking the neoclassical St Anne's Sq development, with its two theatres hosting regular performances of drama, stand-up comedy and talks, including shows for children. The centre's three galleries stage a rolling program of exhibitions, which are generally free. There's also a cafe here.

Belfast Empire — Live Music

(www.thebelfastempire.com; 42 Botanic Ave; entry live bands £5-22.50; ☺11.30am-1am Mon-Sat, 12.30pm-midnight Sun; ⚑Botanic) A converted late-Victorian church (reputed to be haunted) with three floors of entertainment, the Empire is a legendary live-music venue. Look out for stand-up comedy and quiz nights.

Black Box — Arts Centre

(www.blackboxbelfast.com; 18-22 Hill St; ⚑Victoria Sq) Black Box is an intimate venue for live music, theatre, comedy, film and more on buzzy Hill St in the heart of the Cathedral Quarter.

Ulster Hall — Concert Venue

(www.ulsterhall.co.uk; 34 Bedford St; ⚑Bedford St) Dating from 1862, Ulster Hall is a popular venue for a range of events including rock concerts, lunchtime organ recitals

and performances by the Ulster Orchestra (http://ulsterorchestra.com).

An Droichead — Live Music

(www.androichead.com; 20 Cooke St, Lower Ormeau; ⚑University Ave) This Irish cultural centre offers Irish-language courses, stages traditional dance and *céilidh* (traditional music and dancing) workshops, hosts art exhibitions and serves as a live-music venue. It's a great place to hear live Irish folk music performed by big names from around the country, as well as local talent.

INFORMATION

DANGERS & ANNOYANCES

○ Even at the height of the Troubles, Belfast wasn't a particularly dangerous city for tourists.

○ It's still best, however, to avoid the so-called 'interface areas' – near the peace lines in West Belfast, Crumlin Rd and the Short Strand (just east of Queen's Bridge) – after dark. If in doubt about any area, ask at your hotel or hostel.

○ Dissident Republican groups continue a campaign of violent attacks aimed at police and military targets, but have very little public support. Security alerts usually have no effect on visiting tourists (other than roads being closed), but be aware of the potential danger. You can follow the Police Service of Northern Ireland (PSNI) on Twitter (@policeserviceni) and receive immediate notification of any alerts.

○ You will notice a more obvious security presence than elsewhere in the UK and Ireland, such as armoured police Land Rovers and fortified police stations. There are door staff on many city-centre pubs.

○ If you want to take photos of fortified police stations, army posts or other military or quasi-military paraphernalia, get permission first, just to be on the safe side.

○ In Northern Ireland the 12 July public holiday marks the anniversary of the Protestant victory at the 1690 Battle of the Boyne. It is celebrated with bonfires, marching bands and street parades staged by the Orange Order, the biggest taking place in Belfast.

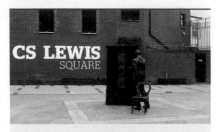

 Van Morrison & CS Lewis

The little explored neighbourhoods of East Belfast were once home to CS Lewis and Van Morrison, whose former haunts have been mapped out in self-guided walking trails.

The star stop on the CS Lewis trail is a new **square** (280 Newtownards Rd; 👶; 🚉Connswater) FREE dedicated to the author, with fabulous sculptures of characters from *The Chronicles of Narnia*.

Fans of 'Van the Man' Morrison can take a 3.5km neighbourhood walk past sights referenced in his lyrics, including the **Hollow** (immortalised in 'Brown Eyed Girl'), **Cypress Avenue** and the modest house where he was born on **Hyndford St** (at number 125).

You can pick up maps at **EastSide Visitor Centre** (📞028-9045 1900; www.eastsidepartnership.com; 278-280 Newtownards Rd; 🕐8am-6pm Mon-Fri, 10am-5pm Sat & Sun; 🚉Connswater), or download them from www.connswatergreenway.co.uk/trails.

CS Lewis Square
DAVID HUNTER/ALAMY STOCK PHOTO ©

Although the 12 July parades have regularly been associated with sectarian stand-offs and outbursts of violence, there has been a concerted effort in recent years to promote the Belfast parade as a cultural celebration, even rebranding it Orangefest.

However, many people still perceive the parades as divisive and confrontational, and with high levels of alcohol consumption among the crowds there is a potential for dangerous situations. Visitors need to be alert for signs of trouble, follow local advice and expect extra security if things escalate in any way.

TOURIST INFORMATION

Queen's Welcome Centre (p227)

Visit Belfast Welcome Centre (📞028-9024 6609; http://visit-belfast.com; 9 Donegall Sq N; 🕐9am-7pm Mon-Sat, 11am-4pm Sun Jun-Sep, 9am-5.30pm Mon-Sat, 11am-4pm Sun Oct-May; 🛜; 🚉Donegall Sq)

Tourist Information Desks George Best Belfast City Airport (📞028-9093 5372; 🕐7.30am-7pm Mon-Fri, 7.30am-4.30pm Sat, 11am-6pm Sun); **Belfast International Airport** (📞028-9448 4677; 🕐7.30am-7pm Mon-Fri, 7.30am-5.30pm Sat, 8-11am Sun)

GETTING THERE & AWAY

AIR

Belfast International Airport (Aldergrove; 📞028-9448 4848; www.belfastairport.com; Airport Rd) Located 30km northwest of the city; flights serve the UK and Europe, and in the USA, New York and Boston.

George Best Belfast City Airport (BHD; 📞028-9093 9093; www.belfastcityairport.com; Airport Rd) Located 6km northeast of the city centre; flights serve the UK and Europe.

BUS

There is an **information point** (Great Victoria St, Great Northern Mall; 🕐8am-6pm Mon-Fri, 8.30am-5pm Sat) at Belfast's **Europa Bus Centre** (📞028-9066 6630; www.translink.co.uk; Great Victoria St, Great Northern Mall; 🕐5am-11pm Mon-Fri, 5.45am-11pm Sat, to 10.15pm Sun), where you can pick up regional bus timetables. Contact **Translink** (📞028-9066 6630; www.translink.co.uk; Europa Bus Centre) for timetable and fares information.

Laganside Buscentre (Oxford St) Near the River Lagan; mainly for buses to eastern County Down, including Bangor and Newtownards.

National Express (📞08717 818 178; www.nationalexpress.com) Runs a daily coach service between Belfast and London via the Cairnryan ferry, Dumfries, Manchester and Birmingham.

Pump House (p223)

Scottish Citylink (0871 266 3333; www.
citylink.co.uk) Operates three buses a day from
Glasgow to Belfast, via the Cairnryan ferry.

TRAIN

For information on train fares and timetables,
contact **Translink**.

Belfast Central Station (East Bridge St) is east
of the city centre; trains run to Dublin and all
destinations in Northern Ireland.

Great Victoria St Station (Great Victoria St,
Great Northern Mall) is next to the Europa Bus
Centre and has trains to Portadown, Lisburn,
Bangor, Larne Harbour and Derry.

Northern Ireland Railways (NIR; 028-9066
6630; www.translink.co.uk/Services/NI-Railways)
runs four routes from Belfast. One links with the
system in the Republic via Newry to Dublin; the
other three go east to Bangor, northeast to Larne
and northwest to Derry via Coleraine.

🛈 GETTING AROUND

Belfast's integrated public-transport system
includes buses linking both airports to the central
train and bus stations.

The **Belfast Visitor Pass** (per one/two/three
days £6.50/11/14.50) allows unlimited travel on
bus and train services in and around Belfast, and
discounts on admission to Titanic Belfast and
other attractions.

Bus Metro (028-9066 6630; www.translink.
co.uk) operates the city's extensive bus network.
Most services depart from various stops on and
around Donegall Sq, at City Hall and along Queen
St. Pick up a free bus map (and buy tickets) from
the **Metro kiosk** (Donegall Sq; 8am-5.30pm
Mon-Fri) at the northwest corner of the square.

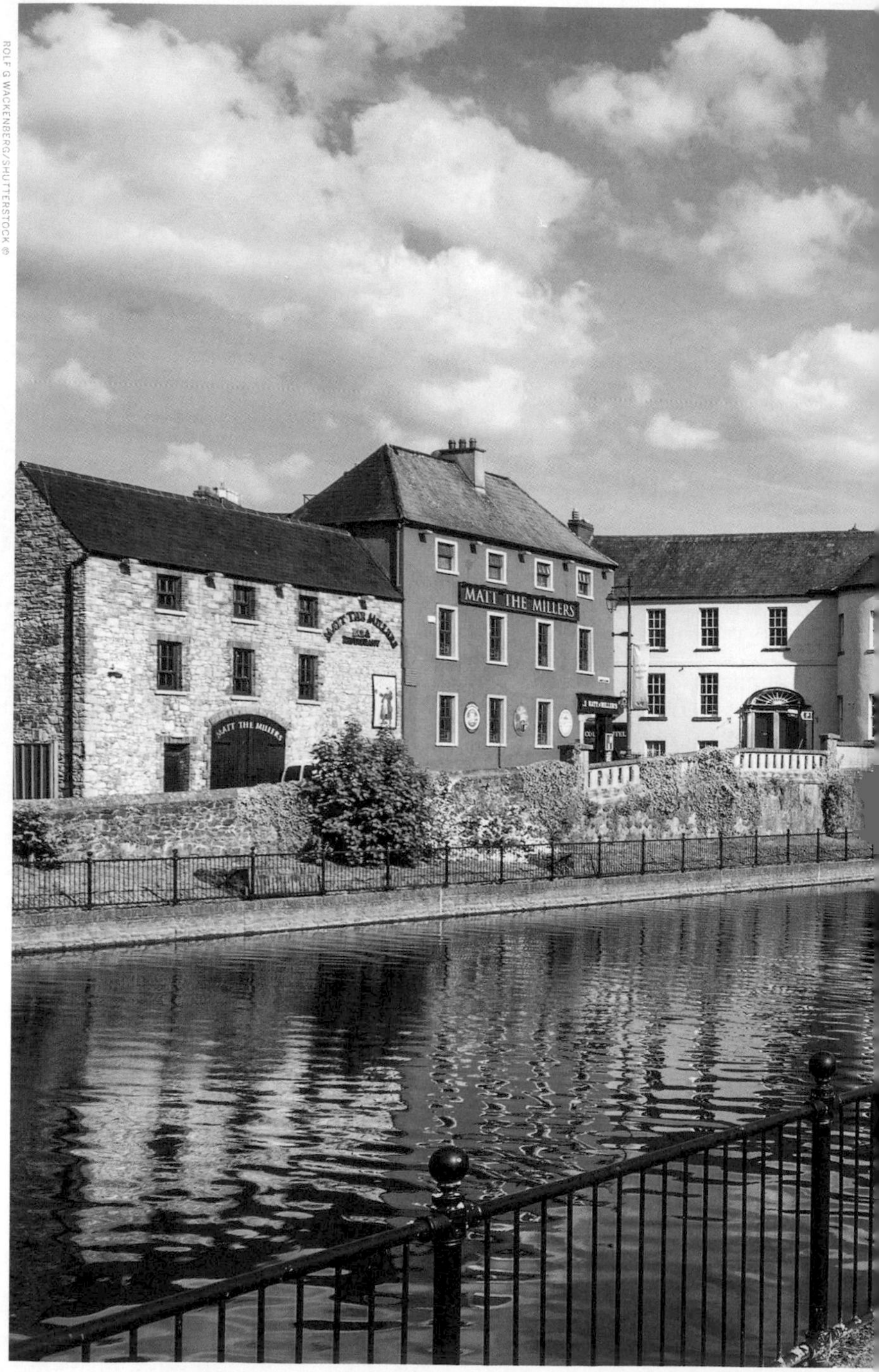
MATT THE MILLERS

KILKENNY CITY

Kilkenny City at a Glance...

Kilkenny is the Ireland of many visitors' imaginations. Built from dark-grey limestone flecked with fossil seashells, Kilkenny (from the Gaelic 'Cill Chainnigh', meaning the Church of St Canice) is also known as 'the marble city'. Its picturesque 'Medieval Mile' of narrow lanes and historic buildings strung between castle and cathedral along the bank of the River Nore is one of the southeast's biggest tourist draws. It's worth braving the crowds to soak up the atmosphere of one of Ireland's creative crucibles – Kilkenny is a centre for arts and crafts, and home to a host of fine restaurants, cafes, pubs and shops.

Kilkenny City in One Day

Spend the morning wandering the aristocratic halls of **Kilkenny Castle** (p243), then cross the road for shopping and lunch at **Kilkenny Design Centre** (p248). In the afternoon explore the **Medieval Mile Museum** (p244) and the historical delights of **St Canice's Cathedral** (p245) before sitting down to a Michelin-starred dinner at **Campagne** (p249).

Kilkenny City in Two Days

On day two visit the **Rothe House & Garden** (p247) museum in the morning, then (if you have a car) pick up a copy of the **Made in Kilkenny** craft trail leaflet from the tourist office and spend the rest of the day travelling the back roads of County Kilkenny, discovering a cornucopia of potteries, crafts studios and glass-blowers' workshops.

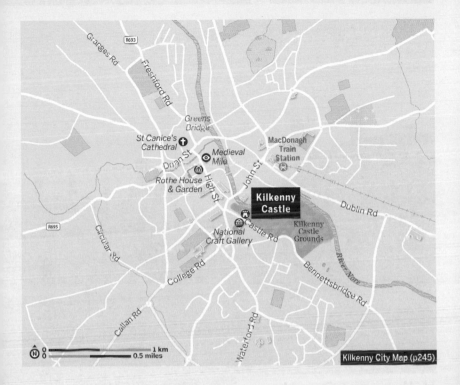

Kilkenny City Map (p245)

Arriving in Kilkenny

Kilkenny city has frequent train and bus links to Dublin and Waterford; for Cork, bus is the only choice.

Kilkenny MacDonagh train station is a 10-minute walk northeast of the town centre.

Bus Éireann services stop at the train station and on Ormonde Rd (nearer the town centre); **JJ Kavanagh** (www.jjkavanagh.ie) buses to Dublin airport stop on Ormonde Rd only.

Sleeping

Kilkenny city has a wide range of accommodation, from camping grounds and backpacker hostels to luxury hotels. Elsewhere in the county there's a more than ample choice of rural B&Bs and country-house hotels.

If you're arriving in town with no room booked (an unwise move at weekends, in summer and during festivals), the **tourist office** (p250) runs an efficient accommodation booking service (€4).

Kilkenny Castle

Rising above the River Nore, Kilkenny Castle is one of Ireland's most visited heritage sites. Stronghold of the powerful Butler family, it has a history dating back to the 12th century, though much of its present look dates from Victorian times.

Great For...

☑ Don't Miss

The superbly sculpted Carrara marble fireplace in the Long Gallery.

History

Kilkenny Castle has a rich – and lengthy – past. The first structure on this strategic site was a wooden tower built in 1172 by Richard de Clare, the Anglo-Norman conqueror of Ireland better known as Strongbow. In 1192, Strongbow's son-in-law, William Marshall, erected a stone castle with four towers, three of which survive. The castle was bought by the powerful Butler family (later earls and dukes of Ormonde) in 1391, and their descendants continued to live there until 1935. Maintaining the castle became such a financial strain that most of the furnishings were sold at auction. The property was handed over to the city in 1967 for the princely sum of £50.

❶ Need to Know

📋056-770 4100; www.kilkennycastle.ie; The Parade; adult/child €8/4; ⏰9.30am-5.30pm Apr-Sep, to 5pm Mar, to 4.30pm Oct-Feb

✕ Take A Break

The Kilkenny Design Centre Restaurant (p249) is right across the street from the castle.

★ Top Tip

A path from the castle grounds leads down to the riverside, where you can walk back into town.

Visiting the Castle

For most visitors, the focal point of a visit is the **Long Gallery**, which showcases portraits of Butler family members, the oldest dating from the 17th century. It is an impressive hall with a 19th-century timber roof vividly painted with Celtic, medieval and Pre-Raphaelite motifs by John Hungerford Pollen (1820–1902), who also created the magnificent Carrara marble fireplace, delicately carved with scenes from Butler family history. During the winter months (November to January) visits are by 40-minute guided tours only, which shift to self-guided tours from February to October. Highlights include the Long Gallery with its painted roof and carved marble fireplace. There's an excellent tearoom in the former castle kitchens, all white marble and gleaming copper.

The castle basement is home to the **Butler Gallery** (📋056-776 1106; www.butlergallery.com; ⏰10am-5.30pm May-Sep, 10am-1pm & 2-4.30pm Oct-Apr) **FREE**, featuring contemporary artwork in temporary exhibitions. You can access the Butler Gallery and cafe without paying admission.

About 20 hectares of **public parkland** (⏰8.30am-8.30pm May-Aug, to 7pm Apr & Sep, shorter hours Oct-Mar) extend to the southeast of Kilkenny Castle, framing a fine view of Mt Leinster, while a Celtic-cross-shaped rose garden lies northwest of the castle.

Kilkenny City

In the Middle Ages Kilkenny was intermittently the unofficial capital of Ireland, with its own Anglo-Norman parliament. In 1366 the parliament passed the Statutes of Kilkenny aimed at preventing the adoption of Irish culture and language by the Anglo-Norman aristocracy – they were prohibited from marrying the native Irish, taking part in Irish sports, speaking or dressing like the Irish or playing any Irish music. Although the laws remained on the books for more than 200 years, they were never enforced with any great effect and did little to halt the absorption of the Anglo-Normans into Irish culture.

During the 1640s Kilkenny sided with the Catholic royalists in the English Civil War. The 1641 Confederation of Kilkenny, an uneasy alliance of native Irish and Anglo-Normans, aimed to bring about the return of land and power to Catholics. After Charles I's execution, Cromwell besieged Kilkenny for five days, destroying much of the southern wall of the castle before the ruling Ormonde family surrendered. The defeat signalled a permanent end to Kilkenny's political influence over Irish affairs.

Today tourism is Kilkenny's main economic focus, but the city is also the regional centre for more traditional pursuits such as agriculture – you'll see farmers on tractors stoically dodging tour buses.

◎ SIGHTS

Medieval Mile Museum   Museum

(☎056-781 7022; www.medievalmilemuseum.ie; 2 St Mary's Lane; adult/child €7/3; ⊙10am-6pm Apr-Oct, 11am-4.30pm Nov-Mar) Dating from the early 13th century, St Mary's Church has been converted into a fascinating modern museum that charts the history of Kilkenny in medieval times. Highlights include the Rothe Chapel, lined with ornate 16th- and 17th-century tombs carved from local limestone, remnants of the 17th-century timber roof above the crossing, and a selection of 13th- and 14th-century grave slabs. A huge interactive map of Kilkenny allows you to explore maps and documents relating to the medieval city.

St Canice's Cathedral

GEORGE MUNDAY/GETTY IMAGES ©

Kilkenny City

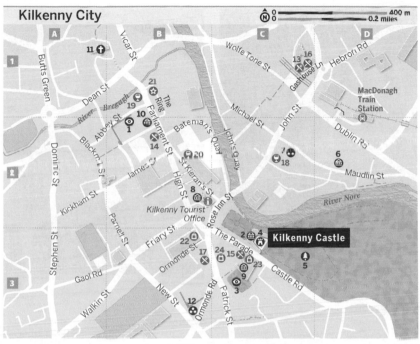

Kilkenny City

St Canice's Cathedral   Cathedral

(☏056-776 4971; www.stcanicescathedral.ie; St Canice's Pl; cathedral/round tower/combined €4/3/6; ⊗9am-6pm Mon-Sat, 1-6pm Sun Jun-Aug, shorter hours Sep-May) Ireland's second-largest medieval cathedral (after St Patrick's in Dublin) has a long and fascinating history. The first monastery was built here in the 6th century by St Canice, Kilkenny's patron saint. The present structure dates from the 13th to 16th centuries, with extensive 19th-century reconstruction, its interior

From left: St Canice's Cathedral (p245); Rothe House; Butler House

housing ancient grave slabs and the tombs of Kilkenny Castle's Butler dynasty. Outside stands a 30m-high round tower, one of only two in Ireland that you can climb.

Records show that a wooden church on the site was burned down in 1087. The existing structure was raised between 1202 and 1285, but then endured a series of catastrophes and resurrections. The first disaster, the collapse of the church tower in 1332, was associated with Dame Alice Kyteler's conviction for witchcraft. Her maid Petronella was also convicted, and her nephew, William Outlawe, was implicated. The unfortunate maid was burned at the stake, but Dame Alice escaped to London and William saved himself by offering to reroof part of St Canice's Cathedral with lead tiles. His new roof proved too heavy, however, and brought the church tower down with it.

In 1650 Cromwell's forces defaced and damaged the church, using it to stable their horses. Repairs began in 1661; the beautiful roof in the nave was completed in 1863.

Inside, highly polished ancient **grave slabs** are set on the walls and the floor.

On the northern wall, a slab inscribed in Norman French commemorates Jose de Keteller, who died in 1280; despite the difference in spelling he was probably the father of Alice Kyteler. The **stone chair of St Kieran** embedded in the wall dates from the 13th century. The fine 1596 monument to Honorina Grace at the western end of the southern aisle is made of beautiful local black limestone. In the southern transept is the handsome black **tomb of Piers Butler**, who died in 1539, and his wife, Margaret Fitzgerald. Tombs and monuments (listed on a board in the southern aisle) to other notable Butlers crowd this corner of the church. Also worth a look is a model of Kilkenny as it was in 1642.

Apart from missing its crown, the 9th-century **round tower** is in excellent condition. Inside is a tight squeeze and you'll need both hands to climb the 100 steps up steep ladders (under 12s not admitted).

Walking to the cathedral from Parliament St leads you over Irishtown Bridge and up **St Canice's Steps**, which date from 1614; the wall at the top contains fragments of

medieval carvings. The leaning tombstones scattered about the grounds prompt you to look, at the very least, for a black cat.

Rothe House & Garden   Museum
([☑]056-772 2893; www.rothehouse.com; Parliament St; adult/child €5.50/4.50; ⊙10.30am-5pm Mon-Sat, noon-5pm Sun Apr-Oct, 10.30am-4.30pm Mon-Sat Nov-Mar) Dating from 1594 this is Ireland's finest example of a Tudor merchant's house, complete with restored medieval garden. Built around a series of courtyards, it now houses a museum with a rather sparse display of local artefacts including a rusted Viking sword and a grinning stone head sculpted by a Celtic artist. The highlight is the delightful walled garden, divided into fruit, vegetable and herb sections and a traditional orchard, as it would have been in the 17th century.

In the 1640s the wealthy Rothe family played a part in the Confederation of Kilkenny, and Peter Rothe, son of the original builder, had all his property confiscated. His sister was able to reclaim it, but just before the Battle of the Boyne (1690) the family supported James II and so lost the house permanently. In 1850 a Confederation ban-ner was discovered in the house; it's now in the National Museum in Dublin.

National Craft Gallery   Gallery
([☑]056-779 6147; www.nationalcraftgallery. ie; Castle Yard; ⊙10am-5.30pm Tue-Sun; [♿]) FREE Contemporary Irish crafts are showcased at these imaginative galleries, set in former stables across the road from Kilkenny Castle, next to the shops of the Kilkenny Design Centre (p248). Ceramics dominate, but exhibits often feature furniture, jewellery and weaving from the members of the Crafts Council of Ireland Family days are held the third Saturday of every month, with a tour of the gallery and free hands-on workshops for children. For additional workshops and events, check the website

Behind the complex, look for the gate that leads into the beautiful **Butler House Gardens** (The Parade; ⊙10am-5pm Mon-Fri, to noon Sat & Sun) FREE, with an unusual water feature constructed from remnants of the British-built Nelson Pillar which once stood in Dublin's O'Connell St but was blown up by the IRA in 1966.

 Kilkenny Arts & Crafts

At least 130 full-time craftspeople and artists work commercially in County Kilkenny – one of the highest concentrations in Ireland – thanks to its fine raw materials and inspirational scenery.

Among the best places to see their work:

Kilkenny Design Centre Has works by more than a dozen local craftspeople.

National Craft Gallery (p247) Features furniture, jewellery and textiles from all over Ireland.

Rudolf Heltzel Goldsmith (📞056-772 1497; http://rudolfheltzel.com; 10 Patrick St; ◷9.30am-1pm & 2-5.30pm Mon-Sat) Fine-art jewellery.

Jerpoint Glass Studio (www.jerpointglass.com; Glenmore, Stoneyford; ◷10am-6pm Mon-Sat, noon-5pm Sun Mar-Oct, shorter hours Nov-Feb) **FREE** Watch skilled glass-blowers at work.

Moth to a Flame (📞056-772 7826; www.mothtoaflame.ie; Kilkenny Rd, Bennettsbridge; ◷9am-6pm Mon-Sat) Handmade art candles.

Clay Creations (📞087 257 0735; www.bridlyonsceramics.com; Low St, Thomastown; ◷10am-5.30pm Wed-Sat, by appointment Mon & Tue) Gallery of original and unusual ceramic pieces.

Pick up a copy of the **Made in Kilkenny craft trail** (www.madeinkilkenny.ie) for a comprehensive list of studios and shops.

National Craft Gallery (p247)
IVICA DRUSANY/SHUTTERSTOCK ©

 TOURS

Pat Tynan Walking Tours Walking
(📞087 265 1745; www.kilkennywalkingtours.ie; €7; ◷11am & 2pm daily mid-Mar–Oct) Entertaining, informative 70-minute walking tours through Kilkenny's narrow lanes, steps and pedestrian passageways. Meet at the tourist office (p250).

Kilkenny Cycling Tours Cycling
(📞086 895 4961; www.kilkennycyclingtours.com; adult/child from €25/16; 🚲) Explore the city and surrounds on a bike over a 2½-hour tour that can include a lunch option; prebooking is essential, at least 48 hours in advance. Bikes are delivered to your accommodation.

 SHOPPING

Kilkenny Design Centre Arts & Crafts
(📞056-772 2118; www.kilkennydesign.com; Castle Yard; ◷10am-7pm) Sells top-end Irish crafts and artworks, from county-wide artisans. Look for John Hanly wool blankets, Cushendale woollen goods, Foxford scarves and Bunbury cutting boards.

Kilkenny Book Centre Books
(📞056-776 2117; http://thebookcentre.ie; 10 High St; ◷10am-5pm Mon-Sat) The largest bookshop in town, stocking plenty of Irish-interest fiction and nonfiction, periodicals and a good range of maps. There's a cafe upstairs.

 EATING

Mocha's Vintage Tearooms Cafe €
(www.facebook.com/thevintagetearoomsbymocha; 4 The Arches, Gashouse Lane; mains €7-14; ◷8.30am-5.30pm Mon-Sat) Cute retro tearoom with picture-cluttered walls and rose-patterned china. As well as tea and cakes, there's a breakfast menu (until 11.30am) with a choice of bagels or a full Irish fry-up, and hot lunch specials including fish and chips.

Zuni   Irish €€

(☑056-772 3999; http://zuni.ie; 26 Patrick St;
mains lunch €8-14, dinner €20-27; ☺12.30-
2.30pm daily, 6-9.30pm Mon-Sat, 6-9pm Sun;
🛜) 🍴 Among Kilkenny's most stylish and
busiest restaurants, Zuni manages to hold
its place on the cutting edge it pioneered
when it opened just before the turn of the
millennium. It's sophisticated yet informal,
with a menu that lends a gourmet touch to
hearty, lip-smacking comfort food such as
strip steak with onions and roast mushroom gravy on focaccia. Yum.

Foodworks   Bistro, Cafe €€

(☑056 777 7696; www.foodworks.ie; 7 Parliament
St; lunch mains €14, 3-course dinner €30; ☺noon-
4.30pm Sun-Wed, noon-9.30pm Thu-Sat; 🛜🚼)
🍴 The owners of this cool and casual bistro
keep their own pigs and grow their own salad leaves, so it would be churlish not to try
their pork belly stuffed with black pudding,
or confit pig's trotter – and you'll be glad
you did. Delicious food, excellent coffee
and friendly service make this a justifiably
popular venue, it's best to book a table.

Kilkenny Design
Centre Foodhall &
Restaurant   Cafeteria €€

(www.kilkennydesign.com; Castle Yard; mains
€7-15; ☺10am-6pm; 🛜🚼) Upstairs from the
craft shops, this arty, organic-oriented,
self-service cafeteria offers home-baked
breads and scones, tasty seafood chowder,
a vast variety of salads, gourmet sandwiches, hot specials and sumptuous desserts.

Campagne   Modern Irish €€€

(☑056-777 2858; www.campagne.ie; 5 Gashouse
Lane; mains €30-33; ☺12.30-2.30pm Fri-Sun,
6-10pm Tue-Thu, 5.30-10pm Fri & Sat) 🍴 Chef
Garrett Byrne was awarded a Michelin star
for this bold, stylish restaurant in his native
Kilkenny. He's passionate about supporting
local and artisan producers, and serves
ever-changing, ever-memorable meals,
adding a French accent to every culinary
creation. The three-course lunch and early

🖼 Kilkenny's City Walls

Parts of Kilkenny's medieval city walls,
mostly dating from the 14th and 15th
centuries, can still be seen in several
places, notably at **Talbot's Tower** (cnr
Ormonde Rd & New St), **Maudlin Tower**
(Maudlin St) and the **Black Freren Gate**
(Abbey St) – the only surviving city gate.
Maudlin Castle (Maudlin St) is a more
substantial tower house that was built
around 1500, and once protected the
eastern approach to the city.

Black Freren Gate
DOUGLAS PFEIFFER/SHUTTERSTOCK ©

bird menu (till 7pm Tuesday to Thursday, till
6pm Friday and Saturday) is €34.

🅾 DRINKING & NIGHTLIFE

John St is a nightlife hub along with Parliament St where there is another clutch of
no-nonsense trad pubs.

Kyteler's Inn   Pub

(☑056-772 1064; www.kytelersinn.com; 27 St
Kieran's St; ☺11am-midnight Sun-Thu, to 2am
Fri & Sat) Dame Alice Kyteler's old house
was built back in 1224 and has seen its
share of history: she was charged with
witchcraft in 1323. Today the rambling bar
includes the original building, complete
with vaulted ceiling and arches. There is
a beer garden, a courtyard and a large
upstairs room for the live bands (nightly
March to October), ranging from trad to
blues.

LITTLENYSTOCK/SHUTTERSTOCK ©

Kyteler's Inn (p249)

John Cleere's   Pub

(☏056-776 2573; www.cleeres.com; 22 Parliament St; ☺11.30am-11.30pm Mon-Thu, to 12.30am Fri & Sat, 1-11pm Sun) One of Kilkenny's finest venues for live music, theatre and comedy, this long bar has blues, jazz and rock, as well as trad music sessions on Monday and Wednesday. Food is served throughout the day, including soup, sandwiches, pizza and Irish stew.

O'Hara's Brewery Corner   Pub

(☏056-780 5081; www.carlowbrewing.com/our-pub; 29 Parliament St; ☺1-11.30pm Mon-Thu, to 12.30am Fri & Sat, to 11pm Sun) Kilkenny's best venue for craft brews is a long, narrow beer hall of a place owned by Carlow Brewing Company. Service can be a bit hit or miss, especially at quiet times, but there's a wide selection of ale to choose from, including Carlow's own IPA.

Bridie's General Store   Pub

(☏056-776 5133; John St; ☺11am-10pm Sun-Wed, 6pm-2am Thu-Sat) Top design talent was employed by the Langton's empire to create this reproduction trad grocery-cum-pub; the results are worth it. The front is a beguiling retail potpourri of souvenirs, jokes, toys, preserves and deli items. Step through the swinging doors to arrive at a new/old pub with beautiful tiles, while outback is a fittingly classy beer garden.

✪ ENTERTAINMENT

Watergate Theatre   Theatre

(☏box office 056-776 1674; www.watergatetheatre.com; Parliament St) Kilkenny's top theatre venue hosts drama, comedy and musical performances. If you're wondering why intermission lasts 18 minutes, it's so patrons can nip into John Cleere's pub for a pint.

ℹ INFORMATION

Kilkenny Tourist Office (☏056-775 1500; www.visitkilkenny.ie; Rose Inn St; ☺9am-6pm Mon-Sat, 10.30am-4pm Sun) Stocks guides and walking maps. Located in Shee Alms House, dating from 1582 and built in local stone by benefactor Sir Richard Shee to help the poor.

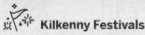

Kilkenny Festivals

Kilkenny hosts several world-class events throughout the year, attracting thousands of revellers.

Cat Laughs Comedy Festival (📞056-776 3837; www.thecatlaughs.com; ⊙May-Jun) An acclaimed gathering of world-class comedians, including Irish stars such as Dara O'Briain and Aisling Bea, in Kilkenny's hotels and pubs over a long weekend in late May/early June.

Kilkenny Arts Festival (📞056-776 3663; www.kilkennyarts.ie; ⊙Aug; 🖼) In August the city comes alive with theatre, cinema, music, literature, visual arts, children's events and street spectacles for 10 action-packed days.

Kilkenny Rhythm & Roots (📞056-776 3669; www.kilkennyroots.com; ⊙Apr-May) More than 30 pubs and other venues participate in hosting this major music festival in late April/early May, with an emphasis on country and 'old-time' American roots music.

🚹 GETTING THERE & AWAY

BUS

Bus Éireann (p302) and **DublinCoach** (http://www.dublincoach.ie/) services stop at the train station and on Ormonde Rd (nearer the town centre); **JJ Kavanagh** (www.jjkavanagh.ie) buses to Dublin airport stop on Ormonde Rd only.

Carlow (€10.40, 35 minutes, four daily) Bus Éireann

Cork (€15, 2½ hours, every two hours) Dublin-Coach M9 Express

Dublin (€14.50, 2¼ hours, two daily) Bus Éireann X4

Dublin airport (€20, two to three hours, seven daily) JJ Kavanagh

Waterford (€5, 40 minutes, every two hours) DublinCoach M9 Express

TRAIN

Kilkenny's **MacDonagh train station** (Dublin Rd) is a 10-minute walk northeast of the town centre, with trains to Dublin Heuston (€25.85, 1½ hours, six daily) and Waterford (€13.85, 40 minutes, seven daily).

COUNTY
TIPPERARY

County Tipperary at a Glance...

Landlocked Tipperary boasts the sort of fertile soil that farmers dream of. The central area of the county is low-lying, but rolling hills spill over from adjoining counties and an upper-crust gloss still clings to traditions here, with fox hunts in full legal cry during the winter season.

Walking and cycling opportunities abound, especially in the Glen of Aherlow near Tipperary town. But the real crowd pleasers are the iconic Rock of Cashel and Cahir Castle. In between, you'll find bucolic charm along pretty much any country road you choose.

County Tipperary in One Day

You'll need two hours to properly explore the **Rock of Cashel** (p256), so devote the morning to that followed by a slap-up lunch at **Cafe Hans** (p261). In the afternoon visit the **Brú Ború** (p260) and **Cashel Folk Village** (p260) museums in town, then take a walk out to the atmospheric ruins of **Hore Abbey** (p260).

County Tipperary in Two Days

On day two head to **Cahir** (p261) for a visit to impressive **Cahir Castle** (p262), followed by a pleasant walk along the wooded banks of the River Suir to the delightful and unexpected **Swiss Cottage** (p262). If you're continuing west to County Clare, then make the most of the afternoon with a scenic drive through the lovely **Glen of Aherlow** (p262)..

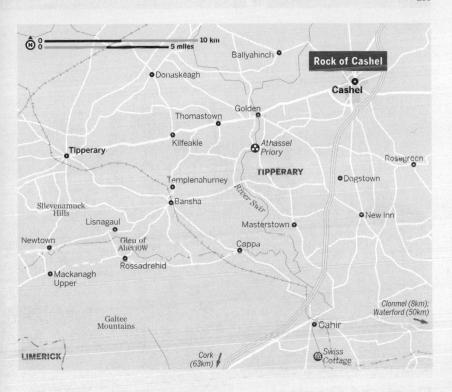

Arriving in County Tipperary

The M8 motorway links Dublin to Cashel, Cahir and Mitchelstown. There are good bus links from Dublin and Cork to Clonmel and the main towns, while rail is really only useful for travelling from Waterford to Clonmel, Cahir and Tipperary town. Bus Éireann runs eight buses daily between Cashel and Cork

Sleeping

The best choice of accommodation is to be found in Tipperary's larger towns such as Clonmel, Cashel and Cahir, but there are some good country inns and lots of rural B&Bs scattered across the county. The best campsites are around Clonmel, and in the Glen of Aherlow to the west.

DAVID MAURER/500PX ©

Rock of Cashel

For more than 1000 years the Rock of Cashel was a symbol of power and the seat of kings and priests. Exploring this monumental complex offers a fascinating insight into Ireland's past.

The Rock of Cashel is one of Ireland's most spectacular historic sites: a prominent green hill, banded with limestone outcrops, rising from a grassy plain and bristling with ancient fortifications. Sturdy walls circle an enclosure containing a complete round tower, a 13th-century Gothic cathedral and the finest 12th-century Romanesque chapel in Ireland, home to some of the land's oldest frescoes.

It's a five-minute stroll from the town centre up to the Rock, from where fantastic views range over the Tipperary countryside.

History

The word 'cashel' is an Anglicised version of the Irish word *caiseal,* meaning 'fortress' (related to the English 'castle', from the Latin castellum). In the 4th century the Rock of Cashel was chosen as a base by

Great For...

☑ **Don't Miss**

The carving of a centaur firing an arrow at a rampaging lion, on Cormac's Chapel.

Rock of Cashel ◎
○ Cashel

❶ Need to Know

www.heritageireland.ie; adult/child €8/4,
◷9am–7pm early Jun–mid-Sep, to 5.30pm
mid-Mar–early Jun & mid-Sep–mid-Oct, to
4.30pm mid-Oct–mid-Mar

✕ Take a Break

Head for Cafe Hans (p261) in the village
immediately below the rock.

★ Top Tip

Download a free audio-guided tour of
the town from the tourist office website (www.cashel.ie/audio-tour).

the Eóghanachta clan from Wales, who
went on to conquer much of Munster and
become kings of the region. For some 400
years it rivalled Tara as a centre of power
in Ireland. The clan was associated with St
Patrick, hence the Rock's alternative name
of St Patrick's Rock. In the 10th century the
Eóghanachta lost possession of the rock to
the O'Brien (Dál gCais) tribe under Brian
Ború's leadership. In 1101 King Muircheart-
ach O'Brien presented the Rock to the
Church to curry favour with the powerful
bishops and to end secular rivalry over possession of the Rock with the Eóghanachta,
by now known as the MacCarthys.

Buildings

Numerous buildings must have occupied the cold and exposed Rock over the
years, but it is the ecclesiastical relics that
have survived even the depredations of
the Cromwellian army in 1647. The vast
medieval **cathedral** was used for worship
until the mid 1700s. Among the graves are
a 19th-century high cross and mausoleum
for local landowners, the Scully family;
the top of the Scully Cross was razed by
lightning in 1976.

But the undoubted highlight of the
Rock is the early 12th-century **Cormac's
Chapel**, an exquisite gem of Romanesque
architecture with beautifully carved door-
ways and the precious remains of colourful
wall paintings. Call ahead for details of the
45-minute guided tours (included in the
admission fee).

Rock of Cashel

A TOUR OF THE COMPLEX

For more than 1000 years the Rock of Cashel was a symbol of power and the seat of kings and clergy men who ruled over the region. Exploring this monumental complex offers a fascinating insight into Ireland's past.

Enter via the 15th-century **① Hall of the Vicars Choral**, built to house the male choristers who sang in the cathedral. Exhibits in its undercroft include rare silverware, stone reliefs and the original St Patrick's Cross. In the courtyard you'll see the replica of **② St Patrick's Cross**. A small porch leads into the 13th-century Gothic **③ cathedral**. To the west of the nave are the remains of the **④ Archbishop's Residence**. From the cathedral's north transept on the northeastern corner is the Rock's earliest building, an 11th- or 12th-century **⑤ Round Tower**. Nestled in the southeast corner of the cathedral is the compelling **⑥ Cormac's Chapel**, Ireland's earliest surviving Romanesque church. It dates from 1127 and the medieval integrity of its trans-European architecture survives. Inside the main door on the left is the sarcophagus said to house King Cormac, dating from between 1125 and 1150. Before leaving, take time for a close-up look at the Rock's **⑦ enclosing walls and corner tower**.

Hall of the Vicars Choral
Head upstairs from the ticket office to see the choristers' restored kitchen and dining hall, complete with period furniture, tapestries and paintings beneath a fine carved-oak roof and gallery.

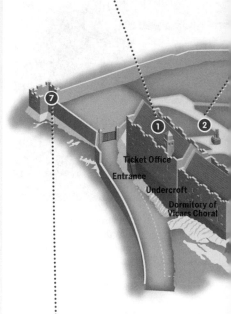

Ticket Office

Entrance

Undercroft

Dormitory of Vicars Choral

TOP TIPS

➡ Good photographic vantage points for framing the mighty Rock are on the road into Cashel from the Dublin Rd roundabout or from the little roads just west of the centre.

➡ The best photo opportunities, however, are from inside the atmospheric ruins of Hore Abbey, 1km to the west.

Enclosing Walls & Corner Tower
Constructed from lime mortar around the 15th century, and originally incorporating five gates, stone walls enclose the entire site. It's thought the surviving corner tower was used as a watchtower.

St Patrick's Cross

In the castle courtyard, this cross replicates the eroded Hall of the Vicars Choral original – an impressive 12th-century crutched cross depicting a crucifixion scene on one face and animals on the other.

Archbishop's Residence

The west side of the cathedral is taken up by the Archbishop's Residence, a 15th-century, four-storey castle, which had its great hall built over the nave, reducing its length. It was last inhabited in the mid-1700s.

Cathedral

A huge square tower with a turret on the southwestern corner soars above the cathedral. Scattered throughout are monuments, a 16th-century altar tomb, coats of arms panels, and stone heads on capitals and corbels

Turret

④

③

⑤

⑥

Choir

Scully Cross

Cormac's Chapel

Look closely at the exquisite doorway arches, the grand chancel arch and ribbed barrel vault, and carved vignettes, including a trefoil-tailed grotesque and a Norman-helmeted centaur firing an arrow at a rampaging lion.

Round Tower

Standing 28m tall, the doorway to this ancient edifice is 3.5m above the ground – perhaps for structural rather than defensive reasons. Its exact age is unknown but may be as early as 1101.

 Athassel Priory

Reached over a stile and across grassy (sometimes muddy) fields, the atmospheric ruins of **Athassel Priory** (Golden; ☉dawn-dusk) sit in the shallow and verdant River Suir Valley, 7km southwest of Cashel. The original buildings date from 1205, and Athassel was once one of the richest and most important monasteries in Ireland. What survives is substantial: the gatehouse and portcullis gateway, the cloister (ruined but recognisable) and large stretches of walled enclosure, as well as some medieval tomb effigies.

To get here, take the N74 to the village of Golden, then head 2km south along the narrow L4304 road signed 'Athassel Abbey'. Roadside parking is limited.

JOE CORNISH/GETTY IMAGES ©

Cashel

It's little wonder that Cashel (Caiseal Mumhan) is such a fabulous draw (the Queen included it on her historic visit in 2011). The iconic religious buildings that crown the blustery summit of the Rock of Cashel (p256) seem to emerge from the rocky landscape itself and the neighbouring market town of Cashel rewards rambles around its charming streets.

◉ SIGHTS

Hore Abbey Ruins
(☉dawn-dusk) **FREE** The formidable ruin of 13th-century Hore Abbey (also known as Hoare Abbey or St Mary's) stands in flat farmland 1km west of the Rock of Cashel. Originally Benedictine and settled by monks from Glastonbury in England at the end of the 12th century, it later became a Cistercian house. Now an enjoyably gloomy wreck, the abbey was gifted to the order by a 13th-century archbishop who expelled the Benedictine monks after dreaming that they planned to murder him.

Brú Ború Museum
(☏062-61122; www.bruboru.ie; The Kiln; adult/child €5/3; ☉9am-5pm Mon-Fri) This privately run cultural centre is next to the car park below the Rock of Cashel, and offers absorbing insights into Irish traditional music, dance and song. The centre's main attraction, the **Sounds of History** exhibition, relates the story of Ireland and its music through imaginative audio displays; various other musical events take place in summer.

Cashel Folk Village Museum
(☏062-63601; www.cashelfolkvillage.ie; St Dominic St; adult/child €5/3.50; ☉9am-7.30pm mid-Jun–mid-Sep, 9.30am-5.30pm mid-Mar–mid-Jun & mid-Sep–mid-Oct, 9.30am-4.30pm mid-Oct–mid-Mar) An engaging exhibition of old buildings, shopfronts and memorabilia from around the town. It's all a bit slipshod, but in a heart-warming way.

Cashel Heritage Centre Museum
(☏062-61333; www.cashel.ie; Main St; ☉9.30am-5.30pm daily Mar-Oct, Mon-Fri Nov-Feb) **FREE** Located in the town hall alongside the tourist office, the displays here include a scale model of Cashel in the 1640s with an audio commentary.

EATING

Apart from the Rock, Cashel is best known in Ireland and beyond for award-winning Cashel Blue farmhouse cheese, Ireland's first-ever blue cheese. Although it's still handmade locally (and only locally), it's surprisingly hard to find in shops and on restaurant menus in town.

Swiss Cottage (p262)

Cafe Hans
Cafe €€

(☑062-63660; Dominic St; mains €13-23; ☺noon-5.30pm Tue-Sat; 🐾) Competition for the 32 seats is fierce at this gourmet cafe run by the same family as Chez Hans next door. There's a fantastic selection of salads, open sandwiches (including succulent prawns with tangy Marie Rose sauce) and filling fish, shellfish, lamb and vegetarian dishes, accompanied by a discerning wine selection and mouth-watering desserts. No credit cards. Enter via Moor Lane.

Arrive before or after the lunchtime rush or plan on queuing.

Chez Hans
Irish €€€

(☑062-61177; www.chezhans.net; Dominic St; 2-/3-course lunch €16/20, 2-/3-course dinner €28/33; ☺6-10pm Tue-Sat) Since 1968 this former church has been a place of worship for foodies from all over Ireland and beyond. Still as fresh and inventive as ever, the restaurant has a regularly changing menu and gives its blessing to all manner of Irish foods, including steamed Galway mussels, goat's cheese tart and pan-fried peppered skate wing. No credit cards.

ℹ️ INFORMATION

Tourist Office (☑062-61333; www.cashel.ie; Town Hall, Main St; ☺9.30am-5.30pm daily Mar-Oct, Mon-Fri Nov-Feb) Helpful office with reams of info on the area.

🚍 GETTING THERE & AWAY

Bus Éireann (www.buseireann.ie) runs eight buses daily between Cashel and Cork (€16, 1¾ hours) via Cahir (€6, 20 minutes, six daily). The bus stop for Cork is outside the Bake House on Main St. The Dublin stop (€16, 2½ hours, six daily) is opposite.

Ring a Link (☑1890 424 141; www.ringalink. ie), a not-for-profit service for rural residents that's also available to tourists, operates a minibus between Tipperary town and Cashel (€3.50, 50 minutes); it must be booked in advance by phone.

Parking in town is cheaper and less crowded than the car park below the Rock.

Cahir

At the eastern tip of the Galtee Mountains, 15km south of Cashel, Cahir (An Cathair;

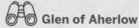 **Glen of Aherlow**

The broad, fertile valley of the Glen of Aherlow, slung between the wooded Slievenamuck Hills and the shapely Galtee Mountains, is the most scenic part of County Tipperary and one of Ireland's hidden delights.

A beautiful and leisurely 25km **scenic drive** through the Glen is signposted from Tipperary town. At the eastern end of the Glen, between Tipperary and Cahir, the village of Bansha (An Bháinseach) marks the start of a 20km trip west to Galbally, an easy bike ride or scenic drive along the R663 that takes in the best of the glen's landscapes.

The R663 from Bansha and the R664 south from Tipperary converge at Newtown at the **Coach Road Inn**, a fine old pub that's popular with walkers. Hidden around the back of the pub, the enthusiastically staffed Glen of Aherlow **tourist office** (☑062-56331; http://aherlow. com; Newtown; ☺9am-5pm Mon-Fri, 10am-4pm Sat Jun-Aug) is an excellent source of information on the area, including walking festivals.

S. MUELLER/SHUTTERSTOCK ©

pronounced 'care') is a compact and attractive town that encircles a sublime castle. Walking paths follow the verdant banks of the River Suir, one of Ireland's finest trout-fishing streams.

◎ SIGHTS

Cahir Castle Historic Site

(☑052-744 1011; www.heritageireland.ie; Castle St; adult/child €5/3; ☺9am-6.30pm mid-Jun–Aug, 9.30am-5.30pm Mar–mid-Jun & Sep–mid-Oct, 9.30am-4.30pm mid-Oct–Feb) Cahir's awesome castle enjoys a river-island site with moat, massive walls, turrets and keep, mullioned windows, vast fireplaces and dungeons. Founded by Conor O'Brien in 1142, and passed to the Butler family in 1375, it's one of Ireland's largest castles. In 1599 the Earl of Essex shattered its walls with cannon fire, an event explained with a large model. With a huge set of antlers pinned to its white walls, the **Banquet Hall** is an impressive sight; you can also climb the **Keep**.

The castle eventually surrendered to Cromwell in 1650 without a struggle; its future usefulness may have discouraged the usual Cromwellian 'deconstruction' – it is largely intact and still formidable. It was restored in the 1840s and again in the 1960s when it came under state ownership.

A 15-minute audiovisual presentation puts Cahir in context with other Irish castles. The buildings within the castle walls are sparsely furnished, although there are good displays, including an exhibition on 'Women in Medieval Ireland'. There are frequent guided tours.

Swiss Cottage Historic Building

(☑052-744 1144; www.heritageireland.ie; Cahir Park; adult/child €5/3; ☺10am-6pm Easter-Oct) A 30-minute walk along a riverside path from Cahir Castle car park leads to this thatched cottage, surrounded by roses, lavender and honeysuckle. A lavish example of Regency Picturesque, the cottage was built in 1810 as a retreat for Richard Butler, 12th Baron Caher, and his wife, and was designed by London architect John Nash, creator of the Royal Pavilion at Brighton. The 30-minute (compulsory) guided tours are thoroughly enjoyable.

The *cottage-orné* style emerged during the late 18th and early 19th centuries in England in response to the prevailing taste for the picturesque. Thatched roofs, natural wood and carved weatherboarding were characteristics and most examples were built as ornamental features on estates. The cottage was restored in the 1980s under the direction of Irish designer Sybil Connolly.

🔒 SHOPPING

Craft Granary   Arts & Crafts
(☎052-744 1473; www.craftgranary.ie; Church St; ⏰10am-6pm Mon-Fri, 9am-5pm Sat) Hundreds of locals toiled away in a notorious linen mill during the 19th century. Almost 200 years later, the once ominous stone building has been reborn as this crafts centre, with local artists creating and selling works including pottery, carvings, paintings and jewellery. It's just north of the square, past the post office.

🍴 EATING

Don't miss the **farmers market** (www.facebook.com/pg/cahirfarmersmarket; Castle car park; ⏰9am-1pm Sat) 🥬 where you can browse some of the county's finest produce.

Galileo   Italian €€
(www.galileocafe.com; Church St; mains €11 24; ⏰noon-10pm Mon-Sat, 1-9pm Sun) Serving fine pizza and pasta to Cahir locals for over a decade, Galileo is a neat and smooth Italian restaurant, with a modern interior and efficient, friendly service. The restaurant has no licence, so BYO.

ℹ️ INFORMATION

Tourist Office (☎052-744 1453; Cahir Castle car park; ⏰9.30am 1pm & 1.45-5.30pm Tue-Sat Apr-Oct) Has information about the town and region.

ℹ️ GETTING THERE & AWAY

BUS

Cahir is a hub for several **Bus Éireann** (www.buseireann.ie) routes, including Dublin–Cork, Limerick–Waterford, Galway–Waterford, Kilkenny–Cork and Cork–Athlone.

There are six buses per day to Cashel (€6, 20 minutes).

Buses stop in the car park beside the castle.

TRAIN

From Monday to Saturday, the train from Waterford to Limerick Junction stops in Clonmel and Cahir (€10.25, one hour, twice daily).

Samuel Beckett Bridge, Dublin

In Focus

Dáil Éireann, Dublin

Ireland Today

*In and out of a deep recession, the Republic of Ireland
continues to embrace the changes of progressive
liberalism: in 2015 it passed marriage-equality legislation granting equal marital status to same-sex couples.
Northern Ireland remains resistant to this kind of change
for now – but it continues along the path of peace with
greater confidence than ever before. Meanwhile, a Brex-
it-shaped shadow lurks in the distance...*

Progressive Conservatism

Although the 2016 elections returned the Fine Gael party to government, their unconvincing show in the campaign and the resulting hung parliament that left them relying on a motley crew of independents to govern eventually led to the resignation of Enda Kenny as Taoiseach (Republic of Ireland prime minister) and party leader in May 2017.

His replacement is Leo Varadkar, who happens to be gay and half-Indian. While much has been written about Ireland's remarkable journey over the last three decades, that has resulted in the ascent to the highest office of the homosexual son of an immigrant, it is perhaps even more remarkable that he did so as a member of Fine Gael, whose conservative values are woven into the party's DNA.

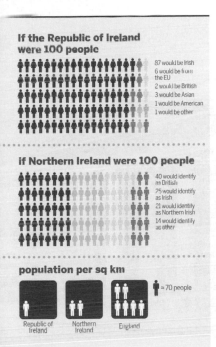

If the Republic of Ireland were 100 people

87 would be Irish
6 would be from the EU
2 would be British
3 would be Asian
1 would be American
1 would be other

if Northern Ireland were 100 people

40 would identify as British
25 would identify as Irish
21 would identify as Northern Irish
14 would identify as other

population per sq km

≈ 70 people

Republic of Ireland
Northern Ireland
England

Varadkar is something of a conundrum. He is charismatic, straight-talking and very much a child of progressive, contemporary Ireland: at 38 he was the youngest person ever to become Taoiseach. But many progressives are troubled by the conservative tone of his politics, and while the new Taoiseach insists that some of his views have evolved (read: softened) over the years, his rise reveals a fascinating dichotomy: he is the product of a social liberalism that he doesn't fully espouse. Or, put another way, his success is down to a mix of political nous and pragmatic conservatism, qualities that make his sexual orientation and ethnic background completely irrelevant.

Repealing the 8th

With same-sex marriage already on the statute books of the Republic, the next big social issue it will have to look at is reform of the country's strict anti-abortion laws, outlined in the 8th amendment to the constitution.

In April 2017 a Citizens' Assembly – a body convened by the government to explore constitutional issues – voted overwhelmingly to extend access to abortion with 'no restriction as to reasons' by a majority of 64%. While a majority of the electorate supports reform of the existing law, polls show that two-thirds would reject legislation allowing abortion on request.

The specific wording of a new law is the main challenge for the government, which has indicated that a referendum is likely at some point in 2018. In the meantime, both sides of the argument have dug in for what promises to be a bitter fight. The pro-choice campaign, which is supported by an overwhelming majority of younger voters, has been especially vocal: you might see people sporting a 'repeal' T-shirt or sweatshirt on your travels.

Brexit & Beyond

What will Brexit bring? At the time of writing, this was the pressing political and economic question. Ireland has close socioeconomic ties with the UK, so most economists believe that 'the harder the Brexit, the worse the outcome', with bilateral trade hit by as much as 20%.

But the biggest impact will be felt by Northern Ireland, which in a post-Brexit landscape will be divided from the Republic by the only land border between the UK and the EU. The majority of its citizens (56% to 44%) voted Remain, but the governing Democratic Unionist Party (DUP) favoured Leave, if only, they argued, to copper-fasten the province's ties to a UK that was out of the EU.

General Post Office (p273)

History

Ireland's history is a search for identity, a search complicated by a long list of invaders, especially the English. Indeed, Ireland's fractious relationship with its nearest neighbour has occupied much of the last 1000 years, and it is through the prism of that relationship that a huge part of the Irish identity is reflected.

10,000–8000 BC

After the last ice age ends, the first humans arrive in Ireland.

550–800

The flowering of early monasticism ushers in Ireland's 'Golden Age' of saints and scholars.

700–300 BC

The Celtic culture and language arrive, ushering in 1000 years of cultural and political dominance.

Rowan Gillespie's *Famine* memorial

Who Are the Irish?

Hunters and gatherers may first have traversed the narrowing land bridge that once linked Ireland with Britain, but many more crossed the Irish Sea in small hide-covered boats

In the 8th century BC, Ireland came to the attention of the fearsome Celts, who, having fought their way across Central Europe, established permanent settlements on the island in the 3rd century BC.

Getting into the Habit

Arguably the most significant import into Ireland came between the 3rd and 5th centuries AD, when Christian missionaries first brought the new religion of Rome. Everyone has heard of St Patrick, but he was merely the most famous of many who converted the local pagan tribes by cleverly fusing traditional pagan rituals with the new Christian teaching, creating an exciting hybrid known as Celtic (Insular) Christianity. The artistic

AD 432–800	795–841	1171
Arrival of St Patrick is followed by the flowering of early Christian monasticism in Ireland.	Vikings plunder Irish monasteries then establish settlements throughout the country.	King Henry II invades Ireland, forcing the Cambro-Norman warlords to accept him as their overlord.

Clonmacnoise (p116)

CORENTIN/SHUTTERSTOCK ©

★ **Monastic Sites**

Rock of Cashel (p256)

Clonmacnoise (p116)

Glendalough (p106)

Skellig Michael (p202)

Monasterboice (p91)

and intellectual credentials of Ireland's Christians were the envy of Europe and led to the moniker 'the land of saints and scholars'.

More Invaders

The Celts' lack of political unity made the island easy pickings for the next wave of invaders, Danish Vikings. Over the course of the 9th and 10th centuries, they established settlements along the east coast, intermarried with the Celtic tribes and introduced red hair and freckles to the Irish gene pool.

The '800 years' of English rule in Ireland began in 1171, when the English king Henry II sent a huge invasion force, at the urging of the pope, to bring the increasingly independent Christian missionaries to heel. It was also intended to curb the growing power of the Anglo-Norman lords, who had arrived in Ireland two years before Henry's army, and who had settled quite nicely into Irish life, becoming – as the old saying went – Hiberniores Hibernis ipsis (more Irish than the Irish themselves). By the 16th century, they had divided the country into their own fiefdoms and the English Crown's direct control didn't extend any further than a cordon surrounding Dublin, known as 'the Pale'.

Divorce, Dissolution & Destruction

Henry VIII's failure to get the pope's blessing for his divorce augured badly for the Irish, who sided with the Vatican. Henry retaliated by ordering the dissolution of all monasteries in Britain and Ireland, and had himself declared King of Ireland. His daughter Elizabeth I went even further, establishing jurisdiction in Connaught and Munster before crushing the last of the rebels, the lords of Ulster, led by the crafty and courageous Hugh O'Neill, Earl of Tyrone.

With the native chiefs gone, Elizabeth and her successor, James I, could pursue their policy of Plantation with impunity. Though confiscations took place all over the country, Ulster was most affected both because of its wealthy farmlands and as punishment for being home to the primary fomenters of rebellion.

1350–1530

Anglo-Norman barons establish power bases, English control recedes to an area around Dublin known as 'the Pale'.

1536–41

Henry VIII declares war on the Irish Church and declares himself King of Ireland.

1601

Following the Battle of Kinsale, Irish rebellion against the English Crown is broken.

Bloody Religion

At the outset of the English Civil War In 1642, the Irish threw their support behind Charles I against the very Protestant parliamentarians in the hope that victory for the king would lead to the restoration of Catholic power in Ireland. When Oliver Cromwell and his Roundheads defeated the Royalists and took Charles' head off in 1649, Cromwell turned his attention to the disloyal Irish. His nine-month campaign was effective and brutal (Drogheda was particularly mistreated); yet more lands were confiscated – Cromwell's famous utterance that the Irish could 'go to hell or to Connaught' seems odd given the province's beauty, but there wasn't much arable land out there – and Catholic rights restricted even more.

St Patrick

Ireland's patron saint, St Patrick (AD 389–461), remembered all around the world on 17 March, wasn't even Irish. This symbol of Irish pride hailed from what is now Wales, which at the time of his birth was under Roman occupation. Kidnapped by Irish raiders when he was 16 and made a slave, he found religion, escaped from captivity and returned to Britain. He returned to Ireland vowing to make Christians out of the Irish, and within 30 years of his return his dream had come true.

So next St Paddy's Day, as you're swilling Guinness, think of who the man really was.

The Boyne & Penal Laws

Catholic Ireland's next major setback came in 1690. Yet again the Irish had backed the wrong horse, this time supporting James II after his deposition in the Glorious Revolution by the Dutch Protestant King William of Orange (who was married to James' daughter Mary!). After James had unsuccessfully laid siege to Derry for 105 days (the Loyalist cry of 'No surrender!', in use to this day, dates from the siege), in July he fought William's armies by the banks of the Boyne in County Louth and was roundly defeated.

The final ignominy for Catholics came in 1695 with the passing of the Penal Laws, which prohibited them from owning land or entering any higher profession. Irish culture, music and education were banned in the hope that Catholicism would be eradicated. Most Catholics continued to worship at secret locations, but some prosperous Irish converted to Protestantism to preserve their careers and wealth. Land was steadily transferred to Protestant owners, and a significant majority of the Catholic population became tenants living in wretched conditions. By the late 18th century, Catholics owned barely 5% of the land.

If at First You Don't Succeed...

With Roman Catholics rendered utterly powerless, the seeds of rebellion against autocracy were planted by a handful of liberal Protestants, inspired by the ideologies of the Enlighten-

1649–53

Cromwell lays waste to Ireland after the Irish support Charles I in the English Civil War.

1690

Catholic King James II defeated by William of Orange in the Battle of the Boyne on 12 July.

1798

The flogging and killing of potential rebels sparks an uprising of the United Irishmen led by Wolfe Tone.

ment and the unrest provoked by the American War of Independence and then the French Revolution.

The first of these came in 1798, when the United Irishmen, led by a young Dublin Protestant, Theobald Wolfe Tone (1763–98), took on the British at the Battle of Vinegar Hill in County Wexford. Their defeat was hastened due to the failure of the French to land an army of succour in 1796 in Bantry Bay.

The Liberator

The Act of Union, passed in 1801, was the British government's vain attempt to put an end to any aspirations towards Irish independence, but the nationalist genie was out of the bottle, not least in the body of a Kerry-born Catholic named Daniel O'Connell (1775–1847).

In 1823 O'Connell founded the Catholic Association with the aim of achieving political equality for Catholics, which he did (in part) by forcing the passing of the 1829 Act of Catholic Emancipation, allowing some well-off Catholics voting rights and the right to be elected as MPs.

O'Connell's campaign now switched to the repeal of the Act of Union, but the 'Liberator' came to a sorry end in 1841 when he meekly stood down in face of a government order banning one of his rallies. His capitulation was deemed unforgivable given that Ireland was in the midst of the Potato Famine.

The Uncrowned King of Ireland

Charles Stewart Parnell (1846–91) was the other great 19th-century statesperson. Like O'Connell, he too was a powerful orator, but the primary focus of his artful attentions was land reform, particularly the reduction of rents and the improvement of working conditions (conveniently referred to as the 'Three Fs': fair rent, free sale and fixity of tenure). Parnell championed the activities of the Land League, which instigated the strategy of 'boycotting' (named after one particularly unpleasant agent called Charles Boycott) tenants, agents and landlords who didn't adhere to the Land League's aims. In 1881 they won an important victory with the passing of the Land Act.

Parnell's other great struggle was for a limited form of autonomy for Ireland. Despite the nominal support of the Liberal leader William Gladstone, Home Rule bills introduced in 1886 and 1892 were uniformly rejected. Like O'Connell before him, Parnell's star plummeted dramatically: in 1890 he was embroiled in a divorce proceeding, and the 'uncrowned king of Ireland' was forced to resign; he died less than a year later.

Rebellion Once Again

Ireland's struggle for some kind of autonomy picked up pace in the second decade of the 20th century. The radicalism that had always been at the fringes of Irish nationalist aspirations was once again beginning to assert itself, partly in response to a hardening of

1801	**1828–29**	**1845–51**
The Act of Union unites Ireland politically with Britain, ending Irish 'independence'.	Daniel O'Connell's election to Parliament leads to the Catholic Relief Act; non-Protestants can now be MPs.	Between 500,000 and one million die during the Potato Famine; two million more emigrate.

attitudes in Ulster. Mass opposition to any kind of Irish independence had resulted in the formation of the Ulster Volunteer Force (UVF), a Loyalist vigilante group whose 100,000-plus members swore to resist any attempt to impose Home Rule on Ireland. Nationalists responded by creating the Irish Volunteer Force (IVF) and a showdown seemed inevitable.

Home Rule was finally passed in 1914, but the outbreak of WWI meant that its enactment was shelved for the duration. For most Irish, the suspension was disappointing but hardly unreasonable, and the majority of the volunteers enlisted to help fight the Germans.

Beyond the Pale

The expression 'beyond the pale' came into use when the Pale – defined as a jurisdiction marked by a clear boundary – was the English-controlled part of Ireland, which stretched roughly from Dalkey, a southern suburb of Dublin, to Dundalk, north of Drogheda. Inland, the boundary extended west to Trim and Kells. To the British elite, the rest of Ireland was considered uncivilised.

The Easter Rising

A few, however, did not heed the call. Two small groups – a section of the Irish Volunteers under Pádraig Pearse and the Irish Citizens' Army led by James Connolly – conspired in a rebellion that took the country by surprise. A depleted Volunteer group marched into Dublin on Easter Monday 1916 and took over a number of key positions in the city, claiming the General Post Office on O'Connell St as its headquarters. From its steps, Pearse read out to passers-by a declaration that Ireland was now a republic and that his band was the provisional government. Less than a week of fighting ensued before the rebels surrendered to the superior British forces. The rebels weren't popular and had to be protected from angry Dubliners as they were marched to jail.

The Easter Rising would probably have had little impact on the Irish situation had the British not made martyrs of the rebel leaders. Of the 77 given death sentences, 15 were executed, including the injured Connolly. This brought about a change in public attitudes; support for the Republicans rose dramatically.

War with Britain

By the end of WWI, Home Rule was far too little, far too late. In the 1918 general election, the Republicans stood under the banner of Sinn Féin and won a large majority of the Irish seats. Ignoring London's Parliament, where technically they were supposed to sit, the newly elected Sinn Féin deputies – many of them veterans of the 1916 Easter Rising – declared Ireland independent and formed the first Dáil Éireann (Irish assembly or lower house), which sat in Dublin's Mansion House under the leadership of Éamon de Valera (1882–1975). The Irish Volunteers became the Irish Republican Army (IRA)

1884	**1916**	**1919–21**
The Gaelic Athletic Association (GAA) is founded to promote Gaelic games and culture.	The Easter Rising rebels surrender to superior British forces in less than a week.	The Irish War of Independence, which ends in a truce; Anglo-Irish Treaty is signed.

The Great Famine

As a result of the Great Famine of 1845–51, a staggering three million people died or were forced to emigrate from Ireland. This great tragedy is all the more inconceivable given that the scale of suffering was attributable to greed as much as to natural causes. Potatoes were the staple food of a rapidly growing, desperately poor population and, when a blight hit the crops, prices soared. The repressive Penal Laws ensured that farmers, already crippled with high rents, could ill afford to sell the limited harvest of potatoes not affected by blight or imported from abroad to the Irish. Mass emigration continued to reduce the population during the next 100 years and huge numbers of Irish emigrants found their way abroad.

and the Dáil authorised it to wage war on British troops in Ireland.

As wars go, the War of Independence was pretty small fry. It lasted two and a half years and cost around 1200 casualties. But it was a pretty nasty affair, as the IRA fought a guerrilla-style, hit-and-run campaign against the British, whose numbers were swelled by returning veterans of WWI known as Black and Tans (on account of their uniforms, a mix of army khaki and police black).

A Kind of Freedom

A truce in July 1921 led to intense negotiations between the two sides. The resulting Anglo-Irish Treaty, signed on 6 December 1921, created the Irish Free State, made up of 26 of 32 Irish counties. The remaining six – all in Ulster – remained part of the UK. The Treaty was an imperfect document: not only did it cement the geographic divisions on the island that 50 years later would explode into the Troubles, it also caused a split among nationalists – between those who believed the Treaty to be a necessary stepping stone towards full independence, and those who saw it as capitulation to the British and a betrayal of Republican ideals. This division was to determine the course of Irish political affairs for virtually the remainder of the century.

Civil War

The Treaty was ratified after a bitter debate and the June 1922 elections resulted in a victory for the pro-Treaty side. But the anti-Treaty forces rallied behind de Valera, who, though president of the Dáil, had not been a member of the Treaty negotiating team (affording him, in the eyes of his critics and opponents, maximum deniability should the negotiations go pear-shaped). De Valera's supporters objected to some of the Treaty's provisions, most notably the oath of allegiance to the British monarch.

Within two weeks of the elections, civil war broke out between comrades who, a year previously, had fought alongside each other. The most prominent casualty of this particularly bitter conflict was Michael Collins (1890–1922), mastermind of the IRA's

1921–22
Treaty grants independence to 26 counties, allowing six Ulster counties to remain part of Great Britain.

1922–23
Brief and bloody civil war between pro-Treaty and anti-Treaty forces results in victory for the former.

1932
De Valera leads his Fianna Fáil party into government for the first time.

campaign during the War of Independence and a chief negotiator of the Anglo-Irish Treaty – shot in an ambush in his native Cork.

The Making of a Republic

The Civil War ground to an exhausted halt in 1923 with the victory of the pro-Treaty side, who governed the new state until 1932. Defeated but unbowed, de Valera founded a new party in 1926 called Fianna Fáil (Soldiers of Ireland) and won a majority in the 1932 elections; they would remain in charge until 1948. In the meantime, de Valera created a new constitution in 1937 that did away with the hated oath of allegiance, reaffirmed the special position of the Catholic Church and once again laid claim to the six counties of Northern Ireland. In 1948 Ireland officially left the Commonwealth and became a republic but, as historical irony would have it, it was Fine Gael, as the old pro-Treaty party was now known, that declared it – Fianna Fáil had surprisingly lost the election that year. After 800 years, Ireland – or at least a substantial chunk of it – was independent.

Growing Pains & Roaring Tigers

Unquestionably the most significant figure since independence, Éamon de Valera made an immense contribution to an independent Ireland but, as the 1950s stretched into the 1960s, his vision for the country was mired in a conservative and traditional orthodoxy that was at odds with the reality of a country in desperate economic straits, where chronic unemployment and emigration were but the more visible effects of inadequate policy.

Partners in Europe

In 1972 the Republic (along with Northern Ireland) became a member of the European Economic Community (EEC). This brought an increased measure of prosperity thanks to the benefits of the Common Agricultural Policy, which set fixed prices and guaranteed quotas for Irish farming produce. Nevertheless, the broader global depression, provoked by the oil crisis of 1973, forced the country into yet another slump and emigration figures rose again, reaching a peak in the mid-1980s.

From Celtic Tiger...

In the early 1990s, European funds helped kick-start economic growth. Huge sums of money were invested in education and physical infrastructure, while the policy of low corporate tax rates coupled with attractive incentives made Ireland very appealing to high-tech businesses looking for a door into EU markets. In less than a decade, Ireland went from being one of the poorest countries in Europe to one of the wealthiest: unemployment fell from 18% to 3.5%, the average industrial wage somersaulted to the top of the European league, and the dramatic rise in GDP meant that the country laid claim

1948	1993	1994
The new Fine Gael declares the Free State to be a republic.	Downing Street Declaration signed by British prime minister John Major and Irish Taoiseach Albert Reynolds.	Sinn Féin leader Gerry Adams announces a cessation of IRA violence on 31 August.

to an economic model of success that was the envy of the entire world. Ireland became synonymous with the term 'Celtic Tiger'.

...to Rescue Cat

From 2002 the Irish economy was kept buoyant by a gigantic construction boom that was completely out of step with any measure of responsible growth forecasting. The out-of-control international derivatives market flooded Irish banks with cheap money, and they lent it freely.

Then American global financial services firm Lehman Brothers and the credit crunch happened. The Irish banks nearly went to the wall, but were bailed out at the last minute, and before Ireland could draw breath, the International Monetary Fund (IMF) and the EU held the chits of the country's midterm economic future. Ireland found itself yet again confronting the familiar demons of high unemployment and emigration, but a deep-cutting program of austerity saw the corner turned by the end of 2014.

It's (Not So) Grim Up North

Making sense of Northern Ireland isn't that easy. It's not because the politics are so entrenched (they are), or that the two sides are at such odds with each other (they are): it's because the fight is so old.

It began in the 16th century, with the first Plantations of Ireland ordered by the English Crown, whereby the confiscated lands of the Gaelic and Hiberno-Norman gentry were awarded to English and Scottish settlers of good Protestant stock. The policy was most effective in Ulster, where the newly arrived Protestants were given an extra leg-up by the Penal Laws, which successfully reduced the now landless Catholic population to second-class citizens with little or no rights.

Irish Apartheid

But fast-forward to 1921, when the notion of independent Ireland moved from aspiration to actuality. The new rump state of Northern Ireland was governed until 1972 by the Protestant-majority Ulster Unionist Party, backed up by the overwhelmingly Protestant Royal Ulster Constabulary (RUC) and the sectarian B-Specials militia. As a result of tilted economic subsidies, bias in housing allocation and wholesale gerrymandering, Northern Ireland was, in effect, an apartheid state, leaving the roughly 40% Catholic and Nationalist population grossly underrepresented.

Defiance of Unionist hegemony came with the Civil Rights Movement, founded in 1967 and heavily influenced by its US counterpart. In October 1968 a mainly Catholic march in Derry was violently broken up by the RUC amid rumours that the IRA had provided 'security' for the marchers. Nobody knew it at the time, but the Troubles had begun.

mid-1990s	**1998**	**2005**
The 'Celtic Tiger' economy transforms Ireland into one of Europe's wealthiest countries.	After the Good Friday Agreement, the 'Real IRA' detonates a bomb in Omagh, killing 29 people and injuring 200.	The IRA orders all of its units to commit to exclusively democratic means.

The Troubles

Conflict escalated quickly, clashes between the two communities increased and the police openly sided with the Loyalists against a Nationalist population made increasingly militant by the resurgence of the long-dormant IRA. In August 1969 British troops went to Derry and then Belfast to maintain law and order; they were initially welcomed in Catholic neighbourhoods but within a short time they too were seen as an army of occupation: the killing of 13 innocent civilians in Derry on Bloody Sunday (30 January 1972) set the grim tone for the next two decades, as violence, murder and reprisal became the order of the day in the province and, occasionally, on the British mainland.

Overtures of Peace

By the early 1990s it was clear to Republicans that armed struggle was a bankrupted policy. Northern Ireland was a transformed society – most of the injustices that had sparked the conflict in the late 1960s had long since been rectified and most ordinary citizens were desperate for an end to hostilities.

A series of negotiated statements between the unionists, nationalists and the British and Irish governments – brokered in part by George Mitchell, Bill Clinton's special envoy to Northern Ireland – eventually resulted in the historic Good Friday Agreement of 1998.

The agreement called for the devolution of legislative power from Westminster (where it had been since 1972) to a new Northern Ireland Assembly, but posturing, disagreement, sectarianism and downright obstinance on both sides made slow work of progress, and the Assembly was suspended four times – the last from October 2002 until May 2007.

During this period, the politics of Northern Ireland polarised dramatically, resulting in the falling away of the more moderate UUP and the emergence of the hardline DUP, led by Ian Paisley; and, on the nationalist side, the emergence of the IRA's political wing, Sinn Féin, as the main torch-bearer of nationalist aspirations, under the leadership of Gerry Adams and Martin McGuinness.

2008

The Irish banking system is declared virtually bankrupt following the collapse of Lehman Brothers.

2010

Ireland surrenders financial sovereignty to IMF and EU in exchange for bailout package of €85 billion.

2015

Ireland becomes the first country in the world to introduce marriage equality for same-sex couples by plebiscite.

Soda bread

Food & Drink

Ireland's recently acquired reputation as a gourmet destination is thoroughly deserved, as a host of chefs and producers are leading a foodie revolution that, at its heart, is about bringing to the table the kind of meals that have always been taken for granted on well-run Irish farms. Coupled with the growing sophistication of the Irish palate, it's now relatively easy to eat well on all budgets.

To Eat

Potatoes Still a staple of most traditional meals and presented in a variety of forms. The mashed potato dishes colcannon and champ (with cabbage and spring onion, respectively) are two of the tastiest recipes in the country.

Meat and seafood Beef, lamb and pork are common options. Seafood is widely available in restaurants and is often excellent, especially in the west. Oysters, trout and salmon are delicious, particularly if they're direct from the sea or a river rather than a fish farm.

Soda bread The most famous Irish bread is made with bicarbonate of soda, to make up for soft Irish flour that traditionally didn't take well to yeast. Combined with buttermilk, it makes a superbly tasty bread, and is often on the breakfast menus at B&Bs.

'The fry' – an Irish cooked breakfast

The fry Who can say no to a plate of fried bacon, sausages, black pudding, white pudding, eggs and tomatoes? For the famous Ulster fry, common throughout the North, simply add fadge (potato bread).

Dare to Try

Ironically, while the Irish palate has become more adventurous, it is the old-fashioned Irish menu that features some fairly challenging dishes. Dare to try the following:

Black pudding Made from cooked pork blood, suet and other fillings; a ubiquitous part of an Irish cooked breakfast.

Boxty A Northern Irish starchy potato cake made with a half-and-half mix of cooked mashed potatoes and grated, strained raw potato.

Carrageen The typical Irish seaweed that can be found in dishes as diverse as salad and ice cream.

Corned beef tongue Usually accompanied by cabbage, this dish is still found on a traditional Irish menu.

Lough Neagh eel A speciality of Northern Ireland, typically eaten around Halloween; it's usually served in chunks with a white onion sauce.

Poitín It's rare enough for you to be offered a drop of the 'cratur', as illegally distilled whiskey (made from malted grain or potatoes) is called here. Still, there are pockets of the country with secret stills – in Donegal, Connemara and West Cork.

★ **Memorable Meals**
Restaurant Patrick Guilbaud (p72)
Bastion (p193)
Nash 19 (p187)
Loam (p121)
Muddlers Club (p232)

Scallops starter at Restaurant Patrick Guilbaud (p72)

STRIKING IMAGES / RF/ALAMY STOCK PHOTO ©

To Drink

Stout While Guinness has become synonymous with stout the world over, few outside Ireland realise that there are two other major producers competing for the favour of the Irish drinker: Murphy's and Beamish & Crawford, both based in Cork city.

Tea The Irish drink more tea, per capita, than any other nation in the world and you'll be offered a cup as soon as you cross the threshold of any Irish home. Taken with milk (and sugar, if you want) rather than lemon, preferred blends are very strong, and nothing like the namby-pamby versions that pass for Irish breakfast tea elsewhere.

Whiskey At last count, there were almost 100 different types of Irish whiskey, brewed by only three distilleries – Jameson's, Bushmills and Cooley's. A visit to Ireland reveals a depth of excellence that will make the connoisseur's palate spin while winning over many new friends to what the Irish call *uisce beatha* (water of life).

Craft Beer Revolution

Although mainstream lagers like Heineken, Carlsberg and Coors Lite are most pubs' best-selling beers, the craft-beer revolution has resulted in dozens of microbreweries springing up all over the island, making artisan beers that are served in more than 600 of Ireland's pubs and bars. Here's a small selection to whet the tastebuds:

Devil's Backbone (4.9% Alcohol by Volume) Rich amber ale from County Donegal brewer Kinnegar.

Surrender to the Void (8.5% ABV) a full-on, tropical Double IPA by Whiplash, the independent side project of brewer Alex Lawes, voted Irish beer of the year by Galway Bay Brewery, Galway City in 2017.

O'Hara's Leann Folláin (6% ABV) Dry stout with vaguely chocolate notes produced by Carlow Brewing Company.

Metalman Pale Ale (4.3% ABV) American-style pale ale by the much-respected Metalman Brewing Company in County Waterford – now available in cans.

Puck Pilsner (4.5% ABV) A light lager brewed by Jack Cody's Brewery in Drogheda, County Louth.

Twisted Hop (4.7% ABV) Blond ale produced by Hilden just outside Lisburn, Ireland's oldest independent brewery.

When to Eat

Irish eating habits have changed over the last couple of decades, and there are differences between urban and rural practices.

Breakfast Usually eaten before 9am (although hotels and B&Bs will serve until 11am Monday to Friday, and to noon at weekends in urban areas), as most people rush off to work. Weekend brunch is popular in bigger towns and cities.

Lunch Urban workers eat on the run between 12.30pm and 2pm (most restaurants don't begin to serve lunch until at least midday). At weekends, especially Sunday, the midday lunch is skipped in favour of a substantial mid-afternoon meal (called dinner), usually between 2pm and 4pm.

Tea Not the drink, but the evening meal – also confusingly called dinner. This is the main meal of the day for urbanites, usually eaten around 6.30pm. Rural communities eat at the same time but with a more traditional tea of bread, cold cuts and, yes, tea. Restaurants follow international habits, with most diners not eating until at least 7.30pm.

Supper A before-bed snack of tea and toast or sandwiches, still enjoyed by many Irish, although urbanites increasingly eschew it for health reasons. Not a practice in restaurants.

Price Ranges

The following price ranges refer to the cost of a main course at dinner.

Budget	Republic	Dublin	Northern Ireland
€	less than €12	less than €15	less than £12
€€	€12–25	€15–28	£12–20
€€€	more than €25	more than €28	more than £20

Vegetarians & Vegans

Ireland has come a long, long way since the days when vegetarians were looked upon as odd creatures; nowadays, even the most militant vegan will barely cause a ruffle in all but the most basic of kitchens. Which isn't to say that travellers with plant-based diets are going to find the most imaginative range of options on menus outside the bigger towns and cities – or in the plethora of modern restaurants that have opened in the last few years – but you can rest assured that the overall quality of the homegrown vegetable is top-notch and most places will have at least one dish that you can tuck into comfortably.

Dining Etiquette

The Irish aren't big on restrictive etiquette, preferring friendly informality to any kind of stuffy to-dos. Still, the following are a few tips on dining with the Irish:

Children All restaurants welcome kids up to 7pm, but some smarter restaurants don't allow them in the evening, and by law children under 18 are not permitted in pubs after 9pm. Family restaurants have children's menus; others have reduced portions of regular menu items.

Returning a dish If the food is not to your satisfaction, it's best to politely explain what's wrong with it as soon as you can; any respectable restaurant will endeavour to replace the dish immediately.

Paying the bill If you insist on paying the bill for everyone, be prepared for a first, second and even third refusal to countenance such an exorbitant act of generosity. But don't be fooled: the Irish will refuse something several times even if they're delighted with it. Insist gently but firmly and you'll get your way!

For advice on tipping, see p296.

The Pub

The pub is the heart of Ireland's social existence, and we're guessing that experiencing it ranks high on your list of things to do while you're here. But let's be clear: we're not just talking about a place to get a drink. Oh no. You can get a drink in a restaurant or a hotel, or wherever there's someone with a bottle of something strong. The pub is far more than just that.

Role

The pub is the broadest window through which you can examine and experience the very essence of the nation's culture, in all its myriad forms. It's the great leveller, where status and rank hold no sway, where generation gaps are bridged, inhibitions lowered, tongues loosened, schemes hatched, songs sung, stories told and gossip embroidered. It's a unique institution: a theatre and a cosy room, a centre stage and a hideaway, a debating chamber and a place for silent contemplation. It's whatever you want it to be, and that's the secret of the great Irish pub.

Spirit Groceries

The 'spirit grocery' is a combined pub and grocer's shop. Found all over Ireland, they usually have a bar counter on one side and a general store counter on the other, a combination that has engendered the international image of the Irish pub as littered with old signs and bric-a-brac. There are pubs today where you can buy a bag of nails, a tin of peas or a pair of wellies as well as a pint.

Talk

Talk – whether it is frivolous, earnest or incoherent – is the essential ingredient. Once tongues are loosened and the cogs of thought oiled, the conversation can go anywhere and you should let it flow to its natural conclusion. An old Irish adage suggests you should never talk about sport, religion or politics in unfamiliar company. But as long as you're mindful, you needn't restrict yourself too much. While it's a myth to say you can walk into any pub and be befriended, you probably won't be drinking on your own for long – unless that's what you want of course. There are few more spiritual experiences than a solitary pint in an old country pub in the mid-afternoon.

Tradition

Aesthetically, there is nothing better than the traditional haunt, populated by flat-capped pensioners bursting with delightful anecdotes and always ready to dispense a kind of wisdom distilled through generations' worth of experience. The best of them have stone floors and a peat fire; the chat harely rises above a respectful murmur save for appreciative laughter; and most of all, there's no music save the kind played by someone sitting next to you. Pubs like these are a disappearing breed, but there are still plenty of them around to ensure that you will find one, no matter where you are.

Etiquette

The rounds system – the simple custom where someone buys you a drink and you buy one back – is the bedrock of Irish pub culture. It's summed up in the Irish saying: 'It's impossible for two men to go to a pub for one drink'. Nothing will hasten your fall from social grace here like the failure to uphold this pub law.

Another golden rule about the system is that the next round starts when the first person has finished (or preferably just about to finish) their drink. It doesn't matter if you're only halfway through your pint – if it's your round, get your order in.

Craft Beer

In the last decade there has been a swing away from the big international brands – even Guinness is now part of the multinational Diageo drinks group – in favour of beers made by small, local breweries – so called 'craft beers'. Many of these have their own pubs, or even combine pub and brewery in one place.

A shamrock

MARCHU STUDIO/SHUTTERSTOCK ©

Irish Mythological Symbols

Ireland's collection of icons serves to exemplify the country – or a simplistic version of it – to an astonishing degree. It's referred to by the Irish as 'Oirishness', which is what happens when you take a spud, shove it in a pint of Guinness and garnish it with a shamrock.

The Shamrock

Ireland's most enduring symbol is the shamrock, a three-leafed white clover known diminutively in Irish as *seamróg*, which was anglicised as 'shamrock'. According to legend, when St Patrick was trying to explain the mystery of the Holy Trinity to the recently converted Celtic chieftains, he plucked the modest little weed and used its three leaves to explain the metaphysically challenging concept of the Father, the Son and the Holy Spirit as being separate but part of the one being. This link is what makes the shamrock a ubiquitous part of the St Patrick's Day celebrations.

The Luck of the Irish?

Nearly a millennium of occupation, a long history of oppression and exploitation, a devastating famine, mass emigration...how exactly are the Irish 'lucky'? Well, they're not or at least not any more so than anybody else. The expression was born in the mid-19th century in the US during the gold and silver rush, when some of the most successful miners were Irish or of Irish extraction. It didn't really seem to matter that the Irish were recent escapees from famine and destitution in Ireland and were over-represented among the miners; the expression stuck. Still, the expression was always a little derisory, as though the Irish merely stumbled across good fortune.

The Leprechaun

The country's most enduring cliché is the myth of the mischievous leprechaun and his pot of gold, which he jealously guards from the attentions of greedy humans. Despite the twee aspect of the legend, its origin predates the Celts and belongs to the mythological Tuatha dé Danann (peoples of the Goddess Danu), who lived in Ireland 4000 years ago. When they were eventually defeated, their king Lugh (the demi-god father of Cúchulainn) was forced underground, where he became known as Lugh Chromain, or 'little stooping Lugh' – the origin of leprechaun.

The Irish can get visibly irritated if asked whether they believe in leprechauns (you might as well ask them if they're stupid), but many rural dwellers are a superstitious lot. They mightn't necessarily believe that malevolent sprites who dwell in faerie forts actually exist, but they're not especially keen to test the theory either, which is why there still exist trees, hills and other parts of the landscape that are deemed to have, well, supernatural qualities, and as such will never be touched.

The Harp

The Celtic harp, or clársach, is meant to represent the immortality of the soul, which is handy given that it's been a symbol of Ireland since the days of Henry VIII and the first organised opposition to English rule. The harp was the most popular instrument at the Celtic court, with the harpist (usually blind) ranked only behind the chief and bard in order of importance. In times of war, the harpist played a special, jewel-encrusted harp and served as the cheerleading section for soldiers heading into battle.

During the first rebellions against the English, the harp was once again an instrument of revolutionary fervour, prompting the crown to ban it altogether. This eventually led to its decline as the instrument of choice for Irish musicians but ensured its status as a symbol of Ireland.

The Claddagh Ring

The most famous of all Irish jewellery is the Claddagh ring, made up of two hands (friendship) clasping a heart (love) and usually surmounted by a crown (loyalty). Made in the eponymous fishing village in County Galway since the 17th century, the symbolic origins are much older and belong to a broader family of rings popular since Roman times known as the *fede* rings (from *mani in fede*, or 'hands in trust'), which were used to symbolise marriage. Nevertheless, their popularity is relatively recent, and almost entirely down to their wearing by expat Americans who use them to demonstrate their ties to their Irish heritage.

Ulysses Rare Books, Dublin (p70)

Literary Ireland

Of all their national traits, characteristics and cultural expressions, it's perhaps the way the Irish speak and write that best distinguishes them. Their love of language and their great oral tradition have contributed to Ireland's legacy of world-renowned writers and storytellers – all this in a language imposed on them by a foreign invader.

The Mythic Cycle

Before there was anything like modern literature there was the Ulaid (Ulster) Cycle – Ireland's version of the Homeric epic – recorded from oral tradition between the 8th and 12th centuries. The chief story is the Táin Bó Cúailnge (Cattle Raid of Cooley), about a battle between Queen Maeve of Connaught and Cúchulainn, the principal hero of Irish mythology. Cúchulainn appears in the work of Irish writers right up to the present day, from Samuel Beckett to Frank McCourt.

Contemporary Fiction

Brooklyn (Colm Tóibín, 2009)

The Thrill of it All (Joseph O'Connor, 2014)

Spill Simmer Falter Wither (Sara Baume, 2015)

The Glorious Heresies (Lisa McInerney, 2015)

The Gamal (Ciarán Collins, 2015)

Modern Literature

From the mythic cycle, zip forward 1000 years, past the genius of Jonathan Swift (1667–1745) and his *Gulliver's Travels;* stopping to acknowledge acclaimed dramatist Oscar Wilde (1854–1900); *Dracula* creator Bram Stoker (1847–1912) – some have claimed that the name of the count may have come from the Irish *droch fhola* (bad blood) – and the literary giant that was James Joyce (1882–1941), whose name and books elicit enormous pride in Ireland.

The majority of Joyce's literary output came when he had left Ireland for the artistic hotbed that was Paris, which was also true for another great experimenter of language and style, Samuel Beckett (1906–89). Beckett's work centres on fundamental existential questions about the human condition and the nature of self. He is probably best known for his play *Waiting for Godot* (1952), but his unassailable reputation is based on a series of stark novels and plays.

Of the dozens of 20th-century Irish authors to have achieved published renown, some names to look out for include playwright and novelist Brendan Behan (1923–64), who wove tragedy, wit and a turbulent life into his best works including *Borstal Boy* (1958), *The Quare Fellow* (first produced in 1954) and *The Hostage* (first performed 1958) before dying young of alcoholism.

Belfast-born CS Lewis (1898–1963) died a year earlier, but he left us *The Chronicles of Narnia* (1949-1954), a series of allegorical children's stories, three of which have been made into films. Other Northern writers have, not surprisingly, featured the Troubles in their work: Bernard MacLaverty's *Cal* (2001; also made into a film) and his more recent *The Anatomy School* are both wonderful.

Contemporary Scene

'I love James Joyce. Never read him, but he's a true genius'. Yes, the stalwarts are still great, but ask your average Irish person who their favourite home-grown writer is and they'll most likely mention someone who's still alive.

They might say Roddy Doyle (1958–), whose mega-successful Barrytown trilogy *The Commitments, The Snapper* (1990) and *The Van* (1991) – have all been made into films; his latest book, *The Guts* (2013), saw the return of *The Commitments* (1987) protagonist, Jimmy Rabbitte older, wiser and battling illness. Doyle's novel *Paddy Clarke, Ha Ha Ha* won the Booker Prize in 1993.

Sebastian Barry (1955–) has been shortlisted twice for the Man Booker Prize, for his WWI drama *A Long Long Way* (2005) and the absolutely compelling *The Secret Scripture* (2008), about a 100-year-old inmate of a mental hospital called Roseanne who decides to write an autobiography.

Anne Enright (1962–) did nab the Booker for *The Gathering* (2007), a zeitgeist tale of alcoholism and abuse – she described it as 'the intellectual equivalent of a Hollywood weepie'. Her latest novel, *The Green Road* (2015), continues to mine the murky waters of the Irish family. Another Booker Prize winner is heavyweight John Banville (1945–), who won it for *The Sea* (2005), we also recommend either *The Book of Evidence* (1989) or the masterful roman à clef *The Untouchable* (1997), based loosely on the secret-agent life of art historian Anthony Blunt. Banville's literary alter ego is Benjamin Black, author of a series of seven hard-boiled detective thrillers set in the 1950s starring a troubled pathologist called Quirke – the latest book is *Even the Dead* (2015).

Another big hitter is Wexford-born Colm Tóibín (1955–), author of nine novels including *Brooklyn* (2009; made into a film in 2015 starring Saoirse Ronan) and, most recently, *Nora Webster* (2014), a powerful study of widowhood.

Emma Donoghue (1969–) followed the award-winning *Room* (2010) with *Frog Music* (2014), about the real-life shooting of cross-dressing *gamine* Jenny Bonnet in late-19th-century San Francisco and *The Wonder* (2016), about a fasting child in 1850s Ireland. John Boyne (1971–) made his name with Holocaust novel *The Boy in the Striped Pyjamas* (2006; the film version came out in 2008); his latest novel, *A History of Loneliness* (2014), explores the thorny issue of child abuse and the Catholic Church.

The Gaelic Revival

While Home Rule was being debated and shunted, something of a revolution was taking place in Irish arts, literature and identity. The poet William Butler Yeats (1865–1939) and his coterie of literary friends (including Lady Gregory, Douglas Hyde, John Millington Synge and George Russell) championed the Anglo-Irish literary revival, unearthing old Celtic tales and writing with fresh enthusiasm about a romantic Ireland of epic battles and warrior queens. For a country that had suffered centuries of invasion and deprivation, these images presented a much more attractive version of history.

Colum McCann (1965–) left Ireland in 1986, eventually settling in New York, where his sixth novel, the post–September 11 *Let the Great World Spin* (2009), catapulted him to the top of the literary tree and won him the National Book Award for fiction as well as the International IMPAC Dublin Literary Award. His next novel, *TransAtlantic* (2013) weaves three separate stories together: the flight of Alcock and Brown, the visit of Frederick Douglass to Ireland in 1845 and the story of the Northern Irish peace process of the late 1990s.

The Troubles have been a rich and powerful subject for Northern Irish writers. Derry native Sean O'Reilly's (1969–) novels are populated by characters freed from sectarianism but irreparably damaged by it: his last novel was *Watermark* (2005), about a young woman on the edge of desire and reason in an unnamed Irish town. Eoin McNamee (1961–) has written a series that explores the conflict directly, teasing out the effects of religion and history on the lives of individuals. His latest novel, *Blue is the Night* (2014) is the final book of a trilogy that also includes *The Blue Tango* (2001) and *Orchid Blue* (2010).

Paul Murray's (1975–) second novel, *Skippy Dies* (2010), about a group of privileged students at an all-boys secondary school, won him lots of critical praise (and an upcoming movie version directed by Neil Jordan) but his follow-up, *The Mark and the Void* (2015), which is set against the backdrop of the financial crisis, met with far more lukewarm praise. Not so Shane Hegarty (1976–), who in 2015 published the first volume of *Darkmouth*, a YA novel set in a fictional Irish town where young Finn is learning about girls and fighting monsters.

Chick Lit

Authors hate the label and publishers profess to disregard it, but chick lit is big business, and few have mastered it as well as the Irish. Doyenne of them all is Maeve Binchy (1940–2012), whose mastery of the style saw her outsell most of the literary greats – her last novel before she died was *A Week in Winter* (2012). Marian Keyes (1963–) is another author with a long line of bestsellers, including *The Woman Who Stole My Life* (2014). She's a terrific storyteller with a rare ability to tackle sensitive issues such as alcoholism and depression, issues that she herself has suffered from and is admirably honest about. Former agony aunt Cathy Kelly turns out novels at the rate of one a year: her latest book is *Between Sisters* (2017), exploring the lives of two very different siblings.

Traditional Music

Irish music (known in Ireland as traditional music, or just trad) has retained a vibrancy not found in other traditional European forms, which have lost out to the overbearing influence of pop music. Although it has kept many of its traditional aspects, Irish music has itself influenced many forms of music, most notably American country music.

Instruments

Despite popular perception, the harp isn't widely used in traditional music but it *is* the national emblem. The bodhrán (*bow*-rawn) goat-skin drum is much more prevalent, although it makes for a lousy symbol. The uillean pipes, played by squeezing bellows under the elbow, provide another distinctive sound, although you're not likely to see them in a pub. The fiddle isn't unique to Ireland but it is one of the main instruments in the country's indigenous music, along with the flute, tin whistle, accordion and bouzouki (a version of the mandolin). Music fits into five main categories (jigs, reels, hornpipes, polkas and slow airs), while the old style of singing unaccompanied versions of traditional ballads and airs is called *sean-nós*.

Traditional bodhrán and stick

★ **Traditional Albums**

The Quiet Glen (Tommy Peoples, 1998)

Paddy Keenan (Paddy Keenan, 1975)

The Chieftains 6: Bonaparte's Retreat (The Chieftains, 1976)

Old Hag You Have Killed Me (The Bothy Band, 1976)

Tunes

The music was never written down, it was passed on from one player to another and so endured and evolved – regional 'styles' only developed because local musicians sought to play just like the one who seemed to play better than everybody else. The blind itinerant harpist Turlough O'Carolan (1670–1738) 'wrote' more than 200 tunes – it's difficult to know how many versions their repeated learning has spawned. This characteristic of fluidity is key to an appreciation of traditional music, and explains why it is such a resilient form today.

Popular Bands

In the 1960s composer Seán Ó Riada (1931–71) tried to impose a kind of structure on traditional music. His ensemble group, Ceoltóirí Chualann, was the first to reach a wider audience, and from it were born The Chieftains, arguably the most important traditional group of them all. They started recording in 1963 – any one of their nearly 40 albums are worth a listen, but you won't go wrong with their 10-album eponymous series.

The other big success of the 1960s were The Dubliners. More folksy than traditional, they made a career out of bawdy drinking songs that got everybody singing along. Other popular bands include The Fureys, comprising four brothers originally from the travelling community (no, not like the Wilburys) along with guitarist Davey Arthur. And if it's rousing renditions of Irish rebel songs you're after, you can't go past The Wolfe Tones.

Since the 1970s, various bands have tried to blend traditional with more progressive genres, with mixed success. The Bothy Band were formed in 1975 and were a kind of trad supergroup: bouzouki player Dónal Lunny, uillean piper Paddy Keenan, flute and whistle player Matt Molloy (later a member of The Chieftains), fiddler Paddy Glackin and accordion player Tony MacMahon were all superb instrumentalists and their recordings are still as electrifying today as they were four decades ago.

Musicians tend to come together in collaborative projects. A contemporary group worth checking out are The Gloaming, who've taken traditional reels and given them a contemporary sound – their eponymous debut album (2011) is sensational. A key member of the group, fiddler Caoimhín Ó Raghallaigh, is also worth checking out in his own right; his latest album, The Gloaming 2, displays both his beautiful fiddle playing and his superb understanding of loops and electronic texturing.

And if you want to check out a group that melds rock, folk and traditional music, you won't go far wrong with The Spook of the Thirteenth Lock, who've released a couple of albums since 2008; in 2017 they released an EP called *The Bullet in the Brick*.

Kylemore Abbey (p125)

VORADCA/SHUTTERSTOCK ©

Survival Guide

Directory A–Z

Accommodation

Accommodation options range from bare and basic to pricey and palatial. The spine of the Irish hospitality business is the ubiquitous B&B, in recent years challenged by a plethora of midrange hotels and guesthouses. Ireland-specific online resources for accommodation include the following:

Daft.ie (www.daft.ie) Online classifieds for short- and long-term rentals.

Elegant Ireland (www.elegant.ie) Specialises in self-catering

Book Your Stay Online

For more accommodation reviews by Lonely Planet authors, check out http://hotels.lonelyplanet.com/dublin. You'll find independent reviews, as well as recommendations on the best places to stay. Best of all, you can book online.

castles, period houses and unique properties.

Imagine Ireland (www.imagineireland.com) Modern cottage rentals throughout the whole island, including Northern Ireland.

Irish Landmark Trust (www.irishlandmark.com) Not-for-profit conservation group that rents self-catering properties of historical and cultural significance, such as castles, tower houses, gate lodges, schoolhouses and lighthouses.

Stay in Ireland (www.stayinireland.com) Lists guesthouses and self-catering options.

B&Bs & Guesthouses

Bed and breakfasts are small, family-run houses, farmhouses and period country houses with fewer than five bedrooms. Standards vary enormously, but most have some bedrooms with private bathroom at a cost of roughly €40 to €60 (£35 to £50) per person per night. In luxurious B&Bs, expect to pay €70 (£60) or more per person. Off-season rates – usually October through to March – are usually lower, as are midweek prices.

Guesthouses are like upmarket B&Bs, but bigger – the Irish equivalent of a boutique hotel. Facilities are usually better and sometimes include a restaurant.

Other tips:

○ Facilities in B&Bs range from basic (bed, bathroom, kettle, TV) to beatific (whirlpool baths, rainforest showers) as you go up in price. Wi-fi is standard and most have parking (but check).

○ Most B&Bs take credit cards, but the occasional rural one might not have facilities; check when you book.

○ Advance reservations are strongly recommended, especially in peak season (June to September).

○ Some B&Bs and guesthouses in more remote regions only operate from Easter to September.

○ If full, B&B owners may recommend another house in the area (possibly a private house taking occasional guests, not in tourist listings).

○ To make prices more competitive at some B&Bs, breakfast may be optional.

Hotels

Hotels range from the local pub to medieval castles. Booking online or negotiating directly will almost always net you a better rate than the published one, especially out of season or midweek (except for business hotels, which offer cheaper weekend rates).

The bulk of the country's hotels are of the midrange variety, with clean rooms and a range of facilities, from restaurants to gyms. The recent trend towards offering free wi-fi is stubbornly resisted by many, who still charge for the privilege.

House Swapping

House swapping can be a popular and affordable way to visit a country and enjoy a real home away from home. There are several agencies in Ireland that, for an annual fee, facilitate international swaps. The fee pays for access to a website and a book giving house descriptions, photographs and the owner's details. After that, it's up to you to make arrangements. Use of the family car is sometimes included.

Homelink International House Exchange (www.home link.ie) Home exchange service running for over 60 years.

Intervac International Holiday Service (www. intervac-homeexchange.com) Long-established, with agents in 45 nations worldwide.

Rental Accommodation

Self-catering accommodation is often rented on a weekly basis and usually means an apartment, house or cottage where you look after yourself. The rates vary from one region and season to another.

Fáilte Ireland (Republic 1850 230 330, the UK 0800 039 7000; www.discoverireland.ie) publishes a guide for registered self-catering accommodation; you can check listings at its website.

Customs Regulations

Both the Republic of Ireland and Northern Ireland have a two-tier customs system: one for goods bought duty-free outside the EU, the other for goods bought in another EU country where tax and duty is paid. There is technically no limit to the amount of goods transportable within the EU, but customs will use certain guidelines to distinguish personal use from commercial purpose. Allowances are as follows:

Duty-free For duty-free goods from outside the EU, limits include 200 cigarettes, 1L of spirits or 2L of wine, 60mL of perfume and 250mL of eau de toilette.

Tax and duty paid Amounts that officially constitute personal use include 3200 cigarettes (or 400 cigarillos, 200 cigars or 3kg of tobacco) and either 10L of spirits, 20L of fortified wine, 60L of sparkling wine, 90L of still wine or 110L of beer.

Accommodation Prices

Accommodation prices vary according to demand – or have different rates for online, phone or walk-in bookings. B&B rates are more consistent, but virtually every other accommodation will charge wildly different rates depending on the time of year, day, festival schedule and even your ability to do a little negotiating. The following price ranges are based on a double room with private bathroom in high season.

Budget	Republic	Dublin	Northern Ireland
€/£	less than €80	under €150	less than £50
€€/££	€80–180	€150–250	£50–120
€€€/£££	more than €180	over €250	more than £120

Electricity

Type G
230V/50Hz

Food

Our cafe and restaurant listings appear in budget order, with the cheapest budget range first. Within the ranges, listings are given in preference order.

For more information, see the Food & Drink chapter (p278)

LGBT Travellers

Ireland is a pretty tolerant place for gays and lesbians. Bigger cities such as

Dublin, Galway and Cork have well-established gay scenes, as do Belfast and Derry in Northern Ireland. In 2015 Ireland overwhelmingly backed same-sex marriage in a historic referendum, whereas Northern Ireland is the only part of the United Kingdom where it's not legal.

While the cities and main towns tend to be progressive and tolerant, you'll still find pockets of homophobia throughout the island, particularly in smaller towns and rural areas. Resources include the following:

Gaire (www.gaire.com) Message board and info for a host of gay-related issues.

Gay & Lesbian Youth Northern Ireland (www.cara-friend.org.uk/projects/glyni) Voluntary counselling, information, health and social-space organisation for the gay community.

Gay Men's Health Project (☎01-660 2189; www.hse.ie/go/GMHS) Practical advice on men's health issues.

National Lesbian & Gay Federation (NLGF; ☎01-671 9076; http://nxf.ie) Publishes the monthly *Gay Community News* (www.gcn.ie).

Northern Ireland Gay Rights Association (☎0771-957 6524; www.nigra.co.uk; Belfast LGBT Centre, 23-31 Waring St) Represents the rights and interests of the LGBTQ community in Northern Ireland. It offers phone and online support, but is not a call-in centre.

Outhouse (Map p74; ☎01-873 4932; www.outhouse.ie; 105 Capel St; ☐all city centre) Top gay, lesbian and bisexual resource centre. Great stop-off point to see what's on, check noticeboards and meet people. It publishes Ireland's free *Pink Pages*, a directory of gay-centric services, which is also accessible on the website.

Health

No jabs are required to travel to Ireland.

Excellent health care is readily available. For minor, self-limiting illnesses, pharmacists can give valuable advice and sell over-the-counter medication. They can also advise when more specialised help is required and point you in the right direction.

EU citizens equipped with a European Health Insurance Card (EHIC), available from health centres or, in the UK, post offices, will be covered for most medical care – but not nonemergencies or emergency repatriation. While other countries, such as Australia, also have reciprocal agreements with Ireland and Britain, many do not.

In Northern Ireland, everyone receives free emergency treatment at accident and emergency (A&E) departments of state-run NHS hospitals, irrespective of nationality.

Insurance

Comprehensive travel insurance to cover theft, loss and medical problems is highly recommended. Worldwide travel insurance is available at www.lonelyplanet.com/travel-insurance. You can buy, extend and claim online anytime – even if you're already on the road.

Internet Access

Wi-fi and 3G/4G networks are making internet cafes largely redundant (except to gamers); the few that are left will charge around €6 per hour. Most accommodations have wi-fi service, either free or for a daily charge (up to €10 per day).

Legal Matters

Illegal drugs are widely available, especially in clubs. The possession of small quantities of marijuana attracts a fine or warning, but harder drugs are treated more seriously. Public drunkenness is illegal but commonplace – the police will usually ignore it unless you're causing trouble. Should you find yourself under arrest, you have the right to remain silent and contact either an attorney or your embassy.

Once you are charged and cautioned you will either be released on bail (known as 'station bail') or, in the event of a more serious offence, transferred from the police station to the District Court as early as possible (usually within 12 hours), where you will either be bailed or remanded in custody by the judge.

Contact the following for assistance.

Legal Aid Board (☏066-947 1000; www.legalaidboard.ie) Has a network of local law centres.

Legal Services Agency Northern Ireland (☏028-9076 3000; www.justice-ni.gov.uk/topics/legal-aid) Administers the statutory legal-aid scheme for Northern Ireland, but cannot offer legal advice.

Climate

Belfast

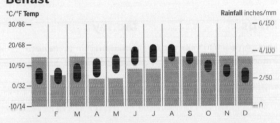

Dublin

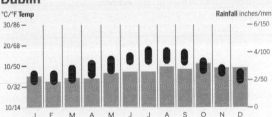

Galway

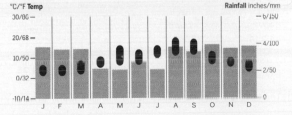

Practicalities

Newspapers *Irish Independent* (www.independent.ie), *Irish Times* (www.irishtimes.com), *Irish Examiner* (www.examiner.ie), *Belfast Telegraph* (www.belfasttelegraph.co.uk).

Radio RTE Radio 1 (88MHz–90MHz), Today FM (100MHz–103MHz), Newstalk 106-108 (106MHz–108MHz), BBC Ulster (92MHz–95MHz; Northern Ireland only).

Smoking It is illegal to smoke indoors everywhere except private residences and prisons.

Weights & Measures The metric system is used; the exception is for liquid measures of alcohol, where pints are used.

Maps

Michelin's 1:400,000-scale Ireland map (No 923) is a decent single sheet map, with clear cartography and most of the island's scenic roads marked. The four maps – North, South, East and West – that make up the Ordnance Survey Holiday map series at 1:250,000 scale are useful for more detail.

The Ordnance Survey Discovery series covers the whole island in 89 maps at a scale of 1:50,000, also available as digital versions. These are all available through Ordnance Survey Ireland (www.osi.ie) and many bookshops around Ireland.

Collins also publishes a range of maps covering Ireland, also available at bookshops.

Money

The Republic of Ireland uses the euro (€), while Northern Ireland uses the pound sterling (£), although the euro is also accepted in many places.

ATMs

Most banks have ATMs that are linked to international money systems such as Cirrus, Maestro or Plus. Each transaction incurs a currency-conversion fee, and credit cards can incur immediate and exorbitant cash-advance interest-rate charges. Watch out for ATMs that have been tampered with; card-reader scams ('skimming') have become a real problem.

Credit & Debit Cards

Visa and MasterCard credit and debit cards are widely accepted; American Express is only accepted by the major chains, and virtually no one will accept Diners or JCB. Chip-and-PIN is the norm for card transactions – only a few places will accept a signature.

Smaller businesses, such as pubs and some B&Bs, prefer debit cards (and will charge a fee for credit cards), and a small number of rural B&Bs only take cash.

Taxes & Refunds

Most goods come with value added tax (VAT) of 21% (20% in Northern Ireland), which non-EU residents can claim back so long as the store in which the goods are purchased operates either the Cashback or Taxback refund program (the Tax-Free Shopping refund scheme in Northern Ireland), usually indicated by a display sticker on the window.

Tipping

Hotels €1/£1 per bag is standard; gratuity for cleaning staff at your discretion.

Pubs Not expected unless table service is provided, then €1/£1 for a round of drinks.

Restaurants For decent service 10%; up to 15% in more expensive places.

Taxis Tip 10% or round up fare to nearest euro/pound.

Toilet Attendants Loose change; no more than €0.50/50p.

Opening Hours

Banks 10am to 4pm Monday to Friday (to 5pm Thursday).

Post offices 9am to 6pm Monday to Friday, 9am to 1pm Saturday.

Pubs 10.30am to 11.30pm Monday to Thursday, 10.30am to 12.30am Friday and Saturday, noon to 11pm Sunday (30 minutes 'drinking up' time allowed); closed Christmas Day and Good Friday.

Restaurants Noon to 10.30pm; many close one day of the week.

Shops 9.30am to 6pm Monday to Saturday (to 8pm Thursday in cities), noon to 6pm Sunday.

Photography

o Natural light can be very dull, so use higher ISO speeds than usual, such as 400 for daylight shots.

o In Northern Ireland, get permission before taking photos of fortified police stations, army posts or other military or quasi-military paraphernalia.

o Don't take photos of people in Protestant or Catholic strongholds of West Belfast without permission; always ask and be prepared to accept a refusal.

o Lonely Planet's *Guide to Travel Photography* is full of helpful tips for photography while on the road.

Public Holidays

Public holidays can cause road chaos as everyone tries to get somewhere else for the break. It's wise to book accommodation in advance for these times.

The following are public holidays in both the Republic and Northern Ireland:

New Year's Day 1 January

St Patrick's Day 17 March

Easter (Good Friday to Easter Monday inclusive) March/April

May Holiday 1st Monday in May

Christmas Day 25 December

St Stephen's Day (Boxing Day) 26 December

St Patrick's Day and St Stephen's Day holidays are taken on the following Monday when they fall on a weekend. In the Republic, nearly everywhere closes on Good Friday even though it isn't an official public holiday. In the North, most shops open on Good Friday, but close the following Tuesday.

Northern Ireland

Spring Bank Holiday Last Monday in May

Orangemen's Day 12 July

August Holiday Last Monday in August

Republic of Ireland

June Holiday 1st Monday in June

August Holiday 1st Monday in August

October Holiday Last Monday in October

Safe Travel

Ireland is safer than most countries in Europe, but normal precautions should be observed.

o Don't leave anything visible in your car when you park.

o Skimming at ATMs is an ongoing problem; be sure to cover the keypad with your hand when you input your PIN.

o In Northern Ireland, exercise extra care in 'interface' areas where sectarian neighbourhoods adjoin.

o Best avoid Northern Ireland during the climax of the Orange marching season on 12 July; sectarian passions are usually inflamed and even many Northerners leave the province at this time.

Telephone

When calling Ireland from abroad, dial your international access code, followed by 353 and the area code (dropping the 0). Area codes in the Republic have three digits, eg 021 for Cork, 091 for Galway and 061 for Limerick. The only exception is Dublin, which has a two-digit code (01).

Useful calling codes

	Republic	Northern Ireland
Country Code	+353	+44
International Access Code	00	00
Directory Enquiries	11811/11850	118 118/ 118 192
International Directory Enquiries	11818	

To make international calls from Ireland, first dial 00, then the country code, followed by the local area code and number. Always use the area code if calling from a mobile phone, but you don't need it if calling from a fixed-line number within the area code.

In Northern Ireland, the area code for all fixed-line numbers is 028, but you only need to use it if calling from a mobile phone or from outside Northern Ireland. To call Northern Ireland from the Republic, use 048 instead of 028, without the international dialling code.

Mobile Phones

○ Both the Republic and Northern Ireland use the GSM 900/1800 cellular phone system, which is compatible with European and Australian, but not North American or Japanese, phones.

○ SMS ('texting') is a national obsession – most people under 30 communicate mostly by text.

○ Pay-as-you-go mobile phone packages with any of the main providers start at around €40 and usually include a basic handset and credit of around €10.

○ SIM-only packages are also available, but make sure your phone is compatible with the local provider.

Time

In winter Ireland is on Greenwich Mean Time (GMT), also known as Universal Time Coordinated (UTC), the same as Britain. In summer the clock shifts to GMT plus one hour, so when it's noon in Dublin and London, it's 4am in Los Angeles and Vancouver, 7am in New York and Toronto, 1pm in Paris, 7pm in Singapore and 9pm in Sydney.

Toilets

There are no on-street facilities in Ireland. All shopping centres have public toilets (either free or €0.20/20p); if you're stranded, go into any bar or hotel.

Tourist Information

In both the Republic and the North there's a tourist office or information point in almost every big town; most can offer a variety of services, including accommodation and attraction reservations, currency-changing services, map and guidebook sales, and free publications.

In the Republic, the tourism purview falls to **Fáilte Ireland** (Republic 1850 230 330, the UK 0800 039 7000; www.discoverireland.ie); in Northern Ireland, it's **Discover Northern Ireland** (head office 028-9023 1221; www.discovernorthernireland.com). Outside Ireland, both organisations unite under the banner Tourism Ireland (www.tourismireland.com).

Travellers with Disabilities

All new buildings have wheelchair access, and many hotels (especially urban ones that are part of chains) have installed lifts, ramps and other facilities such as hearing loops. Many others, particularly B&Bs, have not invested in making their properties accessible.

In big cities, most buses have low-floor access and priority spaces on board, but only 63% of the Bus Éireann coach fleet that operates on Commuter and Expressway services is wheelchair-accessible. Note, too, that many of its rural stops are not accessible.

Trains are accessible with help. Call 1850 366 222 (outside Republic of Ireland +353 1 836 6222) or email access@irishrail.ie 24 hours in advance to arrange assistance.

○ For an informative article with links to accessibility information for getting there and away, getting around and tourist attractions, visit www.ireland.com/en-us/accommodation/articles/accessibility/.

○ Three review sites worth checking out – covering accommodation, eating and drinking, and places of interest – are https://mobilitymojo.com/, whose searchable database is expanding outside its base of Dublin and Galway; http://www.trip-ability.com/, which is expected to soon feature a booking facility; and www.accessibleireland.com/, which also hosts short introductions to public transport.

○ Download Lonely Planet's free Accessible Travel guides from http://lptravel.to/AccessibleTravel

○ The **Citizens' Information Board** (0761-079 000; www.citizensinformationboard.ie) in the Republic and **Disability Action** (028-9029 7880; www.disabilityaction.org) in Northern Ireland can give some advice to travellers with disabilities.

Visas

If you're a European Economic Area (EEA) national, you don't need a visa to visit (or work in) either the Republic or Northern Ireland. Citizens of Australia, Canada, New Zealand, South Africa and the US can visit the Republic for up to three months, and Northern Ireland for up to six months. They are not allowed to work unless sponsored by an employer.

Full visa requirements for visiting the Republic

Border Crossings

Border crossings between Northern Ireland and the Republic are unnoticeable; there are no formalities of any kind. However, this may change once Brexit occurs in 2019.

are available online at www.dfa.ie; for Northern Ireland's visa requirements see www.gov.uk/government/organisations/uk-visas-and-immigration.

To apply to stay longer in the Republic, contact the local *garda* (police) station or the **Garda National Immigration Bureau** (01-666 9100; www.garda.ie; 13-14 Burgh Quay, Dublin; 8am-9pm Mon-Fri; all city centre). To apply to stay longer in Northern Ireland, contact the Home Office (www.gov.uk/government/organisations/uk-visas-and-immigration).

Women Travellers

Ireland should pose no problems for women travellers. Finding contraception is not the problem it once was, although anyone on the pill should bring adequate supplies.
Rape Crisis Network Ireland (091-563 676; www.rcni.ie) In the Republic. App available.

Transport

Getting There & Away

Entering the Country

Dublin is the primary point of entry for most visitors to Ireland, although some do choose Shannon or Belfast.

○ The overwhelming majority of airlines fly into Dublin.

○ For travel to the US, Dublin and Shannon airports operate preclearance facilities, which means you pass through US immigration *before* boarding your aircraft.

○ Dublin is home to two seaports that serve as the main points of sea transport with Britain; ferries from France arrive in the southern ports of Rosslare and Cork.

○ Dublin is the nation's rail hub.

Air

Ireland's main airports:

Cork Airport (☏021-431 3131; www.corkairport.com) Airlines servicing the airport include Aer Lingus and Ryanair.

Dublin Airport (☏01-814 1111; www.dublinairport.com) Ireland's major international gateway airport, with direct flights from the UK, Europe, North America and the Middle East.

Shannon Airport (SNN; ☏061-712 000; www.shannonairport.ie; ☎) Has a few direct flights from the UK, Europe and North America.

Northern Ireland's airports:

Belfast International Airport (Aldergrove; ☏028-9448 4848; www.belfastairport.com; Airport Rd) Has direct flights from the UK, Europe and North America.

Land

Eurolines (www.eurolines.com) has a daily coach and ferry service from London's Victoria Station to Dublin Busáras.

Sea

The main ferry routes between Ireland and the UK and mainland Europe:

○ Belfast to Liverpool (England; eight hours)

○ Belfast to Cairnryan (Scotland; 1¾ hours)

○ Cork to Roscoff (France; 14 hours; April to October only)

○ Dublin to Liverpool (England; fast four hours, slow 8½ hours)

○ Dublin and Dun Laoghaire to Holyhead (Wales; fast two hours, slow 3½ hours)

○ Larne to Cairnryan (Scotland; two hours)

○ Larne to Troon (Scotland; two hours; March to October only)

○ Larne to Fleetwood (England; six hours)

○ Rosslare to Cherbourg/Roscoff (France; 18/20½ hours)

○ Rosslare to Fishguard and Pembroke (Wales; 3½ hours)

Climate Change & Travel

Every form of transport that relies on carbon-based fuel generates CO_2, the main cause of human-induced climate change. Modern travel is dependent on aeroplanes, which might use less fuel per kilometre per person than most cars but travel much greater distances. The altitude at which aircraft emit gases (including CO_2) and particles also contributes to their climate change impact. Many websites offer 'carbon calculators' that allow people to estimate the carbon emissions generated by their journey and, for those who wish to do so, to offset the impact of the greenhouse gases emitted with contributions to portfolios of climate-friendly initiatives throughout the world. Lonely Planet offsets the carbon footprint of all staff and author travel.

Competition from budget airlines has forced ferry operators to discount heavily and offer flexible fares.

A useful website is www.aferry.co.uk, which covers all sea-ferry routes and operators to Ireland.

Main operators include the following:

Brittany Ferries (www.brittanyferries.com) Cork to Roscoff; April to October.

Irish Ferries (www.irishferries.com) It has Dublin to Holyhead ferries (up to four per day year-round); and France to Rosslare (three times per week).

P&O Ferries (www.poferries.com) Daily sailings year-round from Dublin to Liverpool, and Larne to Cairnryan. Larne to Troon runs March to October only.

Stena Line (www.stenaline.com) Daily sailings from Holyhead to Dublin Port, from Belfast to Liverpool and Cairnryan, and from Rosslare to Fishguard.

Getting Around

The big decision in getting around Ireland is whether to go by car or use public transport. Your own car will make the best use of your time and help you reach even the most remote of places. It's usually easy to get very cheap rentals – €10 per day or less is common – and if two or more are travelling together, the fee for rental and petrol can be cheaper than bus fares.

Bus & Train/Ferry Combos

It's possible to combine bus, ferry and train tickets from major UK centres to most Irish towns. This might not be as quick as flying on a budget airline but leaves less of a carbon footprint. The journey between London and Dublin takes about 12 hours by bus, eight hours by train; the London to Belfast trip takes 13 to 16 hours by bus. Both can be had for as little as £29 one way. Eurolines (www.eurolines.com) has bus-ferry combos while Virgin Trains (www.virgintrains.co.uk) has combos that include London to Dublin. For more options, look for SailRail fares.

The bus network, made up of a mix of public and private operators, is extensive and generally quite competitive although journey times can be slow and lots of the points of interest outside towns are not served. The rail network is quicker but more limited, serving only some major towns and cities. Both buses and trains get busy during peak times; you'll need to book in advance to be guaranteed a seat.

Air

Ireland's size makes domestic flying unnecessary, but there are flights between Dublin and Belfast, Cork, Derry, Donegal, Galway, Kerry, Shannon and Sligo aimed at passengers connecting from international flights. Flights linking the mainland to the Aran Islands are popular.

Bicycle

Ireland's compact size and scenic landscapes make it a good cycling destination. However, unreliable weather, many very narrow roads and some very fast drivers are major concerns. Special tracks such as the 42km Great Western Greenway in County Mayo are a delight. A good tip for cyclists in the West of Ireland is that the prevailing winds make it easier to cycle from south to north.

Buses will carry bikes, but only if there's room. For trains, bear the following in mind:

○ Intercity trains charge up to €10.50 per bike.

○ Book in advance (www.irishrail.ie), as there's only room for two bikes per service.

Companies that arrange cycle tours in Ireland include the following:

Go Visit Ireland (☏066-976 2094; www.govisitireland.com) Has guided and independent tours.

Irish Cycling Safaris (☏01-260 0749; www.cyclingsafaris.com; €810 845) Organises numerous tours across Ireland.

Lismore Cycling Holidays (☏087-935 6610; www.cycling-holidays.ie) Runs tours around the southeast.

Boat

Ireland's offshore islands are all served by boat.

Ferries also operate across rivers, inlets and loughs, providing useful short cuts, particularly for cyclists.

Cruises are popular on the 258km-long Shannon–Erne Waterway and on a variety of other lakes and loughs.

Bus

Private buses compete – often very favourably – with Bus Éireann in the Republic and also run where the national buses are irregular or absent.

Distances are not especially long: few bus journeys will last longer than five hours. Bus Éireann bookings can be made online, but you can't reserve a seat for a particular service. Dynamic pricing is in effect on many routes: book early to get the lowest fares.

Note the following:

○ Bus routes and frequencies are slowly contracting in the Republic.

○ The National Journey Planner app by Transport for Ireland is very useful

for planning bus and train journeys.

The main bus services in Ireland are:

Bus Éireann (☑1850 836 6111; www.buseireann.ie) The Republic's main bus line.

Translink (☑028-9066 6630; www.translink.co.uk) Northern Ireland's main bus service; includes Ulsterbus and Goldline.

Car & Motorcycle

Travelling by car or motorbike means greater flexibility and independence. The road system is extensive, and the network of motorways has cut driving times considerably. But also note that many secondary roads are very narrow and at times rather perilous.

All cars on public roads must be insured. If you are bringing your own vehicle, check that your insurance will cover you in Ireland.

Hire

Advance hire rates start at around €20 a day for a small car (unlimited mileage). Shop around and use price-comparison sites as well as company sites (which often have deals not available on booking sites).

Other tips:

○ Most cars are manual; automatic cars are available, but they're more expensive to hire.

○ If you're travelling from the Republic into Northern Ireland, it's important to be sure that your insurance covers journeys to the North.

○ The majority of hire companies won't rent you a car if you're under 23 and haven't had a valid driving licence for at least a year.

Parking

All big towns and cities have covered and open short-stay car parks that are conveniently signposted.

○ On-street parking is usually by 'pay and display' tickets available from on-street machines or disc parking (discs, which rotate to display the time you park your car, are usually provided by rental agencies). Costs range from €1.50 to €6 per hour; all-day parking in a car park will cost around €25.

○ Yellow lines (single or double) along the edge of the road indicate restrictions. Double yellow lines mean no parking at any time. Always look for the nearby sign that spells out when you can and cannot park.

Roads & Rules

Ireland may be one of the few countries where the posted speed limits are often much faster than you'll find possible.

Motoring Organisations

The two main motoring organisations:

Automobile Association (AA; ☑Northern Ireland breakdown 00 800 8877 6655, Republic breakdown 1800 66 77 88; www.theaa.ie)

Royal Automobile Club (RAC; ☑Northern Ireland breakdown 0333 200 0999, Republic breakdown 0800 015 6000; www.rac.ie)

Road Distances (km)

	Athlone	Belfast	Cork	Derry	Donegal	Dublin	Galway	Kilkenny	Killarney	Limerick	Rosslare Harbour	Shannon Airport	Sligo	Waterford
Belfast	242													
Cork	219	424												
Derry	209	117	428											
Donegal	103	180	402	69										
Dublin	127	167	256	237	233									
Galway	93	306	209	272	204	212								
Kilkenny	116	294	148	336	300	120	172							
Killarney	232	436	87	441	407	304	193	198						
Limerick	363	323	105	328	287	202	98	113	111					
Rosslare Harbour	201	330	208	307	201	150	274	98	275	211				
Shannon Airport	133	346	128	351	282	218	93	135	135	25	234			
Sligo	117	206	336	135	66	214	138	245	343	227	325	218		
Waterford	164	333	126	383	357	163	220	48	193	129	82	152	293	
Wexford	184	309	187	378	372	135	253	80	254	190	19	213	307	61

● Motorways (marked by M+number on a blue background): modern, divided highways.

● Primary roads (N+number on a green background in the Republic, A+number in Northern Ireland): usually well-engineered two-lane roads.

● Secondary and tertiary roads (marked as R+number in the Republic, B+number in Northern Ireland): Can be very winding and exceedingly narrow.

● Tolls are charged on many motorways, usually by machine at a plaza. On the M50, pay the automated tolls between junctions 6 and 7 at www.eflow.ie.

● Directional signs are often not in evidence.

● GPS navigation via your smartphone or device is very helpful.

● EU licences are treated like Irish licences.

● Non-EU licences are valid in Ireland for up to 12 months.

● If you plan to bring a car from Europe, it's illegal to drive without at least third-party insurance. The basic rules of the road:

● Drive on the left; overtake to the right.

● Safety belts must be worn by the driver and all passengers.

● Children aged under 12 aren't allowed to sit in the front passenger seat.

● When entering a roundabout, give way to the right.

● In the Republic, speed-limit and distance signs are in kilometres; in the North, speed-limit and distance signs are often in miles.
Speed limits:
Republic 120km/h on motorways, 100km/h on national roads, 80km/h on regional and local roads, and 50km/h or as signposted in towns.

Bus & Rail Passes

There are a few bus, rail and bus-and-rail passes worth considering:

Irish Explorer Offers customers five days of unlimited Irish Rail travel out of 15 consecutive days (adult/child €160/80).

Open Road Pass Three days' travel out of six consecutive days (€60) on Bus Éireann; extra days cost €16.50.

Sunday Day Tracker One day's unlimited travel (adult/child £7/3.50) on Translink buses and trains in Northern Ireland, Sunday only.

Trekker Four Day Four consecutive days of unlimited travel (€110) on Irish Rail.

Note that Eurail's one-country pass for Ireland is a bad deal in any of its permutations.

Northern Ireland 70mph (112km/h) on motorways, 60mph (96km/h) on main roads, 30mph (48km/h) in built-up areas.

○ Drinking and driving is taken very seriously; you're allowed a maximum blood-alcohol level of 50mg/100mL (0.05%) in the Republic, and 35mg/100mL (0.035%) in Northern Ireland.

Local Transport

Dublin and Belfast have comprehensive local bus networks, as do some other larger towns.

○ The Dublin Area Rapid Transport (DART) rail line runs roughly the length of Dublin's coastline, while the Luas tram system has two popular lines.

○ Taxis tend to be expensive: flag fall is daytime/night-time €3.60/4 plus €1.10/1.40 per km after the first 500m.

○ Uber is in Dublin but is not as popular as MyTaxi (www.mytaxi.com), a taxi app.

Tours

Organised tours are a convenient way of exploring the country's main highlights if your time is limited. Tours can be booked through travel agencies, tourist offices, or through the tour companies.

Bus Éireann (☎01-836 6111; www.buseireann.ie) Offers day trips from Dublin and Cork to popular destinations.

CIE Tours International (www.cietours.com) Runs multiday bus tours of the Republic and the North.

Paddywagon Tours (☎01-823 0822; www.paddywagontours.com) Activity-filled tours all over Ireland.

Railtours Ireland (☎01-856 0045; www.railtoursireland.com) All-Ireland tours for train enthusiasts.

Touristy (☎087-631 2682; www.touristy.ie) One- to 14-day custom tours with your own vehicle and driver.

Train

Given Ireland's relatively small size, train travel can be quick and advance-purchase fares are competitive with buses.

○ Many of the Republic's most beautiful areas, such as whole swaths of the Wild Atlantic Way, are not served by rail.

○ Most lines radiate out from Dublin, with limited ways of interconnecting between lines, which can complicate touring.

○ There are four routes from Belfast in Northern Ireland, one links with the system in the Republic via Newry to Dublin.

○ True 1st class only exists on the Dublin–Cork and Dublin–Belfast lines. On all other trains, seats are the same size as in standard class, despite any marketing come-ons such as 'Premier' class.

Irish Rail (Iarnród Éireann; ☎1850 366 222; www.irishrail.ie) Operates trains in the Republic.

Translink NI Railways (☎028-9066 6630; www.translink.co.uk) Operates trains in Northern Ireland.

Language

Irish (Gaeilge) is Ireland's official language. In 2003 the government introduced the Official Languages Act, whereby all official documents, street signs and official titles must be either in Irish or in both Irish and English. Despite its official status, Irish is really only spoken in pockets of rural Ireland known as the Gaeltacht, the main ones being Cork (*Corcaigh*), Donegal (*Dún na nGall*), Galway (*Gaillimh*), Kerry (*Ciarraí*) and Mayo (*Maigh Eo*).

Ask people outside the Gaeltacht if they can speak Irish and nine out of 10 of them will probably reply '*ah, cupla focal*' (a couple of words) – and they generally mean it. Irish is a compulsory subject in schools for those aged six to 15, but Irish classes have traditionally been rather academic and unimaginative, leading many students to resent it as a waste of time. As a result, many adults regret not having a greater grasp of it. In recent times, at long last, a new Irish curriculum has been introduced cutting the hours devoted to the subject but making the lessons more fun, practical and celebratory.

For in-depth language information and a witty insight into the quirks of language in Ireland, check out Lonely Planet's *Irish Language & Culture*. To enhance your trip with this title or a phrasebook, visit **lonelyplanet.com**. Lonely Planet's Fast Talk app is available through the Apple App store.

Pronunciation

Irish divides vowels into long (those with an accent) and short (those without an accent), and distinguishes between broad (**a, á, o, ó, u**) and slender (**e, é, i** and **í**) vowels, which can affect the pronunciation of preceding consonants.

Other than a few odd-looking clusters, like **mh** and **bhf** (both pronounced as 'w'), consonants are generally pronounced as they are in English.

Irish has three main dialects: Connaught Irish (in Galway and northern Mayo), Munster Irish (in Cork, Kerry and Waterford) and Ulster Irish (in Donegal). The pronunciation guides given here are an anglicised version of modern standard Irish, which is essentially an amalgam of the three – if you read them as if they were English, you'll be able to get your point across in Gaeilge without even having to think about the specifics of Irish pronunciation or spelling.

Basics

Hello. (greeting)
Dia duit. — deea gwit
Hello. (reply)
Dia is Muire duit. — deeas moyra gwit
Good morning.
Maidin mhaith. — mawjin wah
Good night.
Oíche mhaith. — eekheh wah
Goodbye. (when leaving)
Slán leat. — slawn lyat
Goodbye. (when staying)
Slán agat. — slawn agut
Excuse me.
Gabh mo leithscéal. — gamoh lesh scale
I'm sorry.
Tá brón orm. — taw brohn oruhm
Thank you (very) much.
Go raibh (míle) maith agat. — goh rev (meela) mah agut
Do you speak Irish?
An bhfuil Gaeilge agat? — on wil gaylge oguht
I don't understand.
Ní thuigim. — nee higgim
What is this?
Cad é seo? — kod ay shoh
What is that?
Cad é sin? — kod ay shin
I'd like to go to ...
Ba mhaith liom dul go dtí ... — baw wah lohm dull go dee ...
I'd like to buy ...
Ba mhaith liom ... a cheannach. — bah wah lohm ... a kyanukh

..., (if you) please.
| *más é do thoil é.* | ... maws ay do hall ay |

Yes.	*Tá.*	taw
No.	*Níl.*	neel
It is.	*Sea.*	sheh
It isn't.	*Ní hea.*	nee heh
another/ one more	*ceann eile*	kyawn ella
nice	*go deas*	goh dyass

Making Conversation

Welcome.
Ceád míle fáilte. kade meela fawlcha
(lit: 100,000 welcomes)

How are you?
Conas a tá tú? kunas aw taw too

I'm fine.
Táim go maith. thawm go mah

What's your name?
Cad is ainm duit? kod is anim dwit

My name is (Sean Frayne).
*(Sean Frayne) is (shawn frain) is
ainm dom.* anim dohm

Impossible!
Ní féidir é! nee faydir ay

Nonsense!
Ráiméis! rawmaysh

That's terrible!
Go huafásach! guh hoofawsokh

Take it easy.
Tóg é gobogé. tohg ay gobogay

Cheers!
Slainte! slawncha

I'm never ever drinking again!
*Ní ólfaidh mé go knee ohlhee mey
gubrách arís!* brawkh ureeshch

Bon voyage!
*Go n-éirí an go nairee on
bóthar leat!* bohhar lat

Happy Christmas!
Nollaig shona! nuhlig hona

Happy Easter!
Cáisc shona! kawshk hona

Days of the Week

Monday	*Dé Luaín*	day loon
Tuesday	*Dé Máirt*	day maart
Wednesday	*Dé Ceádaoin*	day kaydeen
Thursday	*Déardaoin*	daredeen
Friday	*Dé hAoine*	day heeneh
Saturday	*Dé Sathairn*	day sahern
Sunday	*Dé Domhnaigh*	day downick

Numbers

1	*haon*	hayin
2	*dó*	doe
3	*trí*	tree
4	*ceathaír*	kahirr
5	*cúig*	kooig
6	*sé*	shay
7	*seacht*	shocked
8	*hocht*	hukt
9	*naoi*	nay
10	*deich*	jeh
20	*fiche*	feekhe

Behind the Scenes

Writer Thanks

Isabel Albiston

Thanks to all the friendly staff at Northern Ireland's tourist offices who plied me with leaflets while on the road. Thanks in particular to James at Lonely Planet, Victoria Moore at Translink, Barry Flanagan and Caroline Wilson. Lastly, huge thanks to my parents for all your help.

Fionn Davenport

Thanks to everyone in Dublin who helped with research; to Laura for constantly picking me up from the airport; and to LP editors for indulging my every misstep.

Damian Harper

Thanks to everyone who came up with tips and suggestions and helped point me in the right direction along the Wild Atlantic Way. Much gratitude to Shannen, Declan Hassett, Auriel, James Peake, Damien M, Kieron, Fabio, Hans and a raised glass and a tip of the hat to the delightful people of Ireland who made the journey so pleasurable. Daisy, Tim and Emma – thanks as ever.

Catherine Le Nevez

Sláinte first and foremost to Julian, and to all of the Irish locals and fellow travellers throughout County Clare, County Galway, County Kerry and Counties Meath, Louth, Cavan and Monaghan. Huge thanks too to DE James Smart and everyone at LP. As ever, *merci encore* to my parents, brother, belle-sœur and neveu.

Acknowledgements

Climate map data adapted from Peel MC, Finlayson BL & McMahon TA (2007) 'Updated World Map of the Köppen-Geiger Climate Classification', Hydrology and Earth System Sciences, 11, 163344.

Illustrations p88-9, 258-9 by Michael Weldon, p40-1, 52-3, 102-3 by Javier Zarracina

This Book

This 2nd edition of Lonely Planet's *Best of Ireland* guidebook was researched and written by Neil Wilson, Isabel Albiston, Fionn Davenport, Damian Harper and Catherine Le Nevez. This guidebook was produced by the following:

Destination Editor James Smart, Clifton Wilkinson

Product Editor Jessica Ryan

Senior Cartographer Mark Griffiths

Book Designer Gwen Cotter

Assisting Editors Imogen Bannister, Michelle Bennett, Nigel Chin, Michelle Coxall, Andrea Dobbin, Chris Pitts

Cover Researcher Naomi Parker

Thanks to AnneMarie McCarthy, Martin Heng, Stephen Cluskey, Noelle Daly, Katherine Rowan, James Smart, Gabrielle Stefanos, Angela Tinson, Sam Wheeler

Send Us Your Feedback

We love to hear from travellers – your comments keep us on our toes and help make our books better. Our well-travelled team reads every word on what you loved or loathed about this book. Although we cannot reply individually to postal submissions, we always guarantee that your feedback goes straight to the appropriate authors, in time for the next edition. Each person who sends us information is thanked in the next edition, the most useful submissions are rewarded with a selection of digital PDF chapters.

Visit lonelyplanet.com/contact to submit your updates and suggestions or to ask for help. Our award-winning website also features inspirational travel stories, news and discussions.

Note: We may edit, reproduce and incorporate your comments in Lonely Planet products such as guidebooks, websites and digital products, so let us know if you don't want your comments reproduced or your name acknowledged. For a copy of our privacy policy visit lonelyplanet.com/privacy.

Index

000 Map pages

SORINA CHIRITA

LONELY PLANET IN THE WILD

Send your 'Lonely Planet in the Wild' photos to social@lonelyplanet.com
We share the best on our Facebook page every week!

Symbols & Map Key

Look for these symbols to quickly identify listings:

- ◉ Sights
- ✪ Activities
- ✪ Courses
- ✪ Tours
- ✪ Festivals & Events
- ✪ Eating
- ✪ Drinking
- ✪ Entertainment
- ✪ Shopping
- ✪ Information & Transport

These symbols and abbreviations give vital information for each listing:

- ✐ Sustainable or green recommendation
- **FREE** No payment required

☏ Telephone number	▣ Bus
☺ Opening hours	▣ Ferry
Ⓟ Parking	▣ Tram
☺ Nonsmoking	▣ Train
✳ Air-conditioning	▣ English-language menu
@ Internet access	✐ Vegetarian selection
☎ Wi-fi access	
☈ Swimming pool	✦ Family-friendly

Find your best experiences with these Great For... icons.

 Art & Culture

 History

 Beaches

 Local Life

 Budget

 Nature & Wildlife

 Cafe/Coffee

 Photo Op

 Cycling

 Scenery

 Detour

 Shopping

 Drinking

 Short Trip

 Entertainment

Sport

Events

Walking

Family Travel

Food & Drink

Winter Travel

Sights

- ⬤ Beach
- ⬤ Bird Sanctuary
- ⬤ Buddhist
- ⬤ Castle/Palace
- ⬤ Christian
- ⬤ Confucian
- ⬤ Hindu
- ⬤ Islamic
- ⬤ Jain
- ⬤ Jewish
- ⬤ Monument
- ⬤ Museum/Gallery/ Historic Building
- ⬤ Ruin
- ⬤ Shinto
- ⬤ Sikh
- ⬤ Taoist
- ⬤ Winery/Vineyard
- ⬤ Zoo/Wildlife Sanctuary
- ⬤ Other Sight

Points of Interest

- ⬤ Bodysurfing
- ⬤ Camping
- ⬤ Cafe
- ⬤ Canoeing/Kayaking
- • Course/Tour
- ⬤ Diving
- ⬤ Drinking & Nightlife
- ⬤ Eating
- ⬤ Entertainment
- ⬤ Sento Hot Baths/ Onsen
- ⬤ Shopping
- ⬤ Skiing
- ⬤ Sleeping
- ⬤ Snorkelling
- ⬤ Surfing
- ⬤ Swimming/Pool
- ⬤ Walking
- ⬤ Windsurfing
- ⬤ Other Activity

Information

- ⬤ Bank
- ⬤ Embassy/Consulate
- ⬤ Hospital/Medical
- @ Internet
- ⬤ Police
- ⬤ Post Office
- ⬤ Telephone
- ⬤ Toilet
- ⬤ Tourist Information
- • Other Information

Geographic

- ⬤ Beach
- ⬤ Gate
- ⬤ Hut/Shelter
- ⬤ Lighthouse
- ⬤ Lookout
- ▲ Mountain/Volcano
- ⬤ Oasis
- ⬤ Park
-)(Pass
- ⬤ Picnic Area
- ⬤ Waterfall

Transport

- ⬤ Airport
- ⬤ BART station
- ⬤ Border crossing
- ⬤ Boston T station
- ⬤ Bus
- ⬤ Cable car/Funicular
- ⬤ Cycling
- ⬤ Ferry
- ⬤ Metro/MRT station
- ⬤ Monorail
- Ⓟ Parking
- ⬤ Petrol station
- ⬤ Subway/S-Bahn/ Skytrain station
- ⬤ Taxi
- ⬤ Train station/Railway
- ⬤ Tram
- ⬤ Tube Station
- ⬤ Underground/ U-Bahn station
- • Other Transport

Damian Harper

Damian has been writing for Lonely Planet for over two decades, contributing to titles as diverse as *China*, *Beijing*, *Shanghai*, *Vietnam*, *Thailand*, *Ireland*, *London*, *Mallorca*, *Malaysia*, *Singapore & Brunei*, *Hong Kong* and *Great Britain*. A seasoned guidebook writer, Damian has penned articles for numerous newspapers and magazines, including the *Guardian* and the *Daily Telegraph*, and currently makes Surrey, England, his home. A self-taught trumpet novice, his other hobbies include collecting modern first editions, photography and Taekwondo. Follow Damian on Instagram (damian. harper).

Catherine Le Nevez

Catherine's wanderlust kicked in when she roadtripped across Europe from her Parisian base aged four, and she's been hitting the road at every opportunity since, travelling to around 60 countries and completing her Doctorate of Creative Arts in Writing, Masters in Professional Writing, and postgrad qualifications in Editing and Publishing along the way. Over the past dozen-plus years she's written scores of Lonely Planet guides and articles covering Paris, France, Europe and far beyond. Her work has also appeared in numerous online and print publications. Topping Catherine's list of travel tips is to travel without any expectations.

Our Story

A beat-up old car, a few dollars in the pocket and a sense of adventure. In 1972 that's all Tony and Maureen Wheeler needed for the trip of a lifetime – across Europe and Asia overland to Australia. It took several months, and at the end – broke but inspired – they sat at their kitchen table writing and stapling together their first travel guide, *Across Asia on the Cheap*. Within a week they'd sold 1500 copies. Lonely Planet was born.

Today, Lonely Planet has offices in Franklin, London, Melbourne, Oakland, Dublin, Beijing, and Delhi, with more than 600 staff and writers. We share Tony's belief that 'a great guidebook should do three things: inform, educate and amuse'.

Our Writers

Neil Wilson

Based in Perthshire, Neil has been a full-time writer since 1988, working on more than 80 guidebooks for various publishers, including the Lonely Planet guides to Scotland, England, Ireland and Prague. An outdoors enthusiast since childhood, Neil is an active hill walker, mountain biker, sailor, snowboarder, fly fisher and rock climber, and has climbed and tramped in four continents, including ascents of Jebel Toubkal in Morocco, Mount Kinabalu in Borneo, the Old Man of Hoy in Scotland's Orkney Islands and the Northwest Face of Half Dome in California's Yosemite Valley.

Isabel Albiston

After six years working for the *Daily Telegraph* in London, squeezing in as many trips as annual leave would allow, Isabel left to spend more time on the road. A job as writer for a magazine in Sydney, Australia was followed by four years living and working in Buenos Aires, Argentina. Isabel started writing for Lonely Planet in 2014, having been back in the UK just long enough to pack a bag for a research trip to Malaysia, and has contributed to six LP guides. See her pics on instagram: isabel_albiston.

Fionn Davenport

Irish by birth and conviction, Fionn has been writing about his native country for more than two decades. He's come and gone over the years, pulled abroad to escape Dublin's comfortable stasis and by the promise of adventure, but it has cemented his belief that Ireland remains his favourite place to visit, if not always live in. These days, he has a weekly commute home to Dublin from Manchester, where he lives with his partner Laura and their car Trevor. In Dublin he presents Inside Culture on RTE Radio 1 and writes travel features for a host of publications.

◀──── More Writers ────◀

STAY IN TOUCH LONELYPLANET.COM/CONTACT

AUSTRALIA The Malt Store, Level 3, 551 Swanston St, Carlton, Victoria 3053 ☎ 03 8379 8000, fax 03 8379 8111

IRELAND Digital Depot, Roe Lane (off Thomas St), Digital Hub, Dublin 8, D08 TCV4, Ireland

USA 124 Linden Street, Oakland, CA 94607 ☎ 510 250 6400, toll free 800 275 8555, fax 510 893 8572

UK 240 Blackfriars Road, London SE1 8NW ☎ 020 3771 5100, fax 020 3771 5101

 twitter.com/lonelyplanet   facebook.com/lonelyplanet   instagram.com/lonelyplanet   youtube.com/lonelyplanet   lonelyplanet.com/newsletter